Religion and Moral

RELIGION
AND
MORAL REASON

A New Method
for Comparative Study

Ronald M. Green

Dartmouth College

New York   Oxford
OXFORD UNIVERSITY PRESS
1988

Oxford University Press

Oxford   New York   Toronto
Delhi   Bombay   Calcutta   Madras   Karachi
Petaling Jaya   Singapore   Hong Kong   Tokyo
Nairobi   Dar es Salaam   Cape Town
Melbourne   Auckland

and associated companies in
Beirut   Berlin   Ibadan   Nicosia

Copyright © 1988 by Oxford University Press, Inc.

Published by Oxford University Press, Inc.,
200 Madison Avenue, New York, New York 10016

Oxford is a registered trademark of Oxford University Press

Library of Congress Cataloging-in-Publication Data
Green, Ronald Michael.
Religion and moral reason.
Bibliography: p.
Includes index.
1. Religion and ethics.   2. Revelation.
3. Reason   4. Religions.   I. Title.
BJ47.G74   1988   291.5   87-15230
ISBN 0-19-504340-5
ISBN 0-19-504341-3 (pbk.)

Much of chapter 2, "Religion and Morality in the African Traditional Setting," originally appeared in the *Journal of Religion in Africa,* 14 (1983),
1-23. An earlier version of chapter 4 appeared as "Abraham, Isaac, and
the Jewish Tradition" in the *Journal of Religious Ethics,* 10 (1982), 1-21.
Reprinted with permission.

1 3 5 7 9 8 6 4 2

Printed in the United States of America
on acid-free paper

To Julie

Acknowledgments

I am indebted to many people for the insight and assistance they have given me in the preparation of this book. By asking me to serve as Hoover Lecturer at the Disciples Divinity House of the University of Chicago, Don Browning started me thinking about Abraham and Isaac in ways that led to chapters four and five of this book. James Johnson and the staff of the *Journal of Religious Ethics* lent momentum to this by editing and publishing an early version of chapter four, while the students in a graduate seminar I taught in the Department of Religious Studies at Stanford University made a substantial contribution to the thinking that resulted in chapter five.

Cynthia Read at Oxford has been a constant source of support and encouragement. Susan Meigs at Oxford and Sandra Curtis at Dartmouth have both been of major help in transforming a manuscript into a book.

I owe a special debt to my colleagues in Dartmouth's Department of Religion. Fred Berthold, Nancy Frankenberry, Robert Henricks, Arthur Hertzberg, Robert Oden, Hans Penner, Kevin Reinhart, and Charles Stinson have each, in different ways, stimulated the thinking that goes into this book. It is customary in these circumstances to relieve one's colleagues of any responsibility for errors or omissions on the authors' part. But anyone familiar with these individuals will know how unnecessary this is. In seminars and colloquia when aspects of this book were discussed, my colleagues in this extraordinary department have never hesitated to express their scholarly disagreements with me. Despite our specific agreements or disagreements, however, these colleagues have always encouraged my efforts and, through their own work, they have contributed to our common task of understanding religion in rational terms.

Contents

Introduction

My aim in this book is to show that religion has its basis in a process of moral and religious reasoning common to all human beings. I term this process "religious reasoning," and I believe it constitutes a "deep structure" of thought underlying historical religious traditions. But I acknowledge at the outset how doubtful these claims appear to be. Looking at the religious communities around us, we see not similarity but difference: differences in moral codes, in attitudes toward religious authority, in views of the self, and in conceptions of salvation. Moreover, for many religious communities, these differences are matters of life and death. As I write, Jews and Muslims, Catholics and Protestants, Sikhs and Hindus are killing one another partly over differences in religious belief.

I have no intention of denying the reality of these differences. Nor do I plan to show that, despite surface disagreements, religions have a common message of human brotherhood or sisterhood. Like many who are disturbed by religious conflict, I wish this were true. But, while I hope that greater mutual respect might result from my investigation, I know that religions' common moral basis can often be a source of bitter conflict. In any case, my primary aim is not to develop an argument for religious tolerance. My interest is more immediately "scientific" in that I hope to further our understanding of the nature of religious belief and conduct. In this respect, I am somewhat like a molecular biologist investigating the mechanisms of genetic inheritance. Biologists appreciate the diversity of structrures genes can produce, even within a single species or family. They are aware of the differences that can exist at the phenomenal (or "phenotypical") level of expression, and they know that some of these differences may utterly separate one species from the other by rendering interbreeding impossible. Nevertheless, as scientists, they believe that beneath this surface diversity certain basic and universal processes are at work. They also believe that uncovering these processes not only will help explain common features in the biological spectrum but will shed light on just how and why differences arise.

Similarly, I wish to show that the most basic processes of religious reasoning are the same everywhere and give rise, in understandable ways, to diverse forms of religious expression. This process of reasoning has its beginning in a method of moral judgment that, because it reflects the rational constraints on conduct in any communal situation, is common to all human beings and human cultures. Specific moral norms are the complex *outcome* of this process after it has been applied to different circumstances in different contexts, and for this reason specific norms can differ. But the underlying method of decision and judgment is the same everywhere. Moral decision, in turn, poses serious conceptual and personal problems for human beings, which can be addressed only by a further process of "religious reasoning." This process, while it is similar across cultures, is also flexible enough to allow for a wide variety of outcomes, depending on the social and cultural contexts in which it takes place. The result of all these common basic reasoning processes, of this "deep structure" of religious thought[1], is the diverse religious traditions we see around us. Some of these traditions are so opposed to each other's way of viewing the world that understanding between them often seems impossible, and even mutual conversation can be difficult. But these traditions arise, I maintain, out of a similar deep structure of rational thought.

In my previous book, *Religious Reason,*[2] I developed this process of religious reasoning at length and I used it to explain some key beliefs of four major religious traditions: Judaism, Christianity, Hinduism, and Buddhism. My aim in this book is in some ways more general and in others more specific. Instead of developing the full logic of religious reasoning as I did in the first half of that book, I devote a single initial chapter to outlining the basic deep structure of religious reason. This structure is comprehensible by itself and is all we need for the kind of comparative study of religions that follows. The reader interested in exploring the more philosophical questions this structure raises can refer to my earlier discussion.

An understanding of this deep structure, I believe, furnishes us with a powerful new tool for the comparative study of religion. In their surface teachings, religious traditions frequently defy comprehension. Not only do traditions differ enormously in their basic teachings, but in articulating or defending their beliefs, they frequently employ perplexing and paradoxical modes of discourse. This has sometimes led students of comparative religion to believe that religion is essentially nonrational or that it rests on experiences accessible only to those within the tradition. In contrast, we will see that much of the complexity of religious belief stems from tensions inherent within the universal "deep structure" of moral and religious reasoning itself. Understanding this structure is thus a way of entering the seemingly impenetrable world of the beliefs and practices of other traditions.

Subsequent chapters are meant to provide the richest possible illustration of this point. Belief by belief, tradition by tradition, I seek to show how the basic agenda of religious reason affords us insight into the very diverse modes of thought of different traditions. Sometimes the workings of this deep structure are traced in religious traditions other than those I have previously explored; sometimes it is used to examine more complex problems in Judaism, Christianity, Hinduism, and Buddhism. In each case, the effort is made to enhance our understanding of the complexity and richness of religious rationality and of the value of the deep structure as an analytical tool. Chapter 2, for example, traces the presence of this deep structure in the nonliterate, traditional religions of Africa. Since these traditions share many features with other nonliterate religions, including the important role given to ancestors and human spiritual practitioners, this chapter has implications for our understanding of nonliterate, "primal" religions far beyond the African setting.

The examination of Chinese religions in chapter 3 also carries us into a series of new traditions and affords us an opportunity to follow the transition from a nonliterate religion, based on localized spiritual entities and practitioners, to a developed ethical monotheism. The moral intentionality of classical Chinese religion is also so pronounced that the deep structure of religious reasoning lies close to the surface. Paradoxically, the transparency of moral concerns in classical Chinese religion, combined with specific features of Chinese history and civilization, contributed to a relative atrophying of indigenous religious thinking. Religion became ethics, and, as a result, the deeper and fuller

agenda of religious reasoning was cut short. This agenda was picked up
again in China by Buddhism and some forms of Taoism, but the
Chinese experience furnishes the lesson that while religion may be
actuated by moral concerns, it is not reducible to a series of moral
teachings. The development of Chinese religion also vividly illustrates
the way in which the deep structure of religious reasoning interacts with
historical and cultural circumstances to produce diverse religious
outcomes.

The paradox and complexity that are constant features of religious
thought and religious development are nowhere more evident than in
those traditions that trace their moral teaching to a revealed "divine
command." These traditions also pose one of the sharpest challenges to
a view that sees religion as having its foundation in moral reasoning,
since, in their manifest teachings, these traditions seem to deny reason
a significant place in the moral life. In chapters 4 and 5, I explore the
concept of revealed morality as it has been developed in Judaism and
Christianity. Jewish and Christian defenders of divine command
morality often point to the biblical episode of Genesis 22, God's command to Abraham to sacrifice his son Isaac, as concrete proof of the
supremacy of faith over reason in the ethics of these two traditions. By
examining the ways in which this morally problematical text is actually
handled by these traditions, however, I contest this claim and show that
in their ethical teachings, Judaism and Christianity fully respect the primacy owed to moral reason. These faiths undoubtedly emphasize obedience to God's command, and they are prepared to subordinate
human moral understanding to obedience. But this very emphasis
derives from identifiable moral concerns and is never allowed to subvert morality's purposes. Even as thinkers in these traditions stress obedience to God, they display their conviction that God's will can never
really run counter to our deepest moral beliefs. While surface teachings
may appear to violate reason and morality, therefore, the deep structure
of moral and religious reasoning exerts its constant pressure toward fulfillment of its rational agenda. Understanding this structure also illuminates the peculiar course taken by these traditions as they work out
the implications of God's will for the moral life.

If chapters 3 through 5 sometimes take us far into the deep structure of religious thought and away from surface teachings about human
conduct, chapters 6 through 8 return us to identifiable moral territory
and to "normative" aspects of religion that have immediate bearing on
the question of how we should live our lives. In this respect, chapter 6
is transitional, since it develops the moral implications of an aspect of

religion not usually related to ethics or morality: religious ritual. Ritual is not reducible to moral instruction; it is an expressive activity comprising dance, song, poetry, and an intense fellowship. But it also possesses a central and universal moral dimension, one that reaches beyond mere teaching or exhortation. Using an African rainmaking ritual, the Jewish Passover Seder, and early Christian baptism as my principal illustrations, I indicate that religious rituals offer an experiential recapitulation of the moral reasoning process. In diverse ways, they manage to summon participants into "the moral point of view" and give them the experience and insight they need to make sound moral decisions.

Chapter 7 examines a normative issue of worldwide importance: the question of social justice and the moral norms bearing on the fair distribution of wealth. Recent work in social and political philosophy suggests that there is a universal structure to our thinking about this problem. Concepts of "fairness" and "justice," in other words, transcend particular social systems. By examining the social and economic teachings of four very different religious traditions—Judaism, Christianity, Islam, and Buddhism—I lend support to this view. Despite enormous differences in religious teachings (for example, in their respective valuation of material wealth and its relation to human beings' destiny) each of these traditions espouses a remarkably similar social ideal, one that criticizes the uncontrolled private acquisition of wealth, condemns the subjection of people to severe economic hardship, and supports an ongoing ethic of economic redistribution and sharing.

Reasoning about social justice shows that while the procedure of moral choice is simple, it frequently is difficult to apply in actual contexts since it requires one to weigh conflicting rational considerations. Sound moral decision making in general demands a skill of moral judgment not easily acquired. In the final chapter, I try, in a comprehensive way, to provide an illustration of one religious tradition's effort to impart this skill. For millions of Hindus (and for many Buddhists, as well), the Rāmāyaṇa epic has long been a source of moral inspiration. Scholars have often viewed it as imparting a series of moral norms and character ideals. But I think it is a mistake to view the Rāmāyaṇa in such narrowly didactic terms. Instead, I believe this epic is an absorbing presentation of the process of moral reasoning. Episode after episode, choice after choice, its characters are faced with decisions that draw on all their moral and intellectual resources. By following the actors through decisions whose significance and pathos we can all understand,

the epic tutors us in the art of moral judgment. In doing this, the
Rāmāyaṇa is representative of a widespread genre of religious literature. A similar emphasis on the process of reasoned moral deliberation
can be found in the epic literature of Christianity, in narratives surrounding the life of the Buddha, in Jewish midrashim, and in the
hagiography of many other traditions. An encounter with this type of
literature is thus a fitting conclusion to a book whose aim is to demonstrate the deep structure of moral intentionality that animates religious belief everywhere.

I

BASIC ISSUES IN
RELIGION AND REASON

1

The Deep Structure

Religion's deep structure has three essential elements: first, a method of moral reasoning involving "the moral point of view"; second, a set of beliefs affirming the reality of moral retribution; and third, a series of "transmoral" beliefs that suspend moral judgment and retribution when this is needed to overcome moral paralysis and despair. Whatever their surface differences, religions contain these elements. They point their adherents to the method of moral reasoning. They try to assure them that governing one's life by this method is not ultimately self-destructive, that the righteous are rewarded. And, in response to the kind of self-condemnation that inevitably accompanies sensitive moral striving, they are prepared to ease their insistence on judgment and retribution by holding out the promise of a redemption not based entirely on one's deeds.

That this structure contains elements so tensely related to one another—for example, the insistence on retribution and the qualified suspension of retribution—tells us that religious reasoning is complex. In fact, anyone unwilling to tolerate complexity should not undertake the study of religious belief. Religions seek to make reasoned conduct possible in a world that sometimes defies reason, and this effort often pushes them to the limits of human thought. Sometimes religions must resist the claims of experience or make assertions that defy common sense. And sometimes they must even qualify their own beliefs when these yield conclusions that threaten the ultimate rational purposes they have in mind. But none of this means that religions are illogical. Because they are grounded in reason, religions characteristically make painstaking efforts to guarantee the coherency and consistency of their beliefs. Thus, it is paradox, not overt self-contradiction, that characterizes religious thinking.

"The Moral Point of View"

Mention of paradox is an appropriate way of beginning a discussion of the deep structure of religious reasoning, since this structure has its origin in a familiar paradox of the moral life: that self-denial and self-restraint are conditions of human happiness and self-fulfillment. On a purely individual level, this truth impresses itself on us as we mature and learn that the attainment of our most important purposes in life requires self-discipline and the willingness to defer immediate gratification. The genuinely rational person, we know, does not pursue every satisfaction that comes along, but can arrange life's goals in a more or less coherent plan and act on this plan even if it means passing up immediate rewards.

What is true for the individual's personal existence is also true for social and collective life. Human society is predicated on our individual capacity for self-sacrifice and self-restraint. We can imagine a single life based on the impulsive pursuit of pleasure, and we can hypothesize a society whose members take every opportunity to pursue their own interests. But both possibilities eventually produce conflict and anarchy, and neither represents the fullest expression of reason. Only when the individual is prepared to subordinate parts to a whole in matters of personal choice, and self to society in matters that affect others, are conditions established for the harmonious and coherent pursuit of individual ends. The social side of this paradoxical truth is expressed in a hard-won lesson of constitutional democracy: the restraint on arbitrary conduct represented by a firm system of law is the best guarantee of individual freedom. Superficially regarded, law and freedom may seem opposed, but an understanding of the deeper logic of moral life shows they are not.

Three centuries ago, this understanding was expressed by the philosopher Immanuel Kant in a brief treatise on ethics entitled *Foundations of the Metaphysics of Morals*. Few books on ethics have been more widely read than this, and few have been more deeply misunderstood. Part of the blame rests with Kant's poor expression and misleading illustrations, but part of the problem also stems from the difficulty of Kant's pioneering effort to develop systematically the paradoxical truths underlying moral life. Repeatedly, for example, Kant rejects ethics based on "happiness" or the pursuit of any specific human satisfactions (including the satisfactions produced by sympathetic feeling for others). In their place, he sets an ethic based on "duty" and strict adherence to the moral law. These denials that happiness or sympathy have a place in ethics made Kant appear inhuman and led to characterizations of him as a dour misanthrope. In fact, Kant's point is the same as the one made above: happiness or personal satisfaction in any form cannot be people's most basic consideration in making decisions as social beings. For if it were, the result would be anarchy, and in the end, no one's happiness would be served. Instead, Kant argued that private pursuits and desires must always be subordinated to a rule of law whose moral expression he termed "the categorical imperative."

What exactly Kant meant by this imperative is among the most contested issues in moral philosophy. Kant himself had a definite idea of the rule or principle he had in mind. He believed it to be based strictly on reason and, as such, known a priori by all human beings. He believed that it furnished a decisive test of proposed courses of action (what he called "maxims"), enabling us to distinguish right from wrong. And he also believed that this one imperative provided a rational basis for all the more specific moral rules we usually respect (such as those prohibiting lying or cheating). Throughout his writings, Kant gave this imperative several different formulations, the most important of which is "Act only according to that maxim by which you can at the same time will that it should become a universal law."[1]

This imperative is usually viewed as involving a procedure of "universalization" or "generalization." If I propose to undertake some action, such as making a promise I do not intend to keep, I must be prepared to allow others to act this way toward me. "What is sauce for the goose is sauce for the gander." Understood in this way, the categorical imperative seems to be a basic rule of reason. It requires simple consistency and prohibits our doing things we would not want others to do if they were in our position.

Unfortunately, as prevalent as it is, this reading of the categorical imperative has serious problems. Most troublesome, I believe, is the problem posed by someone prepared to do immoral things who would gladly permit others to do the same. For example, a person suffering a terminal disease and able to embezzle funds that will help make his or her last days comfortable might willingly condone others acting the same. Yet we do not ordinarily think that these circumstances and this willingness justify theft. Nor do we think that persons with suicidal or self-destructive tendencies (like some mass murderers) should be allowed to kill or injure others so long as they are willing to put up with mistreatment themselves. Yet that is what the common interpretation of the categorical imperative seems to suggest.[2]

We cannot sort out here all the arguments and counterarguments produced by Kant's ethical theory, but I am convinced that in discussing the categorical imperative, Kant had more in mind than a simple rule of generalization. I believe he was developing something that recent moral philosophers have come to term "the moral point of view." This involves a perspective of radical impartiality or "omnipartiality" before the choices and issues facing us as moral agents. It asks us to choose as though we might be any of the people affected by our conduct. This moral point of view allows self-serving, reasoned choice but always from a standpoint of impartiality. As such, it includes the generalization rule, since what one wills in such circumstances will ordinarily be conduct permissible for the other people one must imagine oneself to be. But it adds to this the requirement that we assess our conduct not just from the egocentric perspective of our own situation but also from the standpoint of the others we might affect. In Kantian terms, what one wills must be capable of becoming "universal law" not only because it must *apply* to all other persons but also because it is something they might "vote for" or accept—a law *for, of,* and *by* everyone.[3]

A contrast with the simpler rule of generalization in cases just mentioned illustrates the importance of this understanding. We saw that the ill-fated embezzler, with little to lose by others' doing the same, might willingly generalize the proposed conduct. But if this person had to regard embezzlement from the viewpoint of all the others it might affect and if others' approval had to be taken into account, the conclusion would be quite different. Then this individual would have to consider the point of view of victims of embezzlement and of survivors in a world where theft and embezzlement had become commonplace. Similarly, however despairing and violent some might be and however willing to relinquish their own lives should they fall victim to the homicide they would permit, it is not enough that they consider this matter from their own perspective. Additionally, they must take into account the viewpoint and interests of all the others they would affect. But surely most people would not want their lives subject to such aberrant and deadly desires. Impartial reasoning about either of these choices appears to furnish overwhelming reasons against them.

Understood in terms of the impartial "moral point of view," the categorical imperative seems to do one of the things Kant says it does: it provides a reasonable and effective test of moral policies. Of course, showing this to be true for every type of choice is the work of a separate book on ethics. But this kind of work is being done. Various contemporary moral philosophers have shown convincingly that when it is strenuously applied, this point of view yields moral judgments consistent with many of our firmest moral intuitions and, more important, it helps us think about new and perplexing choices.[4] The work of these philosophers also indicates that this point of view underlies and justifies many of the ordinary moral rules we respect. However much particular persons might be willing to inflict injury on others, to lie, to steal, or to break solemn promises, none of these practices is likely to be advocated by individuals who must take into account the interests of the many other persons this conduct adversely affects. As Kant believed, therefore, this method of impartial reasoning provides us with a more basic rational justification of our intuitive moral beliefs.

This brief account of the method of moral reasoning leaves many questions unanswered. For example, even if matters are looked at impartially, there will always be conflicts of interest. How are these to be adjudicated? One answer is that a principle of "majority rule" should prevail. Reasoning impartially, one should act in a way that would be acceptable to *most* of the persons whose interests one must consider. In fact, as utilitarian theorists perceived, this will be a sound procedure in many instances of choice.[5] But there will also be instances where it is reasonable to forgo gain for a majority to avoid experiencing serious injury as a member of some minority. This may be why we feel that many basic human rights should not be subject to majority rule and why we believe—against the utilitarians—that certain principles of right and justice should be respected even if they do not always benefit the majority. In any event, these problems of conflict are surmountable. Various general rules for decision are among the first things that impartial persons are called on to work out as they try to think through concrete cases of moral decision.[6]

A more serious objection to this approach is that it assumes human beings capable of reasoning impartially about matters that affect their personal interests. But in our post-Freudian, post-Marxist world, have we not learned too well that our perception of issues and problems is colored by our background, our experiences, and our interests? Can we really expect people to assume the viewpoint of others? Of course, no one can deny that it is extremely difficult to be impartial. We shall see that religious communities invest enormous effort in trying to encourage their adherents to adopt the moral point of view. Failures of impartiality also underlie the problems of sin and wrongdoing that religions seek to address. Nevertheless, this serious practical problem does not lessen the value of the moral point of view as a *standard* for measuring conduct or as an ideal *reference point* for adjudicating disputes. When we try to justify an action morally, we assume it to be one that anyone looking at things impartially and objectively would approve. We may delude ourselves about this, but the need to justify even selfish conduct in this way is an inescapable accompaniment of human reasoning, the homage, as La Rochefoucauld said, that vice offers to virtue. When individuals disagree over the morality of a particular course of conduct, they also appeal to one another's impartial judgment and seek to arouse even keener efforts at impartiality and objectivity. If these efforts fail, individuals or groups commonly resort to other, more impartial persons to help resolve their conflicts. This is the logic of impartial mediation in social disputes and of judges or juries in matters of civil and criminal law. In all these cases, impartiality remains imperfect. But it is the model of reasoned, moral settlement to which the human mind inclines.

Finally, there is the problem posed by the sheer diversity of moral teaching and belief. Recall Kant's claim that this method of moral reasoning is a priori and universal, something known by human beings regardless of their particular beliefs or circumstances. But how can any claim to moral universality be sustained in the face of the great variety of moral teachings that global communication has brought to our attention? In view of this diversity, it seems much more reasonable to accept ethical relativism, the position that moral teachings and beliefs are dependent on one's individual or cultural standpoint.

Ethical relativism undoubtedly remains an attractive and fashionable position in our day. Ironically, this may be partly due to its *moral* appeal: it seems to be a fair alternative to the kind of moral arrogance and cultural imperialism that has often characterized Western civilization. But apart from this appeal, the case for ethical relativism is not impressive. That cultures differ substantially in moral teaching is obvious; that these differences represent fundamentally different ways of thinking about moral choice is far less so. And this is what ethical relativists must prove.

If we consider the method of moral decision, this "moral point of view," or "categorical imperative," as a basic way of thinking that must always be applied in context, we can almost predict diversity in moral conclusions. What is rational for impartial persons to accept in one circumstance, may not be so in another. Classic cases from anthropological lore often taken as proof of ethical relativism merely illustrate the contextual nature of moral reasoning. For example, while most societies regard parricide as a terrible sin, there have been some—including certain Eskimo communities—that once required the killing or abandonment of elderly parents. Examined closely, these cultures displayed similar features: they existed on the edge of survival, counted on the mobility of all their members, and engaged in strenuous pursuits like hunting or fishing. In these societies there was little room for the physically dependent. Not surprisingly, therefore, generations of shared reflection on social norms led all the members of these societies to accept the abandonment of those who could no longer sustain themselves. That this represented an impartially defensible moral decision and one that was freely accepted by all members of these communities was shown by the fact that the elderly regarded such abandonment as an honorable conclusion to their lives, as a duty owed to them that offspring dared not neglect.[7]

What has been true in these extreme cases is also true in other complex areas of moral choice. The sexual realm, for example, reveals a wide variety of different norms and rules across cultural lines. Those of us accustomed by Western religious teaching to regard sexual conduct as almost synonymous with morality may take this as evidence for the utter relativity of morals. However, if we remember that moral reasoning is not reducible to any set of rules but is a basic method of thinking about choices and making decisions, then we must expect this variability of norms. For the fundamental rational considerations underlying the regulation of sexual behavior, considerations such as the ordering of sexual opportunity, the protection of the weak from sexual abuse, and the proper socialization and care of the young can be achieved in a variety of ways. Which specific institutions and norms are selected will depend on the contexts in which these choices are made. Many tribal societies, for example, have found forms of polygamy and (to a lesser extent) polyandry a suitable response to these basic considerations, while other societies facing different circumstances have stressed more or less qualified forms of monogamy. Indeed, as social conditions have changed, cultures have often moved from one specific set of sexual values to another. (Most Western societies, for example, have moved from polygamy to monogamy and now, as aspirations for "personal fulfillment" grow and as the material well-being of women and children becomes less dependent on life-long family stability, these societies seem to be moving toward greater tolerance of serial "monogamy" and nonmarried parenting.)

This same variability of norms is also seen in the realm of supererogatory conduct. Supererogation is that side of the moral life that goes above and beyond the call of duty. For example, while it is usually regarded as obligatory to refrain from injuring other persons, whether or not one should go out of one's way to help others is a matter of supererogation. To this realm belong most of the altruistic, charitable, and self-sacrificial ideals of a society. Obviously, what constitutes "saintly" or "noble" behavior is a matter of dispute even within homogeneous cultures. Most persons would agree that killing is wrong, but just how much risk an individual should take to save another's life can be strenuously debated.[8] But if this is so within cultures, how much more is it likely to be true across cultural lines? We should not be surprised, therefore, to find wide differences in supererogatory ideals among human cultures. Indeed, we shall see that these differences are marked in the religious domain, because supererogation is a special interest of religious communities. This is the sphere in which religions often develop their own unique moral appeal. But these differences (though sustained by seemingly equal conviction on all sides) are not evidence for ethical relativism. In comparing religious ethics, we must look to their basic modes of reasoning and to their basic moral norms, and here we see wide agreement among religions, no matter what their ultimate beliefs or supererogatory teachings. For example, Judaism, Buddhism, and Christianity differ enormously in their respective visions of salvation and they also sharply disagree about the nature of the saintly life. But not one of these traditions permits wanton killing, cheating, or abuse of other persons.

One last point on this matter of moral diversity: Ethical relativists sometimes advance as evidence for their view the fact that conduct between human social groups violates even the most basic norms of our own culture. All over the world, people will deceive, injure, or kill "outsiders" with impunity, often in the belief that this is the "right" thing to do. Centuries ago, Thomas Aquinas, in a classic discussion of the universality of moral norms, attributed this behavior not to the relativity of values but to human beings' "evil persuasions" and "vicious customs."[9] Although Aquinas's words are strong, his point is well taken. Often, human moral community breaks down at cultural or political boundaries and what prevails between communities is a lawless state of violence and aggression. Within each community, moral rules, principles, and ways of thinking prevail. Outside the boundary, a morally lawless realm exists, and strangers are fair game for abuse or mistreatment. Sometimes they are also regarded as evil foes, against whom any form of preemptive self-defense is justified.

Whether they occur on the intertribal or international level, these attitudes are unfortunate. They constitute one of the great problems facing human civilization. But while they may result in part from value differences between human cultures and the tensions they cause, these attitudes are not proof of ethical relativism. What they attest to is either the breakdown of human moral imagination or wanton selfishness and aggression—what Aquinas termed "evil persuasions" and "vicious customs." That human communities often will not treat one another morally almost goes without saying. This reflects the difficulty of being moral and the fact that group life often compounds individual egoism.[10] What the relativist must show, however, is that in their internal standards and principles, including those by which they are sometimes led to "defend" themselves against others, communities fundamentally differ. But neither evidence nor common sense supports this view.

In the chapters ahead, we shall see that this universal structure of moral decision making is a key element of the deep structure of religious thought. Whatever their specific teachings, religions agree on the basic rules of morality. All prohibit wanton killing or injury of other persons (although many permit legitimate self-defense); all condemn deception and the breaking of solemn promises. On the positive side, all require giving some minimum of aid to those in need; all require reparation for wrongs committed; and all ask some expression of gratitude for assistance received. So prevalent are these rules across a variety of religious and cultural traditions that C. S. Lewis once called them "platitudes" of practical reason.[11] More important than these rules, however, is the fact that religions also seek to encourage their adherents to adopt "the moral point of view." Sometimes they take separate paths to this goal. Theistic religions commonly approach the matter very differently from mystical traditions. But despite these differences, the goal of impartiality—the ideal of transcending one's own immediate desires to make choices from a social point of view—is widely shared across religious cultures. Promoting this ideal is among the most important contributions religions make to the moral life.

"Why Should I Be Moral?": The Problem of Moral Retribution and the Justification of Morality

That religions devote so much effort to encouraging their adherents to think and act from the moral point of view partly reflects the difficulty of the task. The kind of self-transcendence that morality requires poses a special problem. Not only is it hard to think and act morally (this follows from the fact that every instance of moral decision requires a measure of self-denial), but a far deeper problem arises at the heart of reasoned reflection about morality: in crucial moments of moral choice, it is simply not rationally compelling that one should be moral. Good arguments can be arrayed both for and against moral choice: for and against adopting the moral point of view. In the context of moral decision, therefore, human reason is at odds with itself and finds itself unable to order a dispute in its own house. Ultimately, this specific conceptual problem leads reason into the realm of religious thought and to the second component of the deep structure of religious reasoning: insistence on the reality of moral retribution.

We can better understand this problem and the ways religions respond to it if we keep in mind the precise mental exercise moral reasoning involves. At the moment of moral choice, each of us is required to regard all the interests lying before us in an impartial or, more precisely, "omnipartial" way. We must allow our own interests no pride of place and we must weigh these evenhandedly alongside those of all the other persons we affect. In some instances, reasoning from the moral point of view may lead us to advocate conduct markedly against our own interests. For example, as a small electronics manufacturer, I may know that I could never impartially agree to waste-disposal practices that endanger water supplies and people's health, but I may also know that halting these practices may jeopardize my firm's financial survival. To think and act morally in this case is to risk my entire welfare and the welfare of some people for whom I care very much (members of my family, my employees). Instances of this sort could by multiplied on the individual or group level. Whether it involves only modest loss or, as in some cases, risk to our very lives and happiness, a willingness to face sacrifice is the essence of morality.

Why, then, should we think and reason morally? When our happiness is on the line, why should we be willing to sacrifice it to the common good? These questions invoke many answers, almost all of which have been offered at one time or another in the course of human thinking about this problem. But closely regarded, most of these answers are inadequate, and the issue remains unresolved. What we have here, in effect, is a conflict between two equally important and equally viable exercises of reason. On the one hand, there is what is termed "prudential" reason: self-serving rationality exercised in the name of personal happiness. On the other hand, there is moral reason, which involves the same self-serving rational choice but now exercised from an impartial point of view. The great similarity between these forms of reason and their common practical goal of human welfare makes it easy to confuse them in justificatory arguments. But individuals sincerely involved in moral choice can detect such confusions and recognize the inadequacy of answers based on them.

For example, in trying to answer these questions, we could point to some of the considerations previously mentioned regarding the general rationality of morality. We can say that the willingness to subordinate private pursuits to moral regulation is the condition of happiness: that a society that allowed unchecked egoism would not be a secure or fulfilling place to live. But while morality is generally conducive to personal happiness, can we commend it to persons whose happiness and welfare are jeopardized by the moral alternative? They will not be misled by linguistic confusions; they may concede that morality yields "happiness," but they want to know why they should decisively forfeit their own happiness when it is in peril.

Again, we can ask individuals torn between these two rational standpoints to regard the conflict impartially. Ordinarily, this is how we reason in conflicts. If I am caught between two desires, I try momentarily to distance myself from each of them to make a "more objective" choice. Or if two persons are in dispute, we ask them to distance themselves from the issues and to look at them impartially (often summoning an impartial mediator to help). Impartial reasoning is our most basic instrument for thinking about conflict. But obviously, this crucial instrument is not available in the case we are now considering. Persons caught between prudential and moral reason cannot be encouraged to look at matters impartially, to distance themselves from their private concerns and to look at matters as would another person affected by their choice. For this is the standpoint of moral reason, and the question before us now is why anyone should bother to look at things this way.

In other words, in this acute conflict between moral and prudential reasoning, our very means of rationally ordering disputes breaks down. There is no "third" or higher use of reason that can settle the dispute, and every effort to commend more strenuous impartiality is biased in the direction of moral reason.[12]

As obvious as this is, it is amazing how often philosophers and others have believed that persons could be rationally encouraged to be moral by pointing them to a more impartial assessment of the issues or by commending to them the "general superiority" of moral norms.[13] Certainly moral norms are superior to lesser considerations. Certainly they take priority over private interests. But where does this superiority come from, and why is it so compelling? We might reply, Because one who looked at matters impartially would agree that moral norms should have this priority. From an impartial standpoint, anything less is self-defeating and rationally unacceptable. We cannot live securely in a world where people fail to respect the moral law this way. But, again, can we really commend this kind of impartial assessment to persons who question why they should be impartial at all? The priority of moral norms makes sense to those who are willing to be impartial and moral. But our questions is, Why one should reason this way in the first place if it is seriously disadvantageous to do so?[14]

We may concede that there is no point in trying to commend morality to one who questions its worth. Since moral reasoning is one ultimate form of rational justification, it cannot in itself be justified. Some thinkers admit this and do not see it as a problem. They argue that one either is or is not moral. The matter rests on choice and nothing more can be said.[15] Presumably, they believe this is a problem only in relation to those who have chosen to be immoral, since these people cannot rationally be persuaded to alter their views. But this oversimplifies the difficulty. For even those who wish to be moral face a dilemma. On the one hand, they know there are good reasons for giving priority to morality, but, on the other hand, they are pulled by powerful prudential considerations in the form of all their natural desires, including the vital concerns they have for particular persons (family or friends). How can those torn by these conflicting attractions adopt the moral point of view without feeling that they are being in some ways irrational, that they are running counter to important dictates of prudential reason that ought to be respected? Can they silence this other voice of reason that counsels self-regard?

The moral life thus poses a painful dilemma for any rational being. On the one hand, moral reason does not speak with absolute authority.

One can be rational and immoral, even if being so involves neglecting an important dimension of reason: morality. Or one can be moral, but even the most morally committed individual must know that this can involve violating another dimension of human reason: prudence. How then is it possible to act rationally at all without doing violence to some facet of our rational life?

Religious belief enters at precisely this point. We can think of religion as the effort by a rational being to act in a fully rational manner. I put matters this way because religion is often associated with the subjective, emotional side of human life, something apart from or opposed to reason. Of course religion has nonrational aspects as well. Any system of religious belief, as a full expression of human capacities, will relate to the affective and even aesthetic dimensions of human experience. But religion is also, and perhaps centrally, a rational enterprise. It is human reason's effort to resolve its own internal dispute and to make possible coherent rational choice.

How is this done? Obviously not be justifying immoral doing and willing. Human reason can never tolerate a subordination of the moral law, since this law, or method of reasoning, is a firm and essential part of our rational structure and is the condition of social life. Neither can reason deny the apparent discrepancy between morality and prudence. Moral commitment appears to entail self-sacrifice. But what a rational person can affirm, and what religions insist, is that this discrepancy is only apparent, not ultimate. Although the individual may appear to run terrible risks in choosing to be moral, these risks are not the last word on the matter. Beyond sacrifice lie possibilities of fulfillment directly proportional to moral effort. Moral retribution is certain. The righteous are rewarded. Those who risk their lives shall gain them.

In the chapter ahead, we will look at some of the subtle and profound ways that religions sustain this claim. Those of us raised in a Western culture are familiar with retributive ideas like heaven, hell, or a future "Kingdom of God," where moral judgment is supposed to take place. These ideas are so firmly embedded in our religious consciousness that we imagine them to be the only ways of thinking about the problem. Nevertheless, religious thought shows surprising creativity and plasticity. The anthropologist Claude Lévi-Strauss maintains that when confronting cultural possibilities, the human mind and human cultures often proceed by filling available "conceptual" boxes on the map of logical possibilities.[16] This is true as well where doctrines of retribution are concerned. In the chapters ahead we will see just a few of the different possibilities that religious traditions have developed.

Overall, however, it is less important to explore all possible retributive concepts than to be aware of the underlying logic, the deep structure, that produces them.

I have stressed how this aspect of religious reasoning arises out of a conflict within reason between reason's prudential and moral employments. This conflict, I have said, points the way to a set of religious beliefs supporting the possibility of ultimate moral retribution. The discovery of these foundational ideas is not new. More than two centuries ago, Kant, pursuing a line of thought revealed by his own insightful analysis of the moral law, developed these ideas into what is sometimes called the "moral proof" of God's existence.[17] In fact, this is an unfortunate appellation (even if Kant sometimes used it himself). Kant understood that he was not proving anything to one who rejected belief in God or a commitment to morality. Rather, he was developing the rational assumptions of those who had already made a commitment to morality and sought to justify this rationally to themselves and to others. Religious beliefs associated with this issue, therefore, are best thought of as *expressions* of a prior commitment to rationality and morality, as the concrete articulations of a series of deep valuations, especially the valuation of rationality itself. This means that religion is an important part of what it means to be a rational human being. It also suggests why religion is a universal and abiding aspect of human experience.

Sin and Its Transcendence

The third element in the deep structure of religious reasoning comes to our attention in two ways. In the course of religious development, this element usually makes its appearance after the breakdown of earlier retributive hopes. It comes to the fore as the effort to make salvation possible in a world where earlier moral confidences have been shaken. But while historically manifested this way, this element also has a place within the basic structure of moral and religious reason. It stems from a genuine rational difficulty that historical religious experience only emphasizes and makes clear.

We can easily trace the appearance of this element in the history of religious traditions, especially those traditions whose course of development is recorded in writing. In the earliest stages of development, religions characteristically affirm the reality of retribution in concrete, this-worldly terms: righteousness finds its reward in this world. The hope of upright persons is to end life surrounded by wealth and progeny, to "come to [the] grave in ripe old age" (Job 5.26). Though the wicked may flourish for a time and the righteous may suffer, there is confidence that more just rewards will soon follow. Religion itself, therefore, reinforces the conviction that the world is ruled by a moral geometry.

Such hopes are usually dashed by experience. No matter how upright the individual or community may be, no matter how attentive individuals are to their religious and moral duties, they suffer. Within the logic of religious belief, this situation demands explanation. Suffering may be viewed as a "trial" or "test" to which the righteous are put before their final, eschatological reward, but another explanation always at hand is that suffering results from sin. Indeed, the more a tradition has insisted on the firmness of retribution, the more it has emphasized the "moral geometry," the more likely it is to equate suffering with sin. Within this thought-world, therefore, the character of the moral and religious problem is changed. No longer is the question simply how the righteous can receive their due reward. Sin is now brought into focus, and because it is seen under penetrating gaze to involve even the most committed persons, the question becomes how one can transcend the penalties attached to wrongdoing, how one who necessarily sins can ever attain salvation. This means that as religious thought develops, the insistence on retribution, though never relinquished, becomes supplemented by teachings that point the way beyond the world of moral reward and punishment. In theistic religious systems, themes of grace and divine mercy appear. In nontheistic systems the hope becomes one of "liberation" to a state beyond our distinctions of good and evil.[18]

But the historical fact of persistent suffering is not the only thing driving this development. At the level of reasoned reflection, this response to experience is supported by close analysis of the moral life. A sense of the omnipresence and inescapability of sin is a concomitant to intense moral striving, and historical religious experience only makes this clear.

We can better understand this if we recall what we said in considering the question of why one should be moral: No one is rationally compelled to be moral. Morality ultimately rests on free choice. This is true not only because moral reason presumes our freedom from physical or psychological determination and our ability to make impartially reasoned choices[19] but, more important, because we are not rationally required to reason morally. Between the two rational perspectives of morality and prudence, we stand utterly undetermined. This truth is picked up by traditional Western religious literature in the observation that human wrongdoing, when it occurs, is not merely the result of a lost struggle between reason and desire, but involves the full complicity of reason.[20] And it has been given expression in our day in the existentialists' emphasis on the primacy of human freedom over reason in matters of moral choice.[21]

Our radical freedom to choose morality or immorality is not in itself the source of an awareness of sin. To this must be added an understanding of the rigor and ideality of the moral demand. To regard ourselves as upright persons, moral reasoning requires that we give unwavering and unexceptional priority to moral willing. Morality is universal not only in the sense that it applies to all persons but also in the sense that it applies to every instant of choosing. If I wish to be moral, I must make a commitment to pass every proposed future action before the bar of impartial reason and to act only in ways that can meet this test. Furthermore, if I am to judge myself to be a moral person, I must be reasonably confident of my own commitment to think and act this way. To doubt the sincerity of my commitment is to call into question my moral worth.

Superficially regarded, this demand may seem too rigorous. Certainly, persons who choose *never* to test their maxims by the method of moral decision cannot be regarded as morally upright. But is it not possible, now and then, to fail to be obedient to the moral law and still be a "good" person? Furthermore, cannot individuals, facing their future realistically, choose obedience to the moral law in *most instances,* while reserving the right on desperate occasions to protect their own interests? Can we not be *mostly* good? And are not mostly good persons better than those who choose never to be good at all?

Once again, I am indebted to Kant for a reply to these difficult questions. Addressing this problem in his *Religion within the Limits of Reason Alone,*[22] Kant considers the possibility that there might be an intermediate position between unwavering obedience to the moral law and systematic disobedience. But he asks us to consider the governing conditions of this intermediate position. If pure self-regard is the principle motive of the amoral or immoral person, what is my motive if I choose to allow myself *occasionally* to violate the moral law? Presumably, I say to myself "I will reason impartially and morally unless it proves seriously disadvantageous for me to do so." But if this is how I think, is it not true that self-interest is really my highest motivating consideration? It serves, after all, as the final reference in each instance of moral choice and it resolves every serious clash between morality and self-interest.

True, one who reserves the right *occasionally* to violate the moral law may have a higher threshold of respect for morality's demands than the crassly immoral person, but this individual still gives self-interest a decisive role in choice. Furthermore, since those who reason this way reserve the right to determine how great the inconvenience must be before they abandon morality, there is no guarantee they will be morally better in practice than amoral or immoral persons, who may be led to act morally in most instances out of enlightened self-interest. In both analytical and in genuinely human terms, in other words, Kant's discussion leads us to see that there really is no intermediate position between moral and immoral willing.[23]

These two insights, the radical nature of the moral demand and our absolutely undetermined freedom to be moral or immoral, work together like jaws of a vise to produce the specific problem that gives rise to religious reasoning's third component: an awareness of the depth and intractability of human wrongdoing, and the need for suspension of moral self-judgment. In moments of honest moral insight, we know ourselves to be called to total moral commitment, but the awareness of our rational freedom to choose otherwise and the powerful attractions of self-interest work together to produce a sense that we may not be up to this demand. As a result, we can never confidently assert our own moral goodness. Furthermore, the fact that in past moments of free choice each of us has invariably neglected the priority due the moral law must convince us that wrongdoing is a recurrent possibility for our willing. Remorse for these past defections from morality thus combines with an honest estimate of their meaning for our future conduct to produce a pervasive sense of moral inadequacy. True, a shallow conscience can evade these facts. We can deny the meaning of our past, relax the rigorous demand of the moral law and perhaps conclude that we are of estimable character. But anyone with a sensitive conscience who is rightly disturbed by past failures must be driven to an awareness of the vast difference between the kind of willing that morality demands and the kind that he or she is able to offer. Indeed, the more sensitive our consciences are on this matter and the more we perceive the possibly deep corruption at the core of our being, the more likely we are to regard ourselves as among the worst of persons, hypocrites who conceal inner selfishness by an outward display of good conduct. We meet here, then, another moral paradox and one that is frequently emphasized by religious traditions: those who think themselves good rarely are. The best persons, the relative saints in our midst, are those who know themselves to be sinners.[24]

Granting this difficulty in the moral life, how can it be overcome? How can morally committed individuals surmount their own sense of moral inadequacy and their corresponding conviction that within a world of strict retribution, a world in which they already have chosen to believe, they merit only condemnation or punishment? If our worth were exclusively measured in terms of the moral judgments we must make about ourselves, there would be no escape from this terrible dilemma. We might carry on with a sense of futility, convinced that our moral striving will only provide further opportunities for wrongdoing, or we might cease trying altogether and expose ourselves directly to the charge of abandoning moral responsibility. Either way, we stand perilously close to moral paralysis and despair.

Here again religious beliefs enter to play a key role in facilitating moral commitment. Just as a belief in retribution eases the apparently insuperable opposition between prudence and morality, so religious beliefs can make it rational to renew our dedication to moral effort even as we realize the difficulty of this task and the failures that loom before us. In their general form the relevant beliefs involve the conviction that our self-imposed moral judgments are not a complete measure of our worth, nor the final determinant of our personal destiny. Ordinarily, these self-judgments must be authoritative for us. But in facing the seeming futility of efforts to attain moral worth, rational persons may allowably entertain the possible reality of a source or standard of judgment that somehow takes into account our moral frailties and confession of sinfulness. This source of judgment is "beyond morality" in the sense that it is not constrained to judge us as we must judge ourselves. It is also "beyond morality" in the positive sense of serving as the ultimate ground of the standards and of the retributive order we accept. The confidence that this supremely authoritative reality governs the evaluative and retributive process frees us from unsparing self-condemnation and despair over the repeated failures of our moral efforts, and it helps us rationally to renew our commitment to the moral conduct our reason otherwise demands.

Religiously expressed, this idea assumes some of the forms mentioned in connection with religious traditions' efforts to confront the fact of sin. In theistic traditions, this idea underlies the important themes of divine grace and forgiveness. Although God upholds morality, he is ultimately not constrained by it, and he is able to suspend punishment and redeem sinners. In some Asian traditions, where retribution is effected by the natural-moral law of karma, we find the belief that the highest levels of spritiual attainment transcend the world of karmic retribution altogether. The Chāndogya Upanishad characteristically describes this as a state "beyond merit and demerit," where evil deeds do not "stain" but depart from the self "even as water rolls off the smooth leaves of the lotus."[25]

These themes admittedly pose some of the most acute problems for religious thought. Superficially regarded, they appear to contradict the very insistence on morality and moral retribution that religions sustain. But this is usually not the case. While sophisticated religious thought permits a subordination of our rational moral standards and a suspension of just retribution, it does so within the framework of a more comprehensive moral vision. For example, although divine forgiveness appears to run counter to justice, this is usually so only with respect to the punitive aspects of the moral code. However, because God is not regarded as motivated by selfishness or weakness, his suspension of punishment is not a morally impermissible evasion of responsibility, as it would be for us, but is an expression of the "higher justice" that seeks to make possible others' moral renewal. Similarly, traditions that point to a domain beyond good and evil do not devalue the lower realm of moral causality ruled by karma. They view it as a necessary preparatory stage for those who aspire to liberation, and they usually insist that the realm beyond karma is open only to those who have first conquered selfish thoughts and impulses. In both theistic and nontheistic traditions, in other words, the higher reality "beyond morality" serves to fulfill and complete, not undermine, moral striving.

Be this as it may, whenever religions develop these themes, they also tend to spawn antinomian, "lawless" responses to their teaching, because some persons are mistakenly led to believe that the ultimate goal of the religion really lies beyond morality in a life free of moral restraints. These conclusions are natural, but as soon as they are voiced, they are repudiated by religious thinkers. Some of St. Paul's less acute readers may have thought that his diatribe against "the Law" and his emphasis on grace meant that Christians were freed from the requirement of moral obedience, that it was allowable "to continue in sin that grace may abound" (Rom. 6.1). But Paul responded to these conclusions with a horrified "By no means!" Similarly, some Hindus and some followers of the Buddha took the teaching that the spiritual adept is "beyond morality" to the antinomian conclusions of Tantra. But these were usually regarded as heretical responses. Against this, it was asserted that genuine enlightenment presupposed and culminated in a life of pure moral commitment, of genuine egolessness and sincere compassion.

The paradoxical aspect of this third element of religious reasoning, this seeming subordination of morality and suspension of retribution side by side with impassioned moral exhortations, illustrates how important it is to approach religious thought with an understanding of the deep structure beneath it. In some ways, the teachings of a religious tradition are like an ocean archipelago. Protruding above the surface, they appear to be a series of disconnected ideas with little relationship to one another. Seeing these surface atolls of thought as part of a deeper structure, however, makes their interconnections and logic more apparent, and allows us to identify and explain the presence of similar surface patterns in a wide variety of traditions.

One further illustration may help make this last point clearer. Paralleling these religious affirmations of both retribution and the suspension of retribution is a related tendency in religious thinking to insist on the reward for righteousness while urging believers not to strive for reward. In the Christian Gospels, for example, we find a puzzling alternation between the encouragement of heedless, self-sacrificial love for others and blatant promises of blessing for the righteous. Rabbinic teaching shows the same alternation, on the one hand admonishing the pious not to be like servants "who serve the master on condition of receiving a gift" while, on the other hand, encouraging them never to doubt the reality of reward.[26] In the Eastern traditions, the stress on the importance of liberation from samsara, the world of karmically conditioned becoming, goes hand in hand with an insistence on the certainty of karmic retribution for those within samsara.

These alternations have sometimes puzzled students of comparative religion and comparative ethics. Is Christian ethics "teleological" and "eudaemonistic" in the sense that it is oriented to the "goal" *(telos)* of happiness *(eudaimonia)* or is it "deontological" in its stress on duty and obligation without regard to any welfare produced?[27] Is it an ethic of self-sacrifice or of reward? The answer, of course, is that it is all these things. Reflecting the tense underlying structure of religious reasoning, Christian thinking stresses both the primacy of moral obligation *and* the benefits produced by moral conduct. It commands selflessness but promises ultimate happiness for self and others. To further complicate matters, Christian thinking (along with that of other major traditions) takes pains to see that the rewards it insists on do not become dominating considerations in the spiritual life. This reflects our deep moral conviction that truly righteous persons should aim at righteousness itself, not the praise or benefits it may reap.[28] Indeed, this issue constitutes a further reason (beyond that produced by the problem of despair over sin) why those at the highest reaches of spirituality are said to go beyond considerations of merit or demerit. In the rarified air of high spirituality, one has no regard for one's own moral worth and any reward this may produce, yet one acts compassionately on others' behalf. Naturally, all this must seem confusing and contradictory to the logically inclined beginning student of religion.[29] But when viewed in terms of the basic tensions within the moral life and the "deep structure" these produce, religious thinking appears coherent, rational, and morally sensitive.

It is one thing to say that religions are morally inclined at their deepest levels and another thing to demonstrate, tradition by tradition, belief by belief, that this is true. Counterevidence is easy to produce: the mutual hostility between traditions, the bouts of intolerance and holy war, the excesses of spirituality that can lead to worldly indifference and neglect.[30] Some of these excesses stem from religions' complexity, the fact that they seek to lead their adherents through a demanding program of moral perfection whose content and meaning is not always clear even to the better minds within the tradition. Other excesses stem from believers' convictions that their tradition alone guarantees the prospect of human righteousness. This can lead to the misguided conviction that these beliefs must be imposed on others. In the intensely moral domain of religious life, the old truism holds that the corruption of the best is sometimes the worst. Yet these difficulties and excesses should not dissuade us from the task of trying to discern and understand the deep moral intentionality underlying religious thought.

The chapters ahead exemplify this task. Across a variety of traditions widely separated in space and time, we will be looking at the ways in which these three elements of the deep structure find expression. In forms that may sometimes surprise us, and by paths that are often strikingly different, we shall see that religions strive in their teachings and in their practices to lead their adherents to a spontaneous and selfless but reasonable commitment to the moral point of view.

2

Religion and Morality in
the African Traditional Setting

African traditional religion poses a major challenge to the claim that religion has a "deep structure" arising from moral and religious reason. This claim makes sense in the context of Western religious culture, where we find ethical monotheisms shaped by moral concerns. But why believe that this structure will also be found in traditions arising in other cultural settings? In the radically different world of African traditional religions, for example, these rationalist claims appear doubtful. Major features of religious life in Africa, including spirit mediumship and ancestor cults, initially seem remote from moral concerns, while other features, like witchcraft practices and accusations, seem opposed to morality.

In this chapter I want to take up this challenge by showing that despite initial appearances, these religious traditions essentially conform to the universal deep structure of religious reason. In Africa, the religious imagination has admittedly struck out on paths of its own, rendering the surface appearance of religion sometimes very different from Western belief. While African traditional religion shows some resemblances to Western religious ideas, these are often superficial, and closer examination reveals that the contrasts between African and Western ways of thinking are greater than the similarities. Nevertheless, despite these differences, I hope to suggest that in their own ways, African traditional religions conform to the deep tripartite structure of religious reason.

The differences between African traditional religions and Western ethical monotheisms can be illustrated by looking at the role of God in various African systems of thought. Many African traditional religions make reference to a high god responsible for the creation or maintenance of the world.[1] In some instances, this creator god or supreme spirit is also considered to be a morally good, omniscient being who cares about humans.[2] But even where this is true, the high god in Africa is usually distanced from human affairs. The Lugbara, for example, as they acknowledge God's goodness, also affirm that he is "far away." He does not punish their sins and there is no moral content in their relationship with him.[3] Much the same could be said of Mbori, the supreme being of the Azande,[4] Nhialic (Divinity) among the Dinka,[5] Tamuno of the Kalabari,[6] Mwari of the Zezuru,[7] Ruhanga of the Ankole[8] and many other high creator divinities in Africa. As commentators have noted, even when he is considered benign, the high god in Africa is morally otiose, having little direct retributive relationship with humankind.[9]

The high god is also sometimes cast in a morally unfavorable light. When God enters human affairs it is often to cause evils. In many African cultures, for example, epidemics, death by wild animals, lightning, and other random events that defy moral explanation are commonly attributed to God.[10] Consequently, a spirit of fatalism marks popular attitudes or mythic and ritual references to the supreme deity. Among the Katanga peoples, God is alluded to as "the father creator who creates and uncreates."[11] A Dinka hymn vividly expresses this same attitude:

> Spring rain in a dry spell, strikes the ants on the head with a
>   club
> And the ants say: My father has seen
> And they do not know whether he helps people
> And they do not know whether he injures people.[12]

As in this hymn, where God is not regarded as a source of support or as a guarantor of moral retribution, the common wish of many African peoples is that the distant God will remain distant. Even the Nuer, whose attitude to the high god among African peoples probably most closely resembles that of Western theists, make repeated and prayerful appeal that God should turn away and not trouble them.[13]

If the idea of God as an active moral presence seems generally lacking in African religion, so too are many of our familiar ideas of religious reward and punishment. Heaven and hell are largely alien notions in non-Islamic Africa. There is no messianic hope, no apocalyptic expectation that God will step in to right wrongs or punish wickedness.[14] It is true that almost all African traditional religions affirm the continuation of life after death. When a person dies, he or she is thought to join a spirit world of ghosts and ancestors and to continue an existence in many ways similar to life before death. But this belief involves no hope for improved existence or for ultimate reward and punishment. A person's moral depravity or moral excellence do not generally count in the beyond, and whatever penalties or rewards these bring have little bearing on life after death.[15]

Taken together, this relative moral indifference of the supreme creator god and the absence of a retributive eschatology have led some observers to conclude that ethical concerns are not central to African traditional religion. Pointing to these absent features in Nupe religion, for example, Siegfried F. Nadel describes the Nupe as living in a world "devoid of moral purpose," and he characterizes their religion as "noncommital and fundamentally amoral."[16] The same conclusion would apply to most African religions if the standard Western religious expressions of moral concern were necessary features of any morally intentioned religion. But morality and religion are not so narrowly related as this. The basic requirements of moral and religious reason can be expressed in ways other than those to which Westerners are accustomed. In what follows I want to show not only that the "deep structure" I have outlined undergirds African religious life but, even more, that Africans live in a morally saturated religious universe. Theirs is a world where all significant interpersonal relationships, including important relationships between humans and spiritual beings, have moral content and are governed by moral considerations. Approached at the right level, African traditional religion can be seen to be powerfully shaped by moral concerns.

The Retributive Order

The important qualification here is that to be understood properly, African religion must be approached *at the right level*. True, the high god is often regarded as morally distant. But this is not evidence for a lack of religious-moral concern so much as a reflection of the belief that God is not the main spiritual and moral agency affecting human life. In Africa, God is distanced from moral affairs because moral retribution and the maintenance of essential norms is ordinarily performed by agents of much lower standing: by spirits of various sorts, by ghosts, and even by human practitioners of spiritual arts. This morally vital work, moreover, is carried out amidst the affairs of living members of the community, and reward and punishment, though mediated by spiritual entities, almost always occur within this life. Thus, while the specific agencies or circumstances of retribution may be unfamiliar to us, the insistence on moral norms and their religious establishment and support are essential to African religion.

To speak of "religion" in Africa is to run a terrible risk of overgeneralization. Because religious culture is so closely tied to tribal identity, Africa has almost as many "religions" as it has tribal groups, and with roughly two thousand different groups, sub-Saharan Africa can offer examples of almost any religious tendency.[17] But, despite this diversity, there are some perspectives widely shared by many African religions. In particular, I would signal two beliefs found almost everywhere in traditional Africa that are crucial to understanding the place of moral reasoning in African religious life. The first is the conviction that the world is populated by a whole array of spiritual entities with various degrees of power and authority, whose presence and conduct impinge on human life. As Mbiti observes, "for African peoples, this is a religious universe." An invisible cosmos of spiritual beings presses in hard upon them, and African peoples 'see' this universe when they look at or feel the visible and tangible world.[18] The second key idea is that human misfortune and suffering are always to be explained in terms of this spiritual world. Misfortune in Africa is never merely a "natural" occurrence in our sense of the word: people do not fall ill, suffer hardship, poverty, or famine, or die just because they have been unlucky or have fallen victim to impersonal natural forces. In Africa, every significant misfortune is caused by a spiritual entity whose malevolence is motivated in some morally understandable way. When this world runs its normal, satisfying course, Africans may or may not engage in religious activity. But if this course is disturbed, as it invariably is, Africans seek an explanation in terms of their morally informed spiritual beliefs.

To say misfortune has a spiritual and moral explanation, however, only begins the characterization of African religious belief. Beyond this, it is important to divide morally understandable agents into two different sorts. One group includes those beings who act legitimately as retributors of moral wrongdoing. While nature spirits and some errant ghosts fit into this category, it chiefly embraces lineage and tribal spirits: the ghosts of parents, grandparents, ancestors, and hero founders of the kin group. These spirits are generally regarded as righteous and concerned with righteousness, and they act as retributive agencies to punish moral wrongdoing among living descendants or community members. A second group of spiritual beings responsible for misfortune are not essentially motivated by legitimate moral concerns. We might term them "malicious" spirits (or spiritual beings). They include some nature spirits, some alien ghosts, but also living malevolent beings with spiritual powers, especially witches and sorcerers. Although these individuals are often not motivated by valid moral indignation, they play an important retributive role and the suffering they cause is sometimes explainable in straightforward terms as something deserved. When suffering is not deserved, these agencies may still be responsible, but their interference in human life elicits a different moral explanation: in these instances misfortune finds its cause in sheer ill will, in the attitudes or conduct of morally reprehensible persons. Either way, whether suffering is caused by lineage spirits or witches, African peoples cannot understand their experience without reference to religious beliefs wholly permeated by vivid judgments of right and wrong.

The moral implications of ancestor cults in the African setting are clear. Once we make the assumption that moral retribution can be effected by independent spiritual beings below the level of a high god, there is little in African relationships with the ancestors to surprise us. We have here what some have termed "morality cults,"[19] tightly knit religious retributive systems in which moral goodness is rewarded, and badness punished. Some common African ideas of personal destiny form a background to understanding these cults. In most African traditional societies, moral authority and social status are a function of age. As an individual (usually the male) matures, he is regarded as more capable of exercising authority for upholding lineage and group values and also more responsible for doing so.[20] This increase in authority and responsibility does not stop at the grave. When a person dies, he passes on to existence as an ancestor who is still responsible for, and concerned with, the conduct of living relations. At death, the individual becomes somewhat idealized: his flaws and faults are forgotton and he is elevated to the status of a moral paradigm whose concern with proper conduct among his relatives is correspondingly enhanced. As Fry points out, ancestor spirits are different from the personalities of living men, and they have special moral authority:

Devoid of essentially personal characteristics they represent the essence of what might be called structural personality. Their significance lies in their genealogical positions and the rights and duties deriving from them. They represent ideal men who, relieved of personal peculiarities and petty jealousies, are able to act as moral and just guardians of pure morality. . . . The ancestors are on the side of group values and openness; free from purely personal interests they stand opposed to the machinations of those who would go against collective ideals and ignore their social obligations for reasons of jealousy or personal advancement.[21]

Although the ancestors are sometimes believed to derive their authority from the high god, they usually act on their own, motivated by moral attitudes and values they previously held as living elders in the community. They represent what amounts to the impartial "moral point of view" in this context and uphold right conduct by punishing moral violations. In some respects, they are merely self-serving; like living elders, ancestors expect service and when they are neglected, they become irate. If a child falls ill, a woman miscarries, or someone suddenly dies, the first instinct of African groups is to prepare a sacrifice for the ancestors. Sometimes, they have been deliberately neglected for a time on the assumption that they are content (as with living persons, it is not always clear just how much the ancestors want). But when misfortune strikes, it is readily attributed to the ancestors' anger at neglect. At these moments, sacrifice—the offering of valued animals or agricultural products—can help repair the wrong. It does so, principally, as a demonstration of selfless devotion to the ancestors' welfare, and as we might expect, serious misfortune demands the very best offerings to set it right.[22] Once propitiated, the ancestors may become benevolently active or even seek help from higher spirits for their living kin.[23] But this is usually more than is required. At a minimum, it is hoped they will feel properly treated and will choose to stay out of the lives of their descendants and cause no further trouble.

African beliefs thus preserve the idea of reciprocity between the living and the dead. Dependence is two-way: the dead need continued respect and support from the living and the living need at least benign neutrality from the dead. This may seem to be a minimally moral relationship, a kind of egoism on one side and fearful propitiation on the other. But this assessment ignores the profound role that respect for age and for the fulfillment of lineage and familial duties plays in the traditional setting. To say that morality virtually equals lineage duties would not overstate the matter. In many African cultures, relationships beyond the local group are tense and filled with mistrust or open conflict. The localized group thus defines the universe of moral relationships, the setting where principle, rather than force, prevails.[24] But within these units, social responsibilities and responsibilities to one's kin are almost the same thing. Since many members of the group are related, lineage obligations comprise most of one's moral duties. In addition, the respect for elders embodied in the attitudes toward ancestors virtually sums up the dispositions required for harmonious and successful group life in this setting. As Middleton observes, "for the Lugbara most of the social interaction of any . . . individual or family is with kinsmen, and these are essentially relations of authority, for which there are more formal sanctions. The network of authority relations must be sustained if Lugbara society is to continue and its members to live in amity and peace."[25] Generous consideration for the needs of ancestors, therefore, is not just a narrowly self-protective measure, nor even a morally understandable expression of gratitude for their past services (although it is also both of these). Above all, it is an affirmation of the essential values of self-discipline and respect for authority that form the moral basis for society as a whole.

This powerful moral role of the ancestors is illustrated by the fact that they do not inflict trouble only when they are personally neglected. They also enforce lineage and social rules. Forms of conduct that disturb the group's peace—enmity, quarreling, incest, failure of specific kinship duties like the support of orphans or the proper distribution of bridewealth—can be severely punished by the ancestors through the infliction of sickness or death.

This process of maintaining group unity and solidarity begins even before the elder crosses to the spirit world. During life, a lineage head may "invoke the ghosts" against refractory kinsmen. It is a sign of an elder's genuine moral integrity that he exercises impartiality in doing this and will not hesitate to call for spirit punishment against his own sons if they break lineage rules or defy authority.[26] On his deathbed, an elder may openly curse kinsmen who have wronged him or who he believes have violated expected standards of conduct. Alternatively, he may remain silent and die with resentment in his heart. Curses or recriminations of this sort are greatly feared and are believed likely to cause a run of misfortune unless the wrong that occasioned them is righted. The morally retributive character of these curses or recriminations is illustrated by the fact that anger or a sense of having been offended are not enough to ensure their efficacy. In addition, the aggrieved party must have justice on his side. One who knows himself to be wrongly accused or blamed need not fear any purely malicious curses. But an individual whose conduct has occasioned legitimate resentment fears trouble even if the public is ignorant of his deed. To avert catastrophe, he must repent and try to make reparation to the individual he has wronged. Should an angered kinsman die before this is done, he is likely to become a pursuing spirit, and misfortune may then be unavoidable.[27]

The importance of ancestor spirits in defending group values is further illustrated by the role these spirits play in morally significant ceremonies and rituals. Sacrificial rituals may be occasioned by the occurrence of any misfortune, or they may be necessitated specifically by feuding or quarreling within the lineage that brings misfortune in its train. During these rites, the ancestors' spiritual presence acts as a general force for group harmony and for active efforts at reconciliation. It is commonly believed, for example, that as spiritual beings, the ancestors communicate with one another, are omniscient and able to penetrate the hearts and minds of the living.[28] As a result, any concealed anger or hatred among kin renders rites of propitiation ineffective. This means that even ordinary rites aimed at eliminating misfortune have the effect of reinforcing the group's unity. But ceremonies specifically occasioned by feuding among kin also have the sterner requirement that outstanding wrongs be righted and that relatives "cool" their angry hearts.[29] In Africa as elsewhere, of course, practice does not always follow theory. Feuding parties often find it difficult to put aside animosities, and in the presence of too much sacrificial beer, a ceremony of reconciliation may turn into a brawl.[30] But even when this happens, there is a strong sense that such behavior is likely to occasion new and more grievous misfortunes.

The spirits play a similar role in vital ceremonies of oath taking and truth determination. False avowal and perjury are in some ways prototypical moral wrongs. They pit the self in its narrowest and most egoistic inclinations against society's necessary interest in veracity. Moreover, whereas all wrongs begin in the deepest recesses of the heart but usually express themselves in public deeds, lies can remain at the inward level and evade ordinary means of detection. In a religious and moral framework, therefore, it is to be expected that these wrongs will be a special province and concern of spiritual retributive agencies who transcend the limits of sensory experience. This is clearly the case in traditional Africa. A variety of ceremonies exist to ensure the truthfulness of factual declarations and the bindingness of oaths. These may involve formal and ritualized avowals before spirits who are believed to grow wrathful if unspoken reservations or falsehood accompany a public declaration. Or they may involve various ordeal ceremonies. Among the Dinka, ashes are placed on the tongue or dissolved in water and drunk during a truth-determination ceremony. It is believed that the individual who lies immediately after ingesting these ashes will fall seriously ill.[31] Among the Azande, a potion that is occasionally lethal may be used in an ordeal to determine whether an individual is guilty of concealing adultery or homicide.[32] As one might imagine, even the threatened use of these poisons serves as an incentive to honesty, but their efficacy in any employment rests on the belief that their effects reveal judgments by the spriits, whose knowledge of the heart is complete and whose power to punish is certain.

Africans thus live in a world populated by spirits who uphold the moral order. Foremost among these are the ancestral and lineage spirits I have been discussing, who operate in specific social contexts, where their will is experienced through misfortune. Other spirits exist who relate directly to individuals outside these contexts. It is commonly believed throughout Africa, for example, that a murder victim's spirit will pursue the killer and will not relent until the malefactor confesses and makes reparation to the deceased's family. Finally, there are some spirits (whether belonging to ancestors or others) who do not act directly but rely on human agents to effect their will. These spirits underlie the power of spirit mediums and some other spiritual practitioners.[33]

Since the medium is an important actor in this retributive setting, a word about him is in order. In societies where he exists, the medium's role is to determine the cause of illness or misfortune. He (less frequently, she) is able to do this by directly communing with the spirits. While in a state of possession, the medium actually becomes the spirit personality of the ancestor or lineage hero whose will he conveys. Much has been written on the psychology and sociology of spirit-mediumship,[34] but what is intriguing in this context is the medium's moral role within the spiritual retributive system. Simply stated, the spirit medium is the human spokesman for the spirits' righteous will. In a state of possession, the medium is believed no longer to be himself; he is the voice of the spirit he represents. This engenders considerable respect for his judgments and makes it possible, as Garbett observes, for the medium to serve as a popular moral teacher and preacher:

> During the course of the public seance the medium, speaking as the spirit-guardian, will urge the congregation to uphold the laws

of the forefathers. He tells them to refrain from sorcery and from committing incest and adultery. Anger with one's neighbours leads to sorcery, which enrages the spirit-guardian, and possibly to homicide, which in addition pollutes the earth. He may also order the congregation to keep the twice-monthly rest days set aside in honour of the spirit.[35]

This authority of the medium in a state of possession also makes him a suitable judge and arbiter when the community faces sharp disagreements and resulting misfortune. The moral explanation for suffering and the remedies the medium offers are not regarded as his but are believed to express the will of the omniscient spirits who represent an unassailably impartial moral judiciary. This "objectivity" of judgment renders the medium's edicts morally and psychologically acceptable. As Field observes, a suppliant to the spirit medium "will accept . . . the same advice that he has rejected from his parents or his wife and he suffers thereby no loss of face."[36] By translating the medium out of his individuality and subjectivity, possession allows him to approximate the status of an impartial moral judge. In view of this role, we might expect that the spirit medium, besides considerable personal charm, psychological discernment, and a sense of theater, also possesses keen moral insight. Observers commonly report that this is so: the success of a spirit medium rests very much on his ability to sense the rights and wrongs of an issue and to articulate latent communal moral judgments.[37] While the phrase *vox populi vox dei* puts matters somewhat incorrectly, since the talented medium does not just vocalize majority sentiment but is able to identify, direct, and articulate the sometimes inchoate moral feelings of a group, it is true that a successful medium serves as the voice of collective moral judgments expressed as the spirits' will. He is thus able to bring moral pressure to bear on a recalcitrant individual without exposing himself or others to the charge of partisanship. Obviously, a medium who repeatedly defies valid group moral sentiments or who imposes wild and idiosyncratic interpretations on events will find himself without a following.[38]

The important moral role of the spirit medium is further reflected in the requirement of moral probity imposed upon him.[39] The common belief is that spirits choose a medium in the first place because of his moral integrity. To retain the spirits' esteem (and their power), the medium must avoid corruption and conduct himself properly. While a medium may receive payment or gifts for his services, the use of these for excessive private gain or for ostentation is frowned upon. In certain groups, theory has it that gifts for successful mediumship belong to the spirit, not the medium. This means that payments are most properly used for ritual paraphernalia or to support destitute clients of the spirit's cult.[40] Similarly, the medium is discouraged from using his powers and resources to benefit close kin. Even the gift of mediumship is not ordinarily regarded as passed along to one's offspring.[41] Because mediumship is a "charismatic" office bestowed by spirits on a morally and psychologically suitable person, efforts to benefit close relations by establishing hereditary claims are viewed with disfavor.

In many ways, the spirit medium is a subordinate agent within the larger retributive order. He is believed to derive his abilities wholly from the spirits and cannot sway their will or enforce the dictates of justice by himself. As an individual, he is regarded as unimportant. But when he is possessed or otherwise under the spirits' influence, he becomes a sacred and morally authoritative personality. His voice and actions connect the community with those moral and spiritual entities who help shape human destiny. In this sense, the spirit medium is the physical embodiment of the religious retributive order in which Africans stand.

Witchcraft and Retribution

Earlier, I said that when misfortune strikes, traditional Africans immediately seek a spiritual and moral explanation. This may lead them to scrutinize their own conduct or the behavior of their kin for flaws. But it may also lead them to wonder whether or not they are innocent victims of the ill will or maliciousness of some other spiritually empowered being: a witch or a sorcerer. If ancestor spirits represent the archetype of moral conduct in the African setting, witches and sorcerers represent the antitype. They are the quintessence of immorality, and their ill will serves to explain nearly all individual suffering not immediately understandable as something deserved.[42] Since few people are initially inclined to regard themselves as being in the wrong, witchcraft and sorcery are often also a first resort in explaining suffering.

African traditional groups exhibit a wide range of beliefs about witches and sorcerers. Sometimes, there is a distinction, witches being thought of as the possessors of an inherent (and inheritable) psychophysical power to harm, and sorcerers as normal people who employ injurious magical techniques or bad "medicines."[43] In other groups, this distinction is not made.[44] In many groups, witches are regarded as keenly aware of their vicious powers, but among some peoples, it is believed that a witch may be unconscious of his or her status. [45] Despite these differences, almost everywhere in Africa it is believed that the active, practicing witch is a morally hateful and "inverted" human being. In every respect, the witch is the opposite of the ideal or even normal human personality. He or she may engage in loathsome practices like cannibalism or incest. It is commonly believed that witches sacrifice or eat their children to magnify their own evil powers. Their inversion is evident even in their physical characteristics and conduct: they vomit or defecate in public places, they are white or gray in color, often physically blemished, go about naked, are active at night, eat salt when thirsty, and—carrying physical inversion to the extreme—are said in some cultures to walk or travel on their heads. [46]

The witch or sorcerer's motivation is also the antitype or inversion of morality. Whatever specific term is used for this motivation—*inona* among the Bakweri, [47] *shanje* among the Zezuru, [48] or *ole'* among the Lugbara [49]—it is thought to involve a combination of envy, jealousy, and unjustified resentment. The witch hates other people and resents their good fortune and happiness. He or she possesses a truly demonic will. Often, without even a clearly selfish motive—the kind that explains ordinary mortals' ill will or misconduct—but simply out of spite, the witch will injure innocent human beings. Morally desirable benevolence or neutrality thus find their antitype here in gratuitous enmity. To compound matters, the witch will actively practice deception. Outwardly, he or she may appear to be an agreeable, concerned neighbor or relative. Inwardly, however, the witch is filled with malice, obsessed with evil designs. Dominique Zahan observes that silence and reticence are widely admired as virtues throughout Africa: loquaciousness is disparaged and self-mastery, displayed in the ability to keep one's thoughts to oneself, esteemed. [50] But the witch inverts even this highly regarded value by turning "closedness" into a cover for aggression. In all respects, witches personify evil.

For all their loathsomeness, witches nevertheless play many morally important roles within the universe of African religious thought. Most obviously, they help explain the suffering that defies clear moral explanation, and they spare ancestors, hero spirits or the high god blame for wrongdoing. In this respect, the very existence of witches presupposes and helps preserve intact the moral goodness of the higher spiritual order. [51] Witchcraft thus forms one response to the "theodicy problem," the question of why, if there are benevolent deities or spirits, the righteous suffer. Like the "free will" defense in Western religion, witchcraft beliefs attribute this suffering to the misuse and perversion of human freedom. God or the ancestors may ultimately be responsible for innocent suffering, but if so, it is because of their failure to punish witches, not because of active involvement in wrongdoing.

Beyond helping to explain morally inexplicable events, witchcraft and sorcery play a direct role in upholding and enforcing the moral order. This is true in several different ways. First, as the antitype of morality, witchcraft highlights the meaning of morally good behavior. As Evans-Pritchard observes, in Azande culture "the notion of witch-craft is not only a function of misfortune and of personal relations, but also comprises moral judgment. Indeed, Zande morality is so closely related to these notions that it may be said to embrace them.[52] To the Azande, according to Evans-Pritchard, a good citizen is one who carries out his obligations, who abhors adultery, who lives charitably and cheerfully with neighbors, who is even-tempered, generous, and just in his dealings with his fellows, good natured, and courteous.[53] The witch is the opposite of this: "A witch acts with malice aforethought. Azande say that hatred, jealousy, envy, backbiting, slander, and so forth go ahead and witchcraft follows after."[54] In all respects, therefore, the witch serves to provide a negative definition of morality. Whether some persons actually behave like witches or not, the concept of the witch has educative value in furnishing a "symbolic representation" of selfish and antisocial behavior.[55]

Beyond this morally definitional and educative role, the presumed existence of witches also exerts a powerful restraining influence on anti-social behavior. Among the Azande, for example, glum, ill-tempered, and unmannerly people invite the suspicion of being witches.[56] Gelfand observes that among the Shona, "anyone who seems to take pleasure in another's suffering or misfortune is also suspected of being a witch."[57] The mere prospect of an accusation of witchcraft is greatly feared. As a result, says Gelfand, witchcraft beliefs encourage good social behavior:

> If an individual harms another, breaks laws, or becomes anti-social, he lays himself open to the suspicion of being a witch. . . .
> The Shona child is indoctrinated with distaste for the terrible attri-butes of the witch and taught about the awful end liable to befall such persons. . . . Having had this fear instilled in him, the average adult Shona chooses good in preference to evil, tries to behave well and endeavours to conform to the ordinary social pattern of his community.[58]

Belief in witchcraft also serves in a direct way to undergird the retributive order. Although their motives are entirely malicious, witches help punish wrongdoing. On the model of "good issuing from evil," witches' malevolence ensures that retribution catches up with wrongdoers. Africans will be careful not to deny hospitality to a stranger or a distant relative, because they fear the visitor may turn out to be a witch.[59] Similarly, a man fears to display partiality to one of his wives, because he then invites witchcraft or sorcery from jealous cowives.[60] It is perhaps not accidental that, throughout Africa, witches are frequently held to be female.[61] Not only do women in these largely polygymous cultures understandably tend to display a great deal of spite and jealousy (often to their own detriment), but they are also relatively powerless to punish wrongs committed against them.[62] Fear of witchcraft thus serves as a powerful incentive to maintaining good relations with all one's wives, kinswomen, and other female acquaintances.

Fear of witchcraft is also an incentive to economic sharing and the redistribution of wealth. In chapter 7, we will see that from the vantage point of impartial reason, economic inequality is always morally suspect and requires justification (usually in terms of its contribution to productivity and the common good).[63] This moral attitude is reflected in many cultures' discomfort with great imbalances in wealth and their encouragement to forms of economic sharing. In traditional Africa, this moral logic is vigorously in force, and it is partly supported by beliefs about witchcraft and sorcery. Conspicuous prosperity, excess wealth not shared with kinsmen or neighbors is almost everywhere regarded as an invitation to aggression by spirits. The Bakweri of West Cameroon provide a good illustration. They are keenly aware of witchcraft envy, *inona,* and to ward it off they periodically redistribute wealth. Among the Bakweri, the accumulation of property—mainly in goats, pigs and dwarf cattle—has traditionally been a means of establishing status. Yet this wealth, as Ardener observes, is collected mainly to be destroyed:

> At a potlatch ceremony known as *ngbaya,* performed only by the very rich, hectacombs of goats, fowls, and cows of a tsetse-free dwarf breed would be killed and distributed among those attending. To receive a great share at *ngbaya* was a mark of status, and also a severe blow, for the recipients would be expected to ruin themselves even more splendidly. . . . The envy of relatives was further stimulated and assuaged by making any riches in livestock that survived a man's death the subject of another *ngbaya*-like ceremony . . .[64]

While the Bakweri are noteworthy for the passion of their accumulative and redistributive efforts, their basic beliefs are widely shared in traditional Africa. Wealth and witchcraft are commonly thought to imply one another. And this is true not only because wealthy, ungenerous persons invite spiritual aggression and must conceive of themselves as living, to use John Beattie's words, in a world peopled by "actual and potential murderers"[65] but also because they are likely to be viewed as witches themselves.[66] This idea sometimes takes form in the African equivalent of a Faustian bargain: witches are believed to exchange the flesh of their own or others' children to earn favor and to procure financial assistance from the society of witches.[67] Sometimes an alleged witch's wealth may be attributed to a nocturnal force of despiritualized slave laborers—zombies—at his disposal.[68] Whatever specific conception is involved, unshared and disproportionate individual prosperity is regarded as having been obtained by inflicting communal suffering. In the economic area as elsewhere, witchcraft is thus a double-edged sword. Immoral behavior can be a sign of witchcraft, or it can stimulate the wrath and resentment of witches. Either way, the net effect is a strong incentive to morally upright conduct.

The sheer wickedness of witchcraft and sorcery therefore presents no bar to our understanding its place in the morally structured African religious universe: witches help (negatively) to define moral conduct, their existence explains misfortune in a morally understandable way and their wrath or the threat of being accused of witchcraft helps deter selfish and immoral conduct. Against the background of these ideas and the conception of benevolent retributive spirits mentioned earlier, we can see that African traditional religion expresses two key elements of the deep structure of moral and religious reason. Africans presume a moral order governed by notions of selflessness, impartiality, and devotion to the common good. And they clearly believe this order to be upheld and enforced by a complex array of spiritual beings.

Transcending Retribution

What, then, of the third and final element in the deep structure, the suspension or qualification of moral condemnation and retribution in the face of persistent human iniquity? Does African traditional religion conform to the deep structure here as well? Africans are certainly alert to human moral failure. Witchcraft and sorcery themselves attest to the possible depths of human wickedness, to the purely gratuitous malevolence that lurks within us. Belief in the existence of witches and sorcerers indicates that at least some persons are viewed as prone to this degree of evil. It is tempting to speculate that witchcraft ideas represent a projection outward of the malign wishes and thoughts all persons know themselves to harbor. But we do not have to speculate about this since Africans are often explicit about the connection between witchcraft and their view of human nature. Among the Lugbara, the evil conduct displayed by living persons, in contrast to ancestors, has a common explanation: "All men have evil hearts."[69] Ganja women, when asked to explain why dangerous witches are often female, unhesitatingly reply, "because we are evil," and they go on to explain how a family situation with cowives brings out jealousy and resentment in everyone.[70] The Azande are among the first to declare that they are "an evil people."[71] They also give this idea virtually physical expression in their belief that an individual can unconsciously possess witchcraft substance. When misfortune occurs to others, the Zande is not surprised to be accused of witchcraft, and rather than denying the charge, he may blow out water to "cool his heart" and display his future good intentions.[72] Other African societies evidence the same highly ambiguous reading of human nature by holding that every person has two spirits, one good and one evil.[73]

Corresponding to this understanding of human nature is a pervasive sense throughout African tribal religions that mechanisms are required for the control and expiation of sin, whose presence otherwise threatens human life. In the previous chapter we saw that within a strict retributive order, suffering, whether it can be traced to specific violations or not, is often thought of as deserved. Famine, illness, and other disasters that strike a tribal community or kin group are usually regarded by Africans as signs of anger on the part of ancestors or other righteous spirits. The natural response is to attempt to turn this anger away through appropriate gestures of repentance and atonement. But the fact that retribution is in the hands of ancestors is itself testimony to the flexibility of the retributive order, since these agencies can be expected to be gracious and merciful to kin whose hearts have been reoriented to the welfare of the group.[74]

Beyond this, there are also concrete instrumentalities for expressing repentance and for winning the spirits' favor. Like many African peoples, the Nuer employ animal sacrifice to propitiate spirits angered by human misconduct, and they regard these animals as substitutes for themselves. Rubbing ashes on the back of the beast before slaughtering it, Nuer explain that what they are doing is placing all the evil in their hearts on the animal so that this evil may flow into the earth with the victim's blood.[75] The fact that the animal's death is regarded as an acceptable substitute for their own testifies to the implicit Nuer belief that the cosmic retributive order is flexible enough to ease human self-judgment and to allow suspension of the merited death penalty for human sin.

It carries this logic a step further to believe, as some African societies do, that even death is not a definitive punishment, but one that has a positive, salutary, and cleansing effect. For example, the Shona believe that death, whether premature or at the end of a long life, helps to pay the price for one's wickedness.[76] It purges one of even the weightiest burden of sin and it affords transit to the domain of the revered and righteous ancestors. Against the background of this belief, the world is ideally constructed: although a penalty for evil exists—and in Africa few deaths are entirely innocent—it is not severe enough to preclude a destiny among the esteemed and the righteous. The prevalence of this belief may also explain why ancestors can be idealized, despite the known flaws in each individual's character, and why an eschatological realm of punishment is largely unnecessary in the African context. The absence of ultimate punishment does not mean that African traditional religion is "amoral," as Nadel and others claim, but rather that it has pursued the logic of moral and religious reason to a rich conclusion: unsparing self-judgment and an unbending order of retribution cannot be tolerated if the dual human ambition of enduring moral virtue *and* well-being is to be realized.

It is striking how many of these ideas are also found in the literate monotheistic religions of the West. The Bible, for example, traces a line of reflection on the problem of suffering beginning with urgent appeals to God to alleviate the suffering of the righteous and ending with a perception of suffering as an unavoidable reality bound up with the problem of sin. In later rabbinic and Christian thinking, we also encounter the idea of suffering and death (whether experienced or vicarious) as an opportunity to atone for human iniquity. Like African religion, biblical thought thus comes full circle on itself, finally accepting suffering in a way the initial impulse in the tradition sought to resist. In all these cases, this thinking is not an unreflective accommodation to experience, but follows on the deepest understanding of the demands and limits of moral life.

The correspondences between African traditional religion and biblical religion also finds expression at less-developed religious levels. Many specific features of African religion—divination, use of ordeals for truth determination, spirit cults, mediumship, and witchcraft beliefs—can also be found in the earliest strata of biblical faith. In the next chapter, we shall see that some of these same institutions and ideas appear in the prehistory of Chinese religion, and they have a presence in many other "primal" religious cultures as well. This suggests a path of religious development, beginning with the more localized spiritual entities we have seen in Africa and moving, as literate reflection increases, to the more unified retributive order of literate traditions.

Both on the surface and in its depths, therefore, African traditional religion reflects the universal structures of human moral and religious thinking. While many surface elements differ from those we are accustomed to, they are typical of many other nonliterate traditions. Beneath even these surface elements, and very much the source of them, is the deep structure of human moral and religious thinking. No less than religious believers everywhere, Africans call on spiritual realities to assist them in grounding and completing the difficult enterprise of human moral life.

3

Morality and the Demise of Ethical Monotheism in China

Nowhere in the ancient world, with the possible exception of Greece, was the essential moral element in religious belief more clearly perceived and addressed than in China. At a very early date, and on the foundation of a simple but vigorous ethical monotheism, China's religious thinkers and philosophers worked out a series of carefully reasoned teachings about the moral life. They were also able to extend and develop these teachings without the heavy reliance on supernatural revelation that characterizes biblical faith of the same period. Yet these pioneering rational efforts to develop the essential moral object of religion carried a price. Because the full complexity of morality's relationship to religion was not perceived, and because simple or limited solutions were sometimes offered for complex problems, cultured Chinese religious thought atrophied. In turn, popular religious life remained both morally and religiously undeveloped. It came to be dominated by magical practices and dependent on foreign religious influences to fill voids left in the structure of religious reasoning. The history of religious development in China thus vividly illustrates the fact that while religion has its basis in morality, it is not reducible to moral teaching alone.

Early Chinese Religion

Chinese religion emerges from the obscurity of prehistory as a nature-fertility-ancestor cult similar to those we met in traditional Africa.[1] The earliest written sources, oracle bones and inscriptions on ritual vessels of the Shang dynasty (ca. 1766–ca. 1122 B.C.), evidence an overriding concern with agricultural abundance, success in war or hunting, and avoidance of natural disasters like floods, droughts, or epidemics.[2] Various nature spirits appear to have been worshipped, including gods of the soil, grain, wind, rain, mountains, and rivers. Additional attention was focused on the spirits of departed ancestors who were conceived as being either powerfully beneficent or malicious, depending on how they were treated by their survivors.[3] Buried carefully, worshipped with ritual, and provided with abundant material goods through sacrifice, they could furnish long life and prosperity for their descendants. Neglected, they could become demonic pursuers.

Although these beliefs and practices may have been shared by all members of ancient Chinese society, they are particularly associated in the earliest records with the ruling classes, especially the king's family.[4] The prosperity and well-being of the realm depended on the king's worship of natural divinities and his maintenance of good relations with his ancestors. Supreme among these was Ti or Shang Ti, (literally, "High God") who oversaw a cult of deceased nobles reigning in heaven, much as his royal descendant ruled over a terrestrial nobility. Shang Ti was the object of the royal cult. Oracle bones and other means were used to discern "Heaven's" intentions towards human beings. Sacrifices properly conducted ensured Shang Ti's favor in the form of natural blessings for the realm, the predominant aim of archaic Chinese religion being harmony between human beings and nature. The ruler was conceived as having a cosmic as well as political responsibility.[5] If he grew lax in his attention to the cult, natural disasters and calamities would ensue. Even something as trifling as a spate of bad weather might be interpreted as a sign of Heaven's displeasure with its Royal Son.

Because of the paucity of our sources for Shang religion, it is hard to say whether specifically moral concerns played a major role in this nature-ancestor cult. Certain key components of a rational religious position may be present. At least at the level of the nobility, some form of personal survival after death was assumed. As in Africa, it might be possible to understand the ancestor cult as an effort to recompense beloved and esteemed parents for their virtuous sacrifices on their children's behalf. Living children here became agents of retribution in an afterlife, while the ancestors and other supernatural agencies were called on in vital ceremonies of oath taking and truth determination.[6] Nevertheless, moral concerns are not pronounced in the oracle bone or inscription literature.[7] What seems predominant is an ancestor and nature cult of hope supplication and fear propitiation.[8] At the political level, a large measure of the ruler's responsibility to Heaven and to his subjects seems to have been not ethical but magical, resting on the precise performance of sacrificial and mortuary ritual in an effort to influence directly the course of nature. Whether it was because they were in fact underdeveloped or merely neglected in the recorded sources, the moral dimensions of religious life are not to the fore in traces of Shang religion.

The Classic Doctrine of Retribution

Against this background, the religious changes instituted by the Chou dynasty (ca. 1122–221 B.C.) were revolutionary. The Chou rulers were the principal chiefs of a fragile coalition of clans from western China who rebelled against their Shang overlords and succeeded in overthrowing the reigning dynasty. Although their victory had been rapid, a difficult task of governing lay ahead. The new rulers had to pacify the country while preventing internecine warfare among their own coalition of governing tribes. The Chou leaders knew they might retain power only if they could elicit the cooperation of the masses and, at the same time, persuade the nobles and administrators who formerly gave Shang allegiance to support the new regime. To achieve these ends, they turned to religion. There was no question of imposing a new religion on the conquered state. That would only aggravate the relationship with the vanquished. But neither could the new rulers merely maintain unchanged the royal cult, for Shang Ti was the ancestor and founder of the Shang dynasty, and to worship him was to affirm Chou's status as usurpers. The new rulers' solution to this dilemma was to retain the outer forms of the older cult but to transform it internally by emphasizing its moral content.[9]

   This transformation proceeded in two steps. First, Shang Ti was identified with T'ien (Heaven), the high god of Chou religion.[10] Second, the ethical dimension of Shang Ti's character was brought to the fore. The righteousness of rulers and just administration were declared to be his principal concerns. Because of this, it was maintained, he had deposed the Shang rulers. Several quotations from the Book of Documents (Shu Ching), a later account of the period heavily colored by Chou (and Confucian) ideology, illustrate this politically motivated moral interpretation:

> The fame of . . . King Wǎn [reputed first ruler of Chou] ascended up to the High God, and God approved. Heaven gave a great charge to Kin Wǎn, to exterminate the great dynasty of Yin [last of the Shang rulers] and receive its great appointment, so that the various States belonging to it and their peoples were brought to an orderly condition.[11]

Again,

> [The king] was greatly excessive in wine. He did not think of ceasing his licentiousness. His heart was malign, and he was unable to fear death. Crimes existed in the city of Shang and in the states of Yin, but for the extinction [of the dynasty] he had no anxiety. It was not (so) that fragrant offerings (made with) virtue ascended and were perceived by Heaven; greatly the people were resentful and the crowds intoxicated themselves, and the rank smell was perceived on high. Therefore, when Heaven sent down destruction on Yin and had no mercy for Yin, it was due to his excesses. Heaven is not tyrannical, people themselves draw guilt upon themselves.[12]

The immediate purpose of this new teaching, of course, was to furnish a justification of Chou rebellion and rule. But in the process of justifying themselves, the Chou leadership forged a political and religious perspective with dramatic implications for all subsequent rulers. In making explicit the moral concerns and character of the high deity, they imposed religious and ethical restraints on the future conduct of government. Henceforth, the sovereign held his commission on sufferance. True, he remained the Son of Heaven (T'ien Tzu) and he ruled by Heaven's mandate (T'ien ming). But this divine authority was his only so long as he evidenced virtue. Should he abuse his powers, act unjustly, or oppress his subjects, he would lose his mandate. "Now that the king has received the mandate," observes the Book of Documents, "Oh, how can he but be careful!"[13] To the ruler's earlier cosmic and natural responsibility, in other words, Chou had added an overriding moral dimension.

Also implicit within this revolutionary teaching was a significant doctrine of moral retribution. The questions, "Why do the wicked flourish and why do the righteous suffer?" received the reply, "They do not—at least not for very long." Because this question was raised at the level of political life, moreover, the answer was convincing. Much like the Deuteronomic writer in ancient Israel or Plato and Aristotle in Greece, early Chou leadership perceived that where statecraft is concerned, virtue is usually profitable and vice is eventually punished. They perceived the connections between Shang's corruption and misrule, its internal dissension, and its susceptibility to overthrow by less powerful neighbors. They also saw that their own continued hold on power was dependent on just rule and the restoration of order and prosperity. Because of their special historical circumstances, in other words, the Chou leaders were able to perceive and raise to the level of state ideology the general truth that there is a strong connection between virtue and happiness.

The authority of this retributive doctrine was further enhanced by an additional feature of Chou belief that reflected the special apologetic interests of the new rulers but which, nevertheless, has a sound moral and experiential basis. This is the conviction that Heaven's displeasure with a ruler is most clearly manifested by the presence of turmoil and sedition among his subjects. "Heaven's hearing and seeing work through our people's hearing and seeing. Heaven's discernment and severity work through our people's discernment and severity," says the Book of Documents.[14] According to this teaching, whenever a people resist the authority of rulers, it is not the people but the rulers who are to blame. A people's restiveness is Heaven's way of responding to misrule.

The political importance of this teaching is obvious. Max Weber characterizes it as a virtual "Magna Charta" of the Chinese masses.[15] But its implications as a retributive doctrine are also significant. One result of this teaching is to remove much of the uncertainty from Heaven's retributive agency. Henceforth, Heaven's will and power are united and manifested in the behavior of the people. The insistence that Heaven surveyed all of a ruler's deeds was already a part of Chou belief. "In its inspection of men below," states the The Book of Documents, "Heaven's first consideration is of their righteousness,"[16] while the Book of Odes warns, "Do not say [Heaven] is very high above; it ascends and descends in its workings, and daily inspects us who are here."[17] This confidence in the watchfulness of Heaven was necessarily strengthened when the masses, who would be quick to respond to misrule, were declared to be the agency of Heaven's wrath.

A further implication of this teaching was what we might call the "humanization" or "rationalization" of Chinese religious concern. Without the presence or power of Heaven being denied, attention was subtly shifted from a distant and perhaps opaque divine will to the realm of political and social life. "The works of Heaven, it is man who carries them out on its behalf," says the Book of Documents.[18] In this context, God's will is potentially easy to discern, and there is little need for a class of charismatic religous virtuosi—prophets or priests—with special insight into the divine will. To understand Heaven is to understand human beings. To respond to Heaven's will is to morally reform political life.

Taken together, these beliefs define the essential Chou contribution to Chinese religious thought. Naturally, they were not long affirmed with great vigor by the Chou rulers themselves. Within the space of a few generations, the need for apology faded, and the caliber of leadership declined from the high level ascribed to the legendary early sage kings, Yao, Shun, and Yü. A slow process of brutalization and refeudalization began that would take China through the bitter strife of the period of Warring States (403–221 B.C.) and culminate in the centralized despotism of the Ch'in Dynasty (221–207 B.C.). Nevertheless, the basic program of the Chou revolution came to form the core of all subsequent cultured Chinese religious reflection. Although scantily honored in practice, Chou religious ideals were handed down from generation to generation and were reasserted by those in and out of power whenever social or political circumstances warranted.

The 'Humanization' of Chinese Religion

These ideas also had powerful impact on the course of subsequent Chinese religious development. At the beginning of this chapter, I observed that in cultured Chinese thought, the specifically moral components of religious belief came to be emphasized, with more typically supernatural "religious" components neglected or downplayed. In the political theology of Chou we can see why this was so. First, there is the "humanization" of religious outlook I just mentioned. By making the behavior of the citizenry the primary locus of divine revelation and retribution, Chou effectively replaced theology with politics and ethics. An important corollary of this was a gradual but significant shift of power from the hands of the magicians and diviners of Shang society to politically trained "religious" counselors. This shift was never complete, and throughout China's history, conflict reigned between ethically trained bureaucrat-advisors and cultic specialists or neocromancers. Understandably, however, this conflict only accentuated the cultured elite's mistrust of both magical and religious practices.

Even more important than this humanistic emphasis in shaping the course of Chinese religious development was the political focus of the Chou doctrine of retribution. The demand for moral retribution is the mainspring of religious thought. The problem of suffering righteousness is an urgent stimulus to religious reflection and leads to the postulation of a power able to overrule the morally bitter facts of experience. But Chou thought tended to minimize this serious problem by approaching it at the level of statecraft, where the discrepancy between virtue and happiness is usually less severe and less evident than it is at the level of an individual's life. On the individual level, there can often be a great disproportion between integrity and reward. Not only are morally upright individual as subject to illness or misfortune as anyone else, but they must often suffer because of their righteousness. In contrast, so long as morally corrupt individuals are willing to practice hypocrisy and create the appearance of integrity, they are in a favorable position to pursue their ends. Unhampered by morality, they can exploit others' moral restraint. But at the level of statecraft, these relations are usually reversed. Justice in rule promotes stability and prosperity, while political and social corruption tend to expose and undo themselves quickly. By focusing on the level of political life, therefore, Chou religious thinkers were confidently able to predict rewards for virtue in terms of stability, security, and prosperity for the nation and for its rulers, while the need to rely on a transcendent, "religious" support in their appeals for justice was minimized. As politics and ethics replaced religion at the forefront of intellectual interest, concern with Heaven's will diminished.

The specific conditions of Chinese political life further contributed to this confidence in moral retribution. Of special importance was the extent and development of the Chinese empire. China's early achievement of substantial cultural uniformity, its early moves toward political unity, and its relative cultural advance over fragmented neighboring tribes and kingdoms tended to minimize the problem of conquest by alien civilizations, so long as the various Chinese states and, later, the unified empire, were well governed. For long periods during the first millennium B.C., the most pressing threats facing Chinese rulers were internecine squabbling, internal disorder, and rebellion, but these were problems wise and benign government could reduce. The Chinese confidence in virtue's inherent rewards and the decline in "supernatural" religious interest, therefore, were supported by this unique conjunction of political, geographical, and historical factors.

A brief comparison with conditions in ancient Israel helps point up the importance of these special factors in shaping Chinese religious development. In Israel, religion also began with political theology. The so-called Deuteronomic writer shared many of the beliefs and much of the confidence of Chou's theology. Like Chou, the Deuteronomist moralized God's will and focused attention on the conduct of political and economic life. Punishment and reward occurred within this world and were strongly linked to the nation's social and religious integrity. During the earliest period of Israel's existence, when the nation was relatively free from external military threat and its unity in the face of scattered indigenous populations was a source of national strength, these confidences were strongly reinforced. But Israel was not China. A tiny state located at the crossroads of large predatory empires, Israel soon found that her destiny was not in her own hands.[19] One might think that this would produce a sense of despair over the divine justice and a weakening of religious fervor. While this response emerged in some later writings (for example, in a text of the "Wisdom" tradition like the Book of Ecclesiastes), the immediate response to national suffering was instead an intense concern with fathoming God's will. The worse the nation fared, the more demanding this will was seen to be. Efforts at religious and moral reform, followed by respites from hardship and new episodes of suffering, only served to intensify the concern with God's activity in history and its relation to human conduct. The result of this centuries-long process are the various eschatological and redemptive doctrines found in Hebraic, rabbinic and Christian thought. These included concepts of bodily resurrection, ultimate judgment in a millennial kingdom, and complex doctrines of human sinfulness and divine grace. Combining all these motifs, Christian thinking presented God's activity as taking its fullest expression through a messianic savior empowered both to redeem and to forgive.[20]

If this development did not take place in China, it is not because of some peculiarity of the Chinese spirit but because the special circumstances of Chinese society, in conjunction with the universal demands of reason, tended to work in an opposite direction. Initially, neither intense doubt nor intense piety characterized Chinese religion. In their place, we find a relatively tranquil confidence in the reality of retribution as manifested by the responses of the people. In the early Chou period, with attention focused on the relationship between the ruler and the people, a sense of active presence of Shang Ti–T'ien diminished. Later, when Chou's early integrity and stability gave way to misrule, strife and disorder, this high god may already have been too far removed from the center of popular or cultured interest to serve as support for a prophetic religious criticism of leadership. A minority of persons who were troubled by this drift of events reacted with an incipient agnosticism or atheism, voicing doubt about T'ien's moral goodness or interest in human affairs,[21] while others sought to reaffirm the older beliefs. But in neither case was impassioned prophecy a natural form of religious expression. No tradition had developed here of a morally demanding God whose will required the closest scrutiny by a class of intensely devoted, charismatic followers. T'ien's will, in contrast, was clearly known and everywhere manifest in the behavior of the people. If leaders would only recall the traditional teaching and cultivate virtue, surely all would again go well in the realm. In other words, the response to this situation most consistent with China's cultural and religious heritage was the rise not of ecstatic religious prophets but of a cultured elite of conservative moral reformers and teachers.

Confucius

In Confucius (551–479 B.C.),[22] China found one such individual. In the Analects, the Master K'ung (Confucius) is reported as offering the following description of himself:

> I for my part am not one of those who have innate knowledge. I am simply one who loves the past and who is diligent in investigating it.[23]

This modest self-characterization is certainly correct. Confucius clearly saw it as his mission to convey to his contemporaries and to embody in his own life the personal and political ideals established by the sage rulers of early Chou, whose reign, for him, was an example of *te* or "absolutely perfect moral power."[24] Amidst the increasing barbarism of life that occurred as later Chou rulers were stripped of power by contending feudal lords, Confucius did not think that reform meant the development of new concepts or ideals, but a return to the neglected older virtues. By "reanimating the Old," he maintained, a teacher can "gain knowledge of the New."[25] In fact, Confucius also added significantly to the moral and religious tradition he received. Without repudiating any of the key tenets of early Chinese faith, as it had developed under Chou rulers, Confucius advanced the process of ethicization and humanization that Chou had begun. When it left his hands, cultured Chinese thought was thoroughly ethicized. Although a deeply spiritual dimension remained, this was stripped of supernatural or transcendent elements and concentrated almost entirely on the individual's moral self-cultivation. Of the older faith, with its relation to Heaven and spiritual agencies, only the exterior ritual forms remained, and these, too, were interpreted largely in humanistic and moral terms.

The Chou conviction that government exists for the benefit of the ruled was the idea of greatest appeal to Confucius. Central to this thinking was the belief that the ruler's primary responsibility was to ensure peace and prosperity for his people. But because of the corruption of the existing feudal nobility, Confucius also knew that mere exhortations to virtue would not suffice. If government was to be returned to the level achieved by the ancients, this required sustained administration by men of the highest integrity, men trained to government service and so devoted to the public welfare that they would prefer to relinquish their own lives rather than act ignobly. Confucius regarded himself as such an administrator. In the Analects he expresses interest in a responsible government post.[26] Denied this opportunity throughout his life, he instead dedicated himself to training others for service in the belief that pedagogy might serve to disseminate and realize his ideals.

The object of Confucius's teaching and the embodiment of his hopes was the *chün-tzu*. Literally a "ruler's son" or "gentleman," the term had usually been applied to the offspring of the nobility. But here, as elsewhere, Confucius filled an older idea with new moral content. This involved ascribing the status of *chün-tzu* not to a hereditary noble, but to any individual, whatever his birth, whose conduct and bearing displayed nobility and virtue. Perhaps informed by his own youth in "humble" circumstances,[27] Confucius prided himself on accepting promising students regardless of their background or family.[28] Merit alone determined fitness to be trained as a gentleman, and the true gentleman would be one whose character showed he deserved the name.[29]

At his best, the *chün-tzu* embodied the two central Confucian ideals, *jen* and *li*. Together, they represented the supreme criteria of moral character.[30] The Chinese ideograph for *jen* combines the symbols for "man" and "two," suggesting its quality as the virtue of human relatedness.[31] It is variously translated as "man-to-manness," "humanness," "humanity," "benevolence," "goodness," and "love." All these translations are correct since, for Confucius, *jen* was really an all-inclusive moral virtue. In the Analects, as Wing-tsit Chan notes, it is identified with filial piety, wisdom, courage, and loyalty to government.[32] It also requires the practice of "earnestness, liberality, truthfulness, diligence and generosity."[33] So central and lofty a place did this virtue hold in Confucius's thinking, that he sometimes presented it as an ideal almost beyond human grasp, or one attained, if at all, only by the sage kings of the past.[34] Nevertheless, pressed by his disciples to provide a concise expression of what goodness means or how it might be attained, Confucius had a simple formula at hand: "Do not do to others what you would not like yourself."[35] *Jen*, therefore, is the attitude and habit of reciprocity in moral thinking.

The appearance of this "golden rule," both in its positive and negative formulations, at the center of the moral teachings of virtually all the major world religious traditions should not surprise us.[36] Formulations of this sort are elliptical expressions for the "moral point of view." Although the full moral-reasoning process requires us to weigh the impact of our decisions on *all* the persons we affect, asking whether we would ourselves be prepared to suffer the actions we impose on others provides a shorthand test of conduct. Emphasis on this test by Confucius indicates that his aim was not to inculcate a specific set of rules so much as encourage the development of the basic moral attitude.

If the habit of reciprocity in thinking is the principal inner feature of the gentleman's character, conformity to *li* is the most important outward manifestation of a morally virtuous disposition. The ideograph for *li* is also composed of two signs, one indicating "communication with the spirits," and the other "sacrificial vessels." Originally, therefore, *li* signified the proper performance of sacrificial rites. Without abandoning the older meaning, Confucius expanded the term to include all the unwritten customary usages regulating relationships in family and society. The translation of *li* as "propriety" is not bad, if one understands by this not only the rules of etiquette and the proper conduct of traditional religious ceremonies but also right conduct in the performance of morally significant social roles. Thus, it is *li* that established and governed the five traditional Chinese relationships, those between ruler and subject, father and child, husband and wife, elder brother and younger brother, friend and friend.[37]

It is hard to overstate the importance of *li* in Confucius's thinking. He repeatedly insists that virtue without *li* is insufficient.[38] The perfect gentleman is not only a morally upright individual but possesses the social graces, cherishes respect for elders and social superiors, and cultivates a full knowledge and appreciation of religious ceremony and ritual. His emphasis on *li* reveals the conservative strain in Confucius's teaching. Clearly, he valued the rites of China's feudal past. At the same time, Confucius also appears to have consistently given priority to the moral dimensions of *li*. He opposed all pomp and ceremony, whether in the social or religious spheres, that was lacking in deep moral feeling. At one point he asks rhetorically: "A man who is not Good, what can he have to do with ritual?"[39] High among the evils he could not bear to see were the forms of mourning observed without grief or dictated by fear rather than reverence.[40]

Ideally, then, *jen* and *li* were complementary and mutually reinforcing.[41] Only the individual displaying both these qualities deserved the title of *chün-tzu,* and only the *chün-tzu* deserved a responsible position in government. Indeed, Confucius was so committed to the idea of government by rulers and administrators of this sort that he occasionally speaks as though the mere example of such men in power would suffice to reverse China's disastrous slide back to feudalism and chaos. It may be, as Creel has suggested, that Confucius believed in a virtual "contagion of character," such that the moral force of virtuous rulers would by itself eliminate division and ensure social and political harmony.[42] He certainly speaks this way at times.[43] It may also be, as Fingarette contends, that this represents an abiding "magical" dimension of Confucius's thought: a belief that moral virtue directly effects change in nature and society.[44] More likely, however, Confucius based his confidence in virtuous rule on an intuitive moral perception of the concrete relationship that existed between a ruler's self-discipline and justice, on the one hand, and domestic tranquility and national security, on the other. He took pains, for example, to impress on his students the self-defeating nature of harsh or repressive policies. Rule the people by severe laws and punishments, he oberved, and you will only render them disobedient or drive them away.[45]

In this teaching, Confucius was repeating the essential moral wisdom of early Chou leadership. That this teaching should have had such an enormous impact on his small band of students probably reflects both his personality and the difficulty of the times. If this teaching also profoundly affected subsequent generations of Chinese, this is partly attributable to the enormous attraction exerted by the ideal of just government in a land where the early achievement of political and cultural unity on such a vast scale raised the hope that enlightened rule could improve the lives of millions.

I have emphasized Confucius's role as a conservative religious-political reformer because I think we must see him in that role to understand his place in the history of Chinese religion. Specifically, we encounter here the issue of Confucius's alleged atheism or agnosticism. It is sometimes said that Confucius actually disbelieved in the objects of traditional Chinese piety, that he denied the reality of the ancestral or other spirits, and that he conceived of the agency of "Heaven" in explicitly naturalistic terms.[46] Some later Confucians drew these conclusions from the master's teaching,[47] and there are many statements in the Analects that can be taken to support this view. For example, it is reported that "the ways of Heaven" figured among the few subjects of which the master would not speak.[48] Nor would he discuss supernatural phenomena, "prodigies, feats of strength, [natural] disorders or spirits."[49] When asked by the disciple Tzu-lu how one should serve ghosts and spirits, he replied emphatically, "Till you have learnt to serve men, how can you serve ghosts. . . . Till you know about the living, how are you to know about the dead?"[50]

While it is possible to view these statements as evidence of Confucius's atheism or agnosticism, it is more correct, I believe, to see them as a sign of the priority he placed on issues of personal or political morality. Like Chou political thinkers, Confucius wanted to stress that the first responsibility of leaders—or those who would instruct them— was to attend to the world of human moral relationships. Because of this priority, Confucius was opposed to magical practices as well as the preoccupation with ritual formalism that marked the religious environment of his day. Historical accounts of the century preceding Confucius's birth carry vivid descriptions of the elaborate sacrificial and mortuary rituals practiced by feudal lords in the effort to gain supernatural support for selfish political ends.[51] In "keeping distance" from the spirits and in urging his disciples to do likewise, therefore, Confucius was not so much denying the spirits' reality, or Heaven's activity, as he was reemphasizing, in a context of religious abuse, the standard Chou belief that geniune political security and strength lie in virtuous leadership, not superstition and religious formalism.

In these respects, Confucius's attitude toward the spirits recalls the Hebrew prophets' polemic against the sacrificial cult. In both cases, there is an insistence that the moral dimensions of a religious-moral whole not be neglected at the expense of ritual formalism. Neither the prophets nor Confucius dismissed religious ritual and religious obligations. For both, moral and ritual requirements were fused together in the normative order in which human beings stood. Problems arose not when human beings followed ritual but only when they favored easy and self-serving aspects of ritual performance over more pressing moral obligations. Of course, there are differences in the way Confucius and the Hebrew prophets express this concern. The prophets characteristically base their demands for moral purity on an explicit appeal to God's will. As a result, the religious foundation of their criticism is never in doubt. The absence of these impassioned religious appeals in Confucius's discussion lends a misleading appearance of nonreligiousness to his thinking when, in fact, it is more accurate to see him as a modest reformer within an established religious-ethical system, but a system whose transcendent revelational dimensions had long been de-emphasized.

If we are to understand the subsequent development of Chinese religious thought, it is valuable to keep in mind this perception of Confucius as a conservative religious reformer, a transmitter of the essential principles of Chou culture. For while Confucius had relatively little supernatural religious interest, the position he defended was the religious system of the cultured Chinese elite. With its implicit but strong doctrine of retribution—the confidence that under Heaven's rule all would prosper if virtue prevailed—it was able to provide moral orientation and motivation to generations of rulers and near rulers. Indeed, as Chinese history shows, it sometimes inspired great personal sacrifices on its behalf, and it was able to do this with only minimal reference to any transcendent ground of support. Later in Chinese history, Confucius himself was made the object of religious veneration as a patron saint of the state bureaucratic religious cult.[52] This was a development he would have abhorred, but it was a natural enough expression of the place his thought and his confidence assumed in the lives of the Chinese upper classes.

Confucianism's Rational Shortcomings

In perceiving the role of Confucius's thought as the sustaining moral and religious ideology of the Chinese elite, however, we can also begin to appreciate its serious deficiencies as a comprehensive or complete system of moral orientation and motivation. Specifically, Confucian thought neglected two important elements of the deep structure of religious reasoning: it subordinated and almost entirely bypassed the question of the individual's personal happiness and destiny; and it ignored the difficult problem of moral failure and sin, even as the facts of egoism and selfishness became more and more apparent in the declining conditions of later Chou civilization.

Neglect of the individual is a corollary of Confucius's primary concern with the realm of politics. Like the early Chou leadership, Confucius tended to address the problem of moral retribution at the macrolevel of political life. But as we have seen the problem of retribution is usually less acute at this level, and the intensity of the problem of suffering righteousness is less severe. When politics is the focus, the welfare of individuals can often be ignored in the belief that a reform of political life will serve to eliminate the most frequent or more grievous cases of individual suffering. Of course, Confucius's sound moral sense led him to the realization that social reform might not be achieved unless some individuals were courageous enough to place duty before their own welfare, and he appears to have stressed this to his disciples.[53] Nevertheless, Confucius's confidence in the efficacy of public virtue limited this problem to, at most, a handful of dedicated public servants.

It is particularly interesting, therefore, that the few utterances with deep religious feeling in the Analects appear in connection with Confucius's personal disappointments. Confucius's intense desire for a responsible governmental post was never satisfied. Although some of his students received important positions during his lifetime, Confucius himself was ignored or, at best, given only titular office. His keen disappointment over this is evident in the Analects, when he asks, "Am I indeed to be forever like the bitter gourd that is only fit to hang up, but not to eat?"[54] In the face of this deep personal disappointment, Confucius sometimes even abandoned his confidence in virtue's reward in this world and sought consolation in a recognizably religious direction. Speaking to his student Tzu-kung, Confucius observed, "The truth is, no one knows me!" and he added, "But the studies of men here below are felt on high, and perhaps after all I am known; not here, but in Heaven!"[55] In this response before personal defeat, Confucius evidenced the very common connection between unmerited suffering and a fervent religious hope. Ironically, in departing from his usual coolness about religious matters, he anticipated the path taken by many later Chinese who were dissatisfied with the impersonal assurances and concerns of Confucian orthodoxy, and who, in various directions, sought a more personal doctrine of salvation.

Confucius's relative neglect of the problem of personal moral reward is also evidenced in the issues that came to preoccupy his immediate intellectual followers. Lacking the concept of a transcendent religious unification of virtue and personal happiness, they were forced to look elsewhere for a possible harmonization of morality and self-interest. Like their approximate contemporaries, the Greek philosophers of

Athens of the fifth and fourth centuries B.C., who also faced the problem of grounding moral obligation following the demise of a more traditional religious faith,[56] the leading Chinese philosophers sought to develop an account of human nature that would support the possibility of reasoned moral commitment. The fact that in both Greece and China these accounts were usually strained and sharply contested only testifies to the difficulty of the task these thinkers faced.

Mencius

These developments are well illustrated in the thought of Confucius's fourth-century B.C. intellectual disciple, Mencius. Although Mencius made many contributions to early Confucian thought, he is best known for his teaching regarding the inherent "goodness" of human nature.[57] According to Mencius, the human heart *(hsin)*, which he regarded as the center of thinking and willing, possessed four incipient moral tendencies or "sprouts" *(tuan)*. The "heart of compassion" was the sprout of benevolence *(jen);* the "heart of shame" was the sprout of dutifulness *(yi);* the "heart of courtesy and modesty" the sprout of the observance of rites *(li);* and the "heart of right and wrong" the sprout of wisdom *(chih)*.[58] In a famous passage, Mencius tries to demonstrate the presence of these inherent moral tendencies, especially benevolence, by offering an example of spontaneous human conduct:

> Suppose a man were, all of a sudden, to see a young child on the verge of falling into a well. He would certainly be moved to compassion, not because he wanted to get in the good graces of the parents, nor because he wished to win the praise of his fellow villagers or friends, nor yet because he disliked the cry of the child. From this it can be seen that whoever is devoid of the heart of compassion is not human, whoever is devoid of the heart of shame is not human, whoever is devoid of the heart of courtesy and modesty is not human, and whoever is devoid of the heart of right and wrong is not human.[59]

Mencius's remark, "Whoever is devoid of the heart of compassion is not human," contains a strong, persuasive definition of "humanity." Drawing on his listeners' assumed wish to live life fully as humans and not as animals or brutes, Mencius would argue that human beings' most distinctive qualities are to be found in these sprouts of moral disposition and conduct.[60] To the question, "Why should I be moral?," Mencius would answer, "If you are not, you forsake your essential humanity and abandon the nature that distinguishes you from the beasts." At times, in more explicitly religious terms, he also sought to identify this distinctively human component with a divine nature immanent in human beings.[61]

These ways of grounding moral conduct are familiar. They bring to mind similar approaches taken by many Greek and Roman philosophers in their efforts to establish an immanent basis for moral commitment. Thinkers of the Stoic school, for example, pointed to human beings' distinctive rational nature in the effort to justify both moral commitment and the respect due other humans. They emphasized the difference between humans and beasts, and they sometimes identified rational capacity as a divine element within us.[62] Somewhat differently, Plato and Aristotle used concepts drawn from existing social hierarchies and redefined them in moral terms to make the morally responsible life appear lofty and attractive. As Confucius had subtly redefined the *chün-tzu* in moral terms, so these Greek thinkers appropriated the older conception of the noble man, the *agathos,* to describe not the esteemed and powerful feudal lord of the past, but the individual marked by the "noble" moral excellences of justice and self-control. And as Mencius sought to brand selfish conduct as subhuman, and "inferior,"[63] Plato and Aristotle reapplied terms like *aischron* (shameful) and *kakon* (base) in the effort to shift the object of older prejudices from lower-class behavior to selfish conduct in any form.[64]

However impassioned they were, these efforts were problematical and recognizably strained. After all, if our most important, and presumably most satisfying, human dimension is expressed only in virtuous conduct, why do so many people refuse to be human or choose to act selfishly? The characteristic Greek answer was to say that people are "ignorant." Misled by false views of human well-being, seduced by bad habits, people allowed passions to obscure their good judgment. Mencius's response was similar. Human beings unthinkingly destroy the source of their power and well being. They are like people who strip bare the richly forested slopes of a mountain: by cutting down the sprouts of goodness they were born with, they lose their "true heart."[65] Why people do this is never clear, although the implicit answer was the same as that found among the Greeks: human beings are ignorant, misled by bad teachers and bad habits. Hence the need for better teachers and more sustained efforts at self-formation. This account clearly justified Mencius's own pedagogical efforts, but it failed to consider that

human beings might have good reasons for being immoral and for sup-
pressing any moral sentiments they possess. It also failed to recognize
that while people naturally wish to be human to avoid being regarded
as lowly animals, it is not clear that they also wish to be "human" if
this means that they must renounce some of their most pressing
"human" desires.

Whether or not it is finally convincing, Mencius's effort was deeply
important in this Chinese setting. For if individuals cannot be persuaded in humanly understandable terms to commit themselves to the
common good, then the remaining alternatives are anarchy or tyranny,
unprincipled egoism on the part of the many or on the part of the few.
That Mencius perceived the stakes here is suggested by the opponents
whose views he felt compelled to refute. On one side, there was the position of Yang Tzu (or Yang Chu) to whom Mencius attributed the opinion that "Even if he could benefit the Empire by pulling out one hair,
he would not do it."[66] Yang Tzu, in other words, was seen to represent
the principle of "egoism" or "everyone for himself." This view was a
natural response to a world where transcendent restraints on self-assertion seemed no longer to exist. It is not accidental that similar sentiments were expressed by many of Socrates' sophist opponents who, like
Yang Tzu, sought to adjust to social change in a context of declining
traditional religious belief. In both cultures, however, this viewpoint
was regarded by ethically inclined humanists as a deadly assault on
social order. In China, this position was seen as opening the way to crass
selfishness by individuals, and as justifying repressive rule as a way of
controlling the resultant anarchy. In all respects, therefore, such egoism
threatened the vision of a harmonious and principled society to which
Confucianism was committed.

It is harder to understand Mencius's polemic against his other
opponent, Mo Tzu (or Mo Ti), but the issues here, though more subtle,
were equally dramatic. Mo Tzu's name is associated with the principle
of "universal love," or what Mencius calls "love without discrimination."[67] According to Mo Tzu, one should treat all one's fellows with
the same degree of moral respect, whatever their special relationship to
oneself. For example, an individual should show as much consideration
to any elder as he shows his own father, and he should confer as much
benefit on any contemporary as he does on his own brother. Mo Tzu,
therefore, would deny the special moral importance of the "five relationships" stressed by Confucian orthodoxy. Indeed, Mo Tzu regarded
the favoritism to kin allowed by orthodox Confucianists as the principal
source of selfishness and dissension in society.[68]

On the surface, it is hard to see why Mencius was so opposed to this teaching. It seems, after all, to be a noble statement of what morality involves: a stress on impartiality and the transcendence of private interests. Is there not deep moral wisdom in Mo Tzu's understanding that familial egoism can be as destructive of social order as individual egoism? Nevertheless, as true as this may be, Mo Tzu's view, in the context of Confucian thought, had morally devastating implications. For one thing, in some respects it simply defied moral common sense: in times of famine, no one feels it right to give a last crust of bread to a stranger rather than to his own father or brother. Since Mencius hoped to stimulate the moral sensibilities of ordinary people, and since his own teaching already stretched people's moral intuitions, he had to avoid advocating extreme positions like Mo Tzu's.

Beyond this, it was vitally important for Mencius to link moral attitudes to the "organic" desires of human beings. Like other thinkers in the Eastern and Western philosophical traditions,[69] he perceived in people's natural instincts of sympathy and fellow feeling a means of forging a connection between the demands of moral reason and our concrete natural desires. Experience testifies that at the family level, individuals are capable of the most intensely selfless conduct. To establish social morality, therefore, it seems necessary only to build on and extend these altruistic sentiments. Various statements by Mencius illustrate this effort to connect morality to human feelings, and then, in typical Confucian fashion, to link both of these to the secure possession of power:

> What a man is able to do without having to learn it is what he can truly do; what he knows without having to reflect on it is what he truly knows. There are no young children who do not know loving their parents, and none of them when they grow up will not know respecting their elder brothers. Loving one's parents is benevolence; respecting one's elders is rightness. What is left to be done is simply the extension of these to the whole Empire.[70]

Again,

> Treat the aged of your own family in a manner befitting their venerable age and extend this treatment to the aged of other families; treat your own young in a manner befitting their tender age and extend this to the young of other families, and you can roll the Empire on your palm.[71]

Of course, there is a significant qualitative difference between persons' natural love of kin and the moral concern owed strangers, but Mencius hoped to minimize this difference. This is why he believed Mo Tzu's "love without discrimination" was such a threat. In a strictly formal sense, Mo Tzu had the stronger case: his understanding of morality embodied the concept of impartiality that is a central aspect of the moral-reasoning process. While morality might permit special obligations to kin, these obligations could not be permitted to take priority over our larger moral duties. (For example, while we may reasonably reserve a last crust of bread for a parent during a famine, we may not ordinarily steal from other starving people on our parents' behalf.) Although Confucianism did not usually carry family obligations this far, it can be said that it was always prone to excessively credit family ties over larger social duties.[72] Mo Tzu thus perceived that the traditional Confucian ethic, by connecting morality so tightly to family feeling, risked legitimating familial egoism and an ethic of private loyalties. Nevertheless, this was a risk that Mencius and other orthodox Confucianists were willing to take in order to identify a concrete basis for moral commitment. That these desperate efforts were made is a sign of Confucianism's essential inability to answer the urgent personal question, "Why should I be moral?"[73] And it is a sign of the insufficiency of Confucianism's humanist doctrine of moral retribution that in China these debates about human nature and our capacity for morality raged on so early and with such force.

The Neglected Problem of Sin

Mencius's emphasis on the essential goodness of human nature points up a second major defect in Confucianism as an embracing system of moral motivation: its near neglect of the problem of moral inadequacy and sin. We know that any complete moral and religious system must come to grips with the persistent problem of human egoism. This is the basis of the third element in religious reason's structure, the "transmoral" suspension of blame and condemnation for those who despairingly attempt to comply with morality's demands but find themselves unable to do so. This element has a complex relationship to the moral life. Pointing backward to human moral and religious performance, it signals the inevitable imperfections and selfishness that mark every achievement. Preliminarily, this sensitizes conscience and further purifies moral effort. But it also leads to a sense of despair that must be alleviated. When properly developed and applied, the third element of religious reasoning addresses all these issues at once. It yields a sharpened sense of one's own moral flaws, sustains the individual through despair, and stimulates ever more selfless forms of moral devotion.

If Confucius neglected this matter, and if Confucianism as a whole did not develop instruments of grace or forgiveness to allow individuals to confront sin and put it behind them, it was not because Confucius was oblivious to the problem of egoism. Indeed, in the Analects he appears somewhat pessimistic about human nature. He confesses, for example, that never in his life had he seen anyone who cared enough about goodness not to put other considerations first or who so abhorred wickedness that he would never permit it to overtake him.[74] More bluntly, he admits that he had never seen anyone whose interest in developing virtue was as strong as his sexual desire.[75]

But despite this impressive realism, the human propensity for wickedness was not something Confucius was likely to stress or make the center of his teaching. His principal concern, after all, was to reform a disordered society, and to achieve this he emphasized the need for and the possibility of virtuous leadership. Confucius's entire program of reform, in other words, rested on two key assumptions that were antagonistic to any doctrine of sin: that genuinely virtuous leaders could be found and developed and that the people could be trusted freely to respond to their examples and initiatives, obviating the need for repressive rule. If these optimistic assumptions were not made explicit by Confucius, they were by Mencius, for whom human goodness was not just a fact but a morally required assumption. Although not all the later Confucianists followed Mencius in this teaching, and some like Hsün Tzu even stressed the "evil" of human nature,[76] no major thinker in the Confucian tradition denied that human beings could be trained to virtue and were capable of moral conduct. Even the pessimistic Hsün Tzu looked back to the model of the sage kings as examples of what human beings are capable of when they commit themselves to *jen* and *li*.[77] He would surely have agreed with Mencius's statement that "The Sage and I are of the same kind. . . . The Sage is simply the man first to discover this common element in my heart."[78]

While this reformative intention may help explain Confucius's and his followers' neglect of the problem of moral failure, it does not excuse it. Their silence on this matter represented an important defect in Confucian thought and one that grew more serious as China moved into the period of the Warring States. During this time, the Confucian confidence in the possibility of rule by an impartial and virtuous elite was shaken by the deteriorating quality of leadership and by the disappointing performance of those Confucians who managed to attain power. In Confucius's own lifetime it had already become clear that successful members of a trained meritocratic elite were more likely to be loyal to the rulers who paid their salaries than to the people they were supposed to serve.[79] These bureaucrats faced a sharp personal dilemma. Would they adhere to their highest ideals and risk losing influence in the affairs of state? Or would they compromise these ideals and succumb to political necessity in order to preserve some capacity to rule? Understandably, more than a few dedicated men chose the latter course and became closely associated with repressive policies. The fact that they continued to be identified as 'virtuous' Confucian bureaucrats (and perhaps regarded themselves as such) could only worsen the popular impression of this teaching.

These developments naturally cast suspicion on Confucius's reformative optimism and his faith in the efficacy of dedicated moral commitment. At the same time, the increasingly perilous circumstances of life accentuated the religious problem facing individuals. Confronted with a crumbling political order and a discredited political-religious hope, people had to turn elsewhere to satisfy their need for happiness, moral recompense, and virtue. Major religious developments in China following Confucius, especially the rise of Taoism and Buddhism, can be viewed as responses to both of the fundamental rational moral problems passed over by early Confucian thought.

The Taoist Revolt

Few major religious movements have more obscure origins than Taoism. The traditional view is that Lao Tzu, the alleged author of one of Taoism's major philosophical works, the Tao te ching, was an older contemporary of Confucius. The Shih chi (Records of the Historian), which dates from the first century B.C., even records a meeting between the two men. According to this account, when Confucius asked to be instructed in the rites, Lao Tzu responded by sharply criticizing him for his excessive concern with the past and for his preoccupation with achieving moral goodness. He then abruptly closed the interview with the following pointed advice: "Rid yourself of your arrogance and your lustfulness, your ingratiating manners and your excessive ambition. These are all detrimental to your person. This is all I have to say to you."[80]

This story is almost certainly apocryphal. Lao Tzu, if there ever was such a person, was probably not a contemporary of Confucius but, like the author of Taoism's other major philosophical text, the Chuang Tzu, a witness to the chaotic events in China sometime during the fourth or third centuries B.C.[81] Nevertheless, this traditional account highlights an important feature of philosophical Taoism as it developed and as it was appreciated by subsequent generations of Chinese: its sharp opposition to the assumptions of Confucian orthodoxy and to the behavior of its representatives. Holmes Welch remarks that the Confucians "bear somewhat the same relationship to the Tao te ching as the Scribes and Pharisees to the New Testament."[82] In fact, neither Confucius nor any of his followers are mentioned by name in the Tao te ching, and while Confucius does appear in the Chuang Tzu, he is no longer the sage of the Analects, but is transformed into a spokesman for Taoist wisdom.[83] Nevertheless, directly or by implication, a critical portrait emerges in the pages of these Taoist works of a type of individual who must certainly represent the Confucian bureaucrat in office. According to the Tao te ching, he is the "loyal minister" of a corrupt state, whose fields are overgrown with weeds, whose granaries are empty, but whose privileged members go about "dressed in fineries, with swords at their sides, filled with food and drink, and possessed of too much wealth."[84] He is preoccupied with "benevolence," "rectitude," and "ritual," but is constantly meddling in people's lives and supporting fiscal and military policies that worsen their lot.[85] Despite these glaring faults, he is boastful of his virtue, always convinced he is right, arrogant and overbearing in his conduct.[86] The Chuang Tzu adds that although he is "after the sham illusion of fame and reputation," his fame has become "something to beat people down with" and his wisdom "a device for wrangling."[87]

This composite portrait is undoubtedly a caricature. Surely not all the representatives of Confucian orthodoxy in public office were this bad. Yet, during the period of the Warring States, the early Confucians who were able to hold onto power must not have been a pretty lot. Some were probably sheer opportunists, bent on using their positions to enrich themselves. Others were possibly more idealistic, but either because they made the choice to remain in positions of influence at any cost or because they became genuinely convinced that ideals had to be accommodated to reality, they tended to acquiesce to many of the cynical and repressive policies of their employers. Whichever course they chose, bureaucratic officials of this sort were a living repudiation of the Confucian ideal of rule by a trained moral elite.[88]

In their attacks on the Confucians, therefore, the Tao te ching and Chuang Tzu were reproaching a class of individuals. More fundamentally, however, they were calling into question the essential Confucian confidence that moral virtue could be wed to political power. The Taoist writers saw projected and magnified against the large screen of public life several moral truths perceived in similar fashion by some of the Hebrew prophets and by New Testament Christian writers. These included the truth that human beings are rarely able to exercise great power without corruption and the truth that striving for moral distinction on the part of political and religious elites breeds a complicated and dangerous form of egoism. Not only does prideful virtue often conceal vice, but, worse, it can lead to smug arrogance and pitiless fanaticism.

The depth of this understanding in both the Tao te ching and the Chuang Tzu is apparent from the fact that neither text confines itself to pointing up some individuals' moral flaws. Such criticism would be perfectly compatible with the Confucian program of reform and could be accepted by any Confucian. But the Taoist writers were not interested in encouraging Confucian bureaucrats to better observe their own ideals: they wished to call into question these very ideals and the dangerous impulses that lurk behind them. Hence, both writings go beyond the criticism of individual conduct to a criticism of "morality" itself. They hold up as the cause of selfishness and social division the making of moral distinctions and the bestowal of moral praise and blame. They trace human evil not merely to moral abuse, but to the gradations of esteem and the subtle forms of self-assertion that "morality" makes possible. Several passages in the Tao te ching and the Chuang Tzu forcefully illustrate this criticism:

> When the great way falls into disuse
> There are benevolence and rectitude;
> When cleverness emerges
> There is great hypocrisy;
> Where the six relations are at variance
> There are filial children
> When the state is benighted
> There are loyal ministers.[89]

Again,

> The sage embraces things. Ordinary men discriminate among
> them and parade their discriminations before others. So I say,
> those who discriminate fail to see.
>
> The Great Way is not named; Great Discriminations are not
> spoken; Great Benevolence is not benevolent; Great Modesty is
> not humble; Great Daring does not attack. If the Way is made
> clear, it is not the Way; if discriminations are put into words, they
> do not suffice.[90]

And again,

> When the way was lost there was virtue: when virtue was lost there
> was benevolence; when benevolence was lost there was rectitude;
> when rectitude was lost there were the rites.
>
> > The rites are the wearing thin of loyalty and good faith
> > And the beginning of disorder.[91]

This criticism of morality is a familiar, if puzzling, feature of
sophisticated religious-ethical systems. We find a form of it in the
Hindu and Buddhist claims that one must extricate oneself from the
lesser domain of karmic good and evil to attain genuine spiritual
enlightenment. And it is found in various Christian denunciations of
the "Law," where this is understood not just as a specific body of biblical norms, but as the very impulse to moral accomplishment.[92] With
deep insight, developed religious systems realize that there is a root
problem in moral striving itself. It is not just that it is impossible to be
fully moral and to attain the level of purity that a sensitive conscience
demands. There is the further terrible problem that at its highest
reaches, morality itself becomes a means of self-assertion. Within a
framework where moral integrity is esteemed, moral accomplishments,
which properly ought to be regarded as deficient in the best of cases,
may become badges of honor. The pride in one's integrity that should
be resisted as vain and unmerited can be subtly turned to advantage
and used as a means of self-aggrandizement.

This problem can be expressed another way by saying that there is
a peculiar paradox to the moral life: the nearer morally sensitive persons approach the very highest levels of achievement, the further they

should feel from their goal and the more they should properly question the depth or sincerity of their moral commitment. Those who fail to do this are incapable of further spiritual progress and may even become morally dangerous, while those who confront these doubts must properly deny themselves any title to further advancement. This paradox, this strange catch-22 of the spirit, is the driving force behind sophisticated religious denunciations of "morality." Negatively, these denunciations serve to criticize those who would exploit their moral achievements for selfish purposes and to highlight the danger such persons represent to themselves and others. Positively, these denunciations alert the religiously and morally adept to the subtle perils that face them in further moral striving. For those insightful enough to understand, they are reminders that moral egoism must be put aside, that the impurity of one's achievements must be recognized, and that one must seek a path beyond self-praise or self-blame if genuine spiritual and moral growth are to continue. Superficially regarded, these advanced maneuvers in religious thinking may appear to be antimoral. But when we consider that they are motivated by impassioned concern for the purity of the moral life, we can understand why they characteristically lead to renewed encouragements to selfless moral dedication.

All these tendencies—the radical devaluation of morality, the criticism of vaunted moral achievements, and the advocacy of a "selfless" state beyond moral distinctions—are clearly present in the classic texts of philosophical Taoism. They are at the heart of the central concept *wu-wei* (nonaction), and they inform the specific Taoist vision of the Way.

'Nonaction' as Selfless Action

Wu-wei was the Taoist substitute for the Confucian ideals of *jen* and *li*. On the surface, it appears to be a negative virtue requiring "stillness" and withdrawal from active moral effort. It has thus sometimes been taken literally as a repudiation of moral striving or as an encouragement to flee worldly responsibility, the ethic of the recluse, not the ruler.[93] But very little in the Tao te ching, where *wu-wei* finds its most explicit Taoist treatment, suggests that it involves an ethic of world renunciation. On the contrary, it appears to represent a definite moral ideal meant to guide the conduct of sage rulers. In contrast to what is perceived to be the selfish and destructive activism advocated by Confucianism, *wu-wei* calls for rulers and administrators to adopt a policy of benevolent abstention from meddling in people's lives. It requires a salutary neglect, a benign laissez-faire that lets people flourish on their own without the constant interference of ostensibly well-intentioned politicians and bureaucrats. A quotation from the Tao te ching conveys this dimension of *wu-wei*:

> The more taboos there are in the empire
> The poorer the people;
> . . . .
> The better known the laws and edicts
> The more thieves and robbers there are.
> Hence the sage says,
>> I take no action and the people are transformed of
>>   themselves;
>> I prefer stillness and the people are rectified of themselves;
>> I am not meddlesome and the people prosper of themselves;
>> I am free from desire and the people of themselves become
>>   simple like the uncarved block.[94]

A further sign that *wu-wei* is primarily political counsel is the fact that the Tao te ching sometimes actually recommends active policies of statecraft, including military ventures when they are required for the security of the state. But in doing so, it places emphasis on the need for modesty and self-effacement in conduct. Indeed, here we find a second and deeper meaning of *wu-wei*: its significance as an antidote to moral pride and destructive moralism. *Wu-wei*, in this sense, is not inaction but moral action free of self-regard, not "nonaction" but "nonselfish action." Like the Hindu and Buddhist concept of "detached action" *(niskama karma)* or St. Paul's conception of *agape* (Christian love), *wu-wei* embodies the ideal of spontaneous and selfless service to others.

This dimension of *wu-wei* is apparent in several different passages in the Tao te ching. It also finds expression in the most explicitly political sections of the Chuang Tzu. For example, speaking of the morally necessary war, Lao Tzu has this advice:

One who is good aims only at bringing his campaign to a conclusion and dare not thereby intimidate. Bring it to a conclusion but do not boast; bring it to a conclusion but do not brag; bring it to a conclusion but do not be arrogant; bring it to a conclusion but only when there is no choice; bring it to a conclusion but do not intimidate.[95]

Elsewhere, the same point is made in more general terms. The sage ruler "acts," but self-effacingly and without personal motives:

> The best of all rulers is but a shadowy presence to his subjects.
>   Next comes the ruler they love and praise;
>   Next comes one they fear;
>   Next comes one with whom they take liberties . . .
> . . . .
> Hesitant, [the sage ruler] does not utter words lightly.
> When his task is accomplished and his work done
> The people all say, 'It happened to us naturally.'[96]
> . . . .
> The sage benefits them yet exacts no gratitude,
> Accomplishes his task yet lays claim to no merit.
> Is this not because he does not wish to be considered a better
>   man than others?[97]

And the Chuang Tzu, in its counsel to rulers, presents the same ideal:

> The government of the enlightened king? His achievements blanket the world but appear not to be his own doing. His transforming influence touches the ten thousand things but the people do not depend upon him. With him there is no promotion or praise . . . [98]

This vision of government by nongovernment and this ethic of selfless service also found expression in the Taoist concept of the Way. The term *Tao* (Way) was not new to either the Tao te ching or Chuang Tzu. By itself or as the "Way of Heaven," it appears repeatedly in the Analects, where it indicates proper human behavior, especially conduct expressive of *jen* and *li*. It also sometimes refers to the cosmic moral order in which Confucius believed human beings to stand.[99] Without abandoning the conception of Tao as a "way" or "path" of moral conduct, the Taoist texts accentuate the cosmic meaning of the term. For both, Tao is more than a guide to human conduct; it is the mysterious, transcendent ground of all reality. "Before Heaven and earth existed it was there, firm from ancient times."[100] It is the "nameless" something that gave birth to the world and served as "mother of the myriad creatures."[101] It supports all creatures, "nurses them" and "brings them to fruition and maturity."[102] Without it, "limpid heaven might split," the "earth might sink," the gods might lose their potencies and the "leaders, lands and princes might fall."[103] Beyond all distinctions, "without action or form," it sustains the world.[104]

Clearly, there is much in this description that escapes simple analysis. The Taoist Way is not just a set of moral rules. Among other things, it may refer cosmologically to the undifferentiated primordial state from which the phenomenal world emerged.[105] There are also scattered passages in the Tao te ching and Chuang Tzu that can be read as allusions to techniques of breath control and trance, suggesting that *the Way* may refer to a mystically discerned ground of consciousness.[106] But whatever additional esoteric meanings the Way has, it is also visibly identified by these Taoist writers with the order of nature around us, and this identification gives the Way its most distinctive moral significance. To understand this, we should keep in mind that nature, for these writers, was not "red in tooth and claw" but was more like our "mother nature," an order characterized by maternal nurturance and generosity. This order, and the ultimate Way on which it depends, together exemplify the Taoist ideal of spontaneous and selfless service to others. They also hold out the model of a reality beyond moral distinctions that is nevertheless consummately moral. Several representative quotations illustrate this use of nature and the Way:

Highest good is like water. Because water excels in benefiting the myriad creatures without contending with them and settles where none would like to be, it comes close to the way.[107]

The way never acts yet nothing is left undone.[108]

The myriad creatures rise from it yet it claims no authority;
It gives them life yet claims no possession;
It benefits them yet exacts no gratitude;
It accomplishes its task yet lays claim to no merit.
It is because it lays claim to no merit
That its merit never deserts it.[109]

This Teacher of mine, this Teacher of mine—he passes judgment on the ten thousand things but he doesn't think himself righteous; his bounty extends to ten thousand generations but he doesn't think himself benevolent. He is older than the highest antiquity but he doesn't think himself long-lived; he covers heaven, bears up the earth, carves and fashions countless forms, but doesn't think himself skilled. It is with him alone I wander.[110]

In looking to nature and the cosmic ground of nature as the basis of its special moral teaching, Taoist thinking revealed its continuity and discontinuity with the earlier Chinese tradition. A basic tenet of Chinese religious and moral thought, we know, was the essential relationship between the human and natural orders. For Chou thought and for Confucianism, moral and ritual effort were required to sustain nature's productivity. Human responsibility within this cosmic-moral order involved active moral striving and the creation of disciplined individuals within a morally structured (and elitist) state. But Taoism saw this very effort as the problem. Reacting against this program and against the hierarchy, pride, and corruption to which they believed it led, Taoists would stress nonaction and nonvirtue, not as moral indifferentism, but as consummately moral action purged of self-regard.[111] In doing so, however, they also looked to nature, finding there not an encouragement to moral activism but the gentle example of nature's own selfless, generous sustenance of its creatures. Just as Christian thought had sought to resolve the problem of sin and despair by replacing the emphasis on human beings' responsibility to God with an emphasis on God's gracious redemption of human beings, so Taoism, working within a nontheistic context, would fundamentally reverse the lines of initiative in the relation between human beings and nature.

Against this background, we can regard Taoism as an effort, within the special world of Chinese thought, to respond to the third element in the deep structure of religious reason: the recognition of human moral inadequacy and the necessary subordination of human moral judgment. Whereas Confucianism, by developing the content of moral obligation and by nourishing a confidence in virtue's reward, sought to respond to the first and second elements in reason's structure, Taoism, by emphasizing conformity to a "Way" beyond "virtue," sought both to highlight and to relieve the destructive pursuit of moral distinction and the egoism that taints even the best moral efforts. In its criticism of "morality" and in its idealization of a nonjudgmental nature, it emphasized the reality of human selfishness and effected the transmoral subordination of morality needed to combat moral despair and empower purified moral devotion.

This is one important reason, I think, why Confucianism and Taoism, as opposing schools of thought, have been so closely linked in China's history. Barely an epoch has passed without these two struggling with one another at the highest levels of political life. Some of this struggle was nothing more than a conflict over power, and some was occasioned by later Taoism's role as a messianic folk religion, whose opposition to the Confucian elite and whose vision of a Perfect Ruler spurred popular uprisings against Confucian rule during the Han dynasty.[112] But, if, as some have thought, these two perspectives form "two halves of the Chinese soul," and if they often have been led into political conflict over essentially different visions of just rule, this is also because each represented a side of religious reason's important interior dialogue.

The vigor of the engagement between Confucian and Taoist thought within China testifies to the force religious and moral reasoning exerts toward the accomplishment of its full agenda. Had early Confucianism developed within itself a sensitivity to the moral frailty of even the "best" human beings, it is unlikely that there would have been an audience for Taoism's sharp critique. As it was, cultured Chinese religion was probably impoverished by the fact that this essential dialogue within religious reasoning was expressed through two opposing religious movements. It is hard enough to relate the moral and transmoral dimensions of religious thought within a single religious system, but this problem was bound to be worsened when these tensely related elements in reason's structure were expressed and embodied in two very different and antagonistic religions. Relieved of the responsibility of elaborating a full ethic combining moral striving with moral self-criticism, each of these separate systems exhibited some of the worst features of the pole it represented: if Confucianism characteristically displayed moralism, rigidity, and excessive hierarchy, Taoism was given to flights from responsibility and utopianism.[113]

The Problem of the Individual

A further difficulty is that while Confucianism and philosophical Taoism may have formed "two halves of the Chinese soul," this was largely true only of China's public or political soul. In their classical expressions, both these traditions were primarily concerned with the realm of politics. Each offered political counsel and addressed itself to the ruler who would be a sage. As a result, neither perspective had much to say to the isolated individual. As we saw, Confucianism's tranquil confidence in a reward for virtue was tenable only at the political level, and, amidst suffering, Confucianism offered the righteous only the faint consolation of support by a remote and religiously undeveloped "Heaven." Similarly, Taoism's advocacy of selfless action was most firmly grounded in the realm of political life where, as the *Tao te ching* recognizes, genuine selflessness may paradoxically be conducive to self-preservation.[114] But for individuals concerned with their own well-being and not securely in possession of political power, self-effacement may seem a risky option.

It is true that there are strands of Taoist thinking that sought to offer individuals a response to the realities of unmerited suffering. In their mystical dimensions, the classic Taoist writings furnished later generations of intellectuals frustrated by the corruption and reverses of public life a rationale for retirement from the world.[115] The classic texts also provided some foothold for an individual response to suffering. In the Chuang Tzu, for example, criticism of moral discriminations is sometimes associated with an ethical relativism that calls into question the judgmentalism, certitude, and arrogance of the Confucians.[116] In some passages, this relativism is also applied to the basic value distinctions of life, the goods and evils that stimulate human desire or aversion, and an effort is made to suggest that one who possesses wisdom may be able to transcend these distinctions.[117] For example, in one famous passage we read of lady Li, who, when captured and taken to the state of Chin, "wept until tears drenched the collar of her robe." But after going to live in the palace of the ruler and after sharing his couch and eating the delicacies of his table, Lady Li came to wonder why she ever wept. "How do I know," concludes the narrator, "that the dead do not wonder why they ever longed for life?"[118]

Elsewhere in the Chuang Tzu, this perception of the relativity of values is fused with a sense of the cyclicity of nature to produce an attitude of equanimity in the face of life's hardships. Death, loss, and failure, we are told, form part of the "alternations of the world, the workings of fate" and should not be allowed to destroy one's harmony or enter the storehouse of one's spirit.[119] The true sage does not weep before death or mutilation but sees it as part of a ceaseless process of change. In another passage, we read of Master Lai, near death, surrounded by his crying wife and children. Master Li, who had come to visit, admonishes the family, "Shoo! Get back! Don't disturb the process of change!" Then, leaning against the doorway, he comments to his friend, "How marvelous the Creator is! What is he going to make of you next? Where is he going to send you? Will he make you into a rat's liver? Will he make you into a bug's arm?"[120]

This kind of equanimity before painful change and this stoic acceptance of suffering is a refined product of the human spirit. In the East and the West, in various forms, it has sometimes provided a measure of comfort and orientation to individuals confronted with seemingly insurmountable problems of suffering and injustice. But because it offers no prospect of positive well-being and no ultimate consolation for those who wrongly suffer, this position is usually incapable of motivating sustained commitment to larger moral purposes and goals. Its appeal is ordinarily confined to a small class of intellectuals committed to high moral standards but unable or unwilling to accept a more vivid religious hope. And even among these groups, stoic resolve of this sort often breaks down in the face of unrelieved and unjustified suffering. The fact that philosophical Taoism held out only this meager consolation was a sign of the spiritual vacuum left in Chinese culture by the religious-moral reflections of Chinese intellectuals.

But religious and moral life, no less than nature, abhors a vacuum. Where indigenous cultured religion fails to meet the conceptual needs dictated by reason's deep structure, the void is typically filled by alternative movements and tendencies. This was the case in ancient Greece and Rome where a corresponding series of failures in cultured indigenous religion on the one hand inspired many religiously and morally undeveloped popular movements and on the other hand paved the way for Christianity.

A similar development occurred in China. On the popular level, the urgent question of the fate of the individual inspired the development of quasi-magical efforts to ward off hardship, secure prosperity, and prolong life. Animism, geomancy, and alchemy all flourished in this environment and supplemented older and continuing traditions of ancestor worship. In time, Taoism itself came to reflect and to nourish this popular piety. Partly because of suggestions in the Tao te ching and Chuang Tzu of certain quasi-magical powers possessed by the sage[121] and partly because the Taoists were always closer to the masses than the Confucian bureaucrats, Taoism, during the Ch'in and Han dynasties (221 B.C.–220 A.D.), became identified with a magical quest for personal immortality. Respiratory, dietary, sexual, and alchemical practices were developed for this purpose, and one position that emerged, esoteric Taoism, even enjoyed a brief popularity at the imperial court.[122] In time, with many of its dedicated practitioners the victims of political intrigue, esoteric Taoism declined in importance. But some of its elements, especially its affinity for magic, were carried on. They reappeared in popular culture as religious Taoism, a syncretic faith characterized by animism, nature polytheism, ancestor worship, and various forms of necromancy.[123] The persistence of these forms of Taoism at the popular level was a sign of Chinese elite culture's inability to speak to the religious and moral needs of individuals. With an "Apollonian" high culture of ethical rationalism, Chinese folk religion assumed a "Dionysiac" quality that continued up to the modern period.[124]

Chinese Buddhism: The Imported Faith

The same failure of indigenous culture underlay the ardent reception given Buddhism in China. This is no place to rehearse the long and complex history of Chinese Buddhism.[125] It is enough to say that Chinese civilization entered into a long, fruitful, but always stormy, relationship with this imported faith. In the end, China perhaps transformed Buddhism as much as Buddhism transformed China. Certain aspects of Buddhism, especially its relative pessimism about the human condition and its subordination of the values of family and kin, constantly impeded its progress in China and contributed to its episodic persecution. Nevertheless, despite these difficulties, Buddhism flourished and spread for centuries in China because of the way it spoke to needs neglected by the indigenous religions. In Buddhism's doctrine of karma, China found the sophisticated personal eschatology it lacked. Buddhism's elaborate scheme of heavens and hells assured retribution to the righteous and wicked, and the doctrine of rebirth offered hope to those whose present worldly fate was disappointing.[126] At the same time, without qualifying its stress on retribution for those preoccupied with reward, Buddhism pointed to the abiding problem of egoism and held out for those who perceived this problem the promise of redemption to a state beyond the distinctions of good and evil and beyond the strict causality of the moral law. For a disciplined elite, this was the promise of nirvana, and for a wider public it was the hope of salvation through immediate enlightenment or through the mercy of a compassionate bodhisattva. As we might expect, movements mediating these advanced religious ideas to the masses, such as Ch'an and Pure Land Buddhism, had special appeal and popularity.[127]

Religious Development: The Lesson of China

The inquiry of this chapter thus ends at the beginning of one of China's most religiously creative and fertile periods. My aim, however, has not been to trace the full course of Chinese religious history, but to identify those factors in early Chinese religion that led, on the one hand, to the apparent demise of native ethical monotheism and on the other, to the adoption of a sophisticated but alien religious culture.

What conclusions can we draw from this investigation? For one thing, we see illustrated the point made earlier that religious reasoning, though rooted in morality and fundamentally actuated by problems of the moral life, cannot be reduced to moral teaching. Religion is not moral philosophy. It is the effort to locate a full understanding of moral responsibility in a context of beliefs that justify moral commitment and sustain it through its own most self-critical moments. In view of this, we can see why the intensely moral quality of early Chinese religion did not contribute to a deepening of indigenous religious-moral culture but led, on the contrary, to its stultification. Lacking balanced development of the other elements of religious reason's deep structure, the specific moral teachings of early Chinese religion were isolated and left without support. This caused the whole tradition they represented to fall into disfavor.

Second, we learn how complex is the process of rational religious development. The three elements of religious reasoning's deep structure are simple, but they work themselves out in the complex materials of a culture, and their expressions are constantly shaped by historical circumstances. Like genetic inheritance in a living organism, these universal structural elements impart momentum and directionality to the process of religious development. But just as a biological organism is finally the product of its genetic inheritance *and* its environment (an environment that can frustrate aspects of its growth or even cause its death), so a religious system results from the interaction of reason's requirements with the culture that surrounds it. This accounts for both the enormous diversity of historical religious traditions as well as some of the surprising similarities they display. In China it explains why a religious culture beginning so much like that found in the Ancient Near East of the same period underwent decline and was largely replaced by a series of very different religious alternatives.

4

Revelation and Reason in Biblical Faith: Genesis 22 and Traditional Judaism

If classical Chinese thought appears to sever the necessary connection between religion and morality because of its humanistic ethics and relative lack of appeal to supernatural revelation, the religious traditions rooted in the Bible pose an opposite problem. Here, rational morality often seems to be given no place at all. In these traditions, human life stands under a revealed "divine command" that sometimes is communicated directly by supernatural means and may require conduct that violates reasoned morality and conscience.

"Divine command" morality of this sort poses some very practical problems. Because biblical faith has shaped our culture, we daily encounter the challenge revealed ethics presents to reasoned ways of approaching moral choice. We meet this problem, for example, whenever parents risk the life of a child in the belief that medical treatment is prohibited by the Bible. We see it in the vehement debates over forms of sexual conduct, from premarital sex to homosexuality, that many believe are explicitly prohibited by biblical teaching. And it makes its most troubling appearance in the episodes of violence, the "holy wars" engaged in by those who look to revelation to support territorial aspirations or claims of racial and religious superiority.

Beyond these practical problems, divine command morality also raises several sharp questions for anyone committed to the view that religion finds its human basis in moral reasoning. Emphasis on the divine command, for example, appears to give human reason a subordinate place in the moral life. Must not those who obey the divine command "humiliate" their intellects if God's command runs counter to the dictates of reason and conscience? But, if so, what becomes of my theoretical claim that religion is essentially animated by moral reasoning? Does not this claim disintegrate before the fact that major world religions inspired by the Bible have flourished and grown for centuries while adhering to a model of revealed morality?

One way of responding to these questions is to contend that the divine command is not really the center of biblical ethics or the ethics of the traditions it has inspired. One might try to argue that these traditions are not limited to revelation, that in addition they respect the existence of a common human ethic accessible to all rational persons. For example, in Judaism, one might point to the so-called Noachide laws, the set of norms incumbent on all the "children of Noah," that include such things as the prohibitions on homicide and injustice. Or one might point to the other teachings in scripture and Jewish writings which presume that human beings possess a basic moral common sense.[1] In Christianity, one might allude to the ancient concept of "natural law" as evidence that this tradition recognizes an ethic independent of divine revelation.[2] Nevertheless, as important as these ideas are, they are dwarfed by the authority and importance of revelation in the life of these religions. Not only is the pious Jew called to the "higher," "revealed" standard of Torah or *halakhah*, the laws received by Moses at Sinai, but even the moral laws applicable to all human beings attain their authority for the Jew only by the subsequent fiat of divine legislation.[3] Christian natural-law teaching, for all its importance and authority, has always taken second place to the dictates of the Bible and has even been deeply influenced by biblical teaching, as Catholic teaching on sexuality shows.[4]

Understanding these religions, therefore, requires accepting that they are essentially divine command traditions. If we are to situate them within a framework of moral reasoning, what is needed is not a denial of this fact but a more penetrating understanding of how a divine command ethic relates to religious rationality in general. In this chapter and the next, I hope to develop this understanding by looking closely at how the concept of a divine command has worked within Judaism and Christianity. The key idea I wish to propose is that an insistence on the primacy of the divine command is not only permitted by the moral reasoning process underlying religious belief, but is also a very natural outcome of that process. To state this paradoxically, there is a deep moral and rational intentionality behind religious claims that the content and authority of the moral code is based not on human reason but on God's will.

Rationality and the Divine Command

To begin to understand this, we need only recall how difficult it is to justify individual moral commitment. While the value of moral norms is easily demonstrated in general rational terms, no entirely persuasive answer can be given to the question, "Why should I be moral?" This problem underlies and leads to the retributive element of religious reason's deep structure, which knits the conflicting voices of prudential and moral reason together by affirming that righteousness will somehow be rewarded and wickedness punished.

While religious beliefs of this sort may be voluntarily assumed and developed by persons seeking to provide a coherent basis for their own sense of moral commitment, they are more commonly picked up as part of an existing religious culture. Here they serve as a powerful ground and support for the moral code. But in these contexts, religious claims about morality are rarely limited to the view that God is only the sustainer of an independent and rationally comprehensible system of moral norms. He is usually also held to be the source of these norms: they proceed from his will and reflect his deepest wishes and purposes. This extension of religious ideas into morality is thoroughly understandable. When all prescriptions for human life are traced to God's will, morality obtains enormous authority. No longer is God a detached enforcer of norms whose main reason for being is their instrumental value in human life. If that were so, if morality's principal value were seen to lie in its utility to the human community, many of the reasoned objections to being moral we already noted would reappear. Though a person might fear punishment for selfish choices, it remains natural in moments of conflict to wonder why one's own welfare should be subordinated to some "common good," or why, if human happiness is the object of the moral life, it should be disbursed so unevenly in the course of moral experience. It might even seem reasonable to question the justice of a God who sustains what may seem to be a "tyranny of the majority." But when God is introduced as the author of a code whose being and purpose derive from his will alone, a will not entirely subject to human interrogation or comprehension, questions of personal welfare fade. Their place is taken by an intense focus on God's will, which is regarded as being backed by a supreme creative and destructive power and motivated by value concerns that comprise but also transcend considerations of human welfare.

The authority lent morality by tracing it to God's will can be expressed another way by saying that this approach breaks the tie we noted earlier between impartial and prudential reasoning. God is precisely that "third" standpoint, or "interest," beyond the prudential or moral uses of reason, a standpoint that human rationality cannot validate or attain by itself. As a center of reasoned willing, God is worthy of attention and respect, and he is not subject to the charge of partiality to either side in reason's internal dispute. Although on the side of group values and morality, God is not one member of a "crowd" of self-concerned finite beings banded together against the individual, and although he is an individual, God is not motivated by crassly selfish concerns. Both individual and social, God—or the concept of God—comprises the seeming contradictions that beset human experience and rational choice. When the moral law is objectified as expressing God's will, therefore, that law ceases to be subject to any of the reasoned criticisms provoked by regarding it as an instrument of human reason alone.

Outlining in this way the rational value of locating the source of morality in a transcendent divine will and seeing this effort as a complex move within an overall rational strategy of grounding moral commitment also suggests the important rational constraints on this idea. Most obviously, it is not allowable that God, when thought of in these terms, be regarded as a source of purely self-centered or *immoral* willing. God is to be obeyed, precisely because he is righteous and because his will, whatever other dimensions it may possess, always highlights and sustains the moral code. If this were not true, the whole purpose of tracing morality to God's will would be lost, and divine authority would serve to encourage merely slavish or wicked behavior. This is the point of long-standing philosophical objections to those divine command moralities that emphasize obedience to God based on fear of his power rather than respect for his moral integrity.[5]

The insistence that God's commands not violate morality does not mean, however, that a concrete religious system based on divine command morality is unacceptable if it fails to be "rational" in every sense of this term. For one thing, a religious position of this sort need not openly trace its norms to human beings' rational, moral judgment, and it need not expose the reasons behind its strategy of relying on God's command. We just saw that there are good reasons for not doing this. Furthermore, from the perspective of impartial reason, what is crucial is not the nature of the source of moral norms, but that this source be one that never conceivably permits violations of what reasoned morality requires.

This openness to different bases of authority for the moral life is possible because morality is, above all, a practical matter; as impartial, rational persons we care less about the intrinsic nature or even credibility of the beliefs others hold than we do about the bearing of their beliefs on their moral conduct. The nature of a religious authority is, therefore, relatively unimportant in this context. The only requirement morality strictly imposes is that people's beliefs—religious or otherwise—not lead them to immoral behavior. Of course, it may seem difficult to imagine a source of authority not identifiable with human reason or not actuated by reason which, at the same time, never conceivably violates the dictates of reason. But religious traditions offer important illustrations of this possibility. For example, where God is viewed as a "father" of all human beings, who loves all persons equally as parents love their children, his moral wishes for humankind, even though they are not traceable to human reason, but to an intense "divine" affection, will directly parallel those of the community of impartial human beings. Or, if God is viewed as a just judge who abhors selfish conduct on the part of human beings, his moral will again becomes coterminous with the domain of impartial human willing. The popularity of these conceptions in various Western and Eastern theistic traditions illustrates how well religious traditions are able to elaborate independent bases for morality without necessarily violating reason's moral commands.[6]

To hold that a religious tradition may not violate rational morality also does not mean that each and every norm of an historical religious system must be clearly and immediately justifiable in rational moral terms. No human cultural system can meet such a rigorous test. For one thing, as motivating systems that seek to shape human life, religions incorporate a variety of norms, not all of which are generically moral. It is common, for example, for ritual commandments to exist side by side in religious systems with requirements more recognizably moral. We will see in chapter 6 that ritual often plays a vital role in the moral life of a religious community. For this reason and because ritual has independent significance within the totality of a religious system, it is normal for ritual requirements to be taken very seriously. From the point of view of impartial reason, this is fully acceptable, unless these requirements lead to serious violations of the moral rules. In rational religious traditions, conflicts on this level may occur and they will usually be resolved in favor of morality.

Religious traditions also sometimes incorporate immoral norms. As products of human reason operating in specific historical contexts, religions are imperfect or "ragged" cultural creations. Like any moral system, they reflect the time-bound and culture-bound assumptions of those who help fashion them. It is not accidental, for example, that Judaism and Christianity count among their oldest teachings forms of racial or sexual discrimination that are no longer acceptable to more sensitive and experienced modern consciences. Nevertheless, isolated moral violations of this sort should not be made the measure of the overall rationality of a "revealed" religious system. In assessing the rationality of a divine command tradition, what is important is the *general* tendency of its normative requirements. This counsels us to ask several specific questions of such a tradition: Are its norms and teachings generally congruent with reasoned morality? Do most of its norms conform to our sense of right and wrong? If there are exceptions that appear to defy moral justification, do they, when subjected to closer scrutiny and when situated properly in their historical context, reveal a more basic moral intentionality? If not, are these exceptions abiding aspects of the tradition or are they rather among the norms that are subject to revision and change as the tradition develops and deepens its processes of moral reflection? Indeed, have these teachings or norms spawned conflict and given rise to schisms or sectarian movements of protest against them? Like bodies of scientific knowledge or political institutions, in other words, religions must be viewed as evolving rational systems that strain over time to move toward greater sensitivity to reason's agenda. This insight is especially important in assessing the teachings of any single divine command tradition.

Rational Theory and Genesis 22

Hard cases may make bad law, but they are essential to the test of theories. A view of religion incapable of explaining the most typical and most difficult evidence from the traditions it hopes to study is of little value. Where the biblically inspired religious traditions are concerned, the hardest case of all for any view stressing the underlying rational and moral basis of religion is presented by Genesis 22, the episode in which God commands Abraham to sacrifice his son Isaac. Here is the divine command at its starkest, requiring the slaughter of an innocent child. If this episode were peripheral to biblical religion, perhaps deliberately "forgotten" as were other embarrassing teachings from the earliest traditions (such as the frequent recourse to the death penalty or the harsh punishment for juvenile delinquency[7]), we might dismiss it. But Genesis 22 is at the heart of biblical religion. Abraham's willingness to sacrifice his son on Mt. Moriah is not only frequently commented on by Jewish and Christian writers, but it is consistently regarded as the archetypical expression of faith. Genesis 22, therefore, is the hard case against which any claim that revealed religion has an essentially rational basis must be measured.

In what follows, I want to look closely at the ways Jewish commentators comprehended and communicated the lessons of this difficult text. In the next chapter, I shall look at Christian treatments of the same episode. In both cases, my focus will be on the postbiblical traditions of commentary and exegesis rather than on the original "meaning" of the biblical text itself. Biblical scholars' opinions on Genesis 22 vary widely, some perceiving it simply as an imaginative etiological tale designed to "explain" the name of a venerated cultic site, and others as a historically based narrative recalling a transition in Israel's history from human to animal sacrifice.[8] But, as I have indicated, whatever the original meaning, I believe it is a mistake in trying to come to terms with the rational and moral intentionality of a religious tradition to focus primarily on early narratives of this sort. Even a tradition as powerfully shaped by moral concerns as biblical faith contains within its earliest strata isolated texts or teachings that defy rational or moral explanation. In seeking to understand a tradition, therefore, the meaning of this earliest material is far less important than what is subsequently done with it. A tradition reveals its deepest impulses not in single texts, but in the ongoing ways these texts are interpreted and handled.

As we look at discussions of Genesis 22 in Jewish and Christian teaching, one question comes to the fore: according to either tradition, did the command issued Abraham by God violate our ordinary human sense of right and wrong? Not at issue is whether Abraham's conduct was viewed as an instance, even a supreme instance, of obedience to the divine command. Nor is it important that these traditions regarded such obedience as morally praiseworthy. Both assumptions are expected where ethics is based on divine revelation. Rather, the content and nature of this command draws our attention. Did God act wrongly, by our own best conscientious standards, in issuing this command, and did Abraham act immorally in obeying it? If the predominant answer to these questions in the recorded history of commentary is yes, then we are presented with ethics making appeal to a standard that defies moral reason, and we will be hard pressed to explain how these traditions reflect requirements of reason's deep structure. But if the conduct of God and Abraham is understood and presented as morally justifiable, as an expression of humanly understandable righteousness, then the gap between reason and revelation disappears and, in this most challenging of instances, the divine command shows itself to be an instrument of reasoned morality.

The 'Kierkegaardian' Reading of Genesis 22

Perhaps the most vehement denial that Genesis 22 can be interpreted in moral terms is found in *Fear and Trembling,* the brilliant treatment of this text by the nineteenth-century Danish theologian, Søren Kierkegaard. In his poetic rendition of Genesis 22, Kierkegaard presents Abraham as the devout believer called to a fearful test in which, to obey the will of God, he must subordinate all human feelings and moral obligations.[9] So powerful is Kierkegaard's reading of Genesis 22 that, although it is a very late entry in the commentary tradition, it has shaped the thinking of subsequent generations of readers. Representing the divine command at its most antirational and antimoral, Kierkegaard's discussion serves as a touchstone we can use to evaluate more traditional Jewish and Christian responses to this text. We might begin, therefore, by looking closely at Kierkegaard's presentation of the episode.

The distinguishing feature of Kierkegaard's reading of Genesis 22 is not his emphasis on the divine command, since even die-hard rationalists are able to counsel obedience to God's commandments when these conform to the dictates of conscience. Instead, it is the vast chasm he perceives between Abraham's conduct and any possible moral justification of it. In Kierkegaard's view, Abraham's actions not only run counter to a father's natural sentiment, but they violate the highest parental duty. In ethical terms, says Kierkegaard, "Abraham's relation to Isaac is quite simply this: the father shall love his son more than himself."[10] But Abraham rejects this duty and places himself and his own relationship to God before his son's welfare. As a result, we can only conclude that Abraham is morally guilty of homicide: "the ethical expression for what Abraham did," says Kierkegaard, "is that he meant to murder Isaac."[11]

Of course, the killing of one's child is not necessarily immoral. In extreme circumstances, even the slaughter of an innocent person may be morally justified. Kierkegaard himself makes reference to three classic cases where he believes such killing can be morally defended: Agamemnon's sacrifice of Iphigenia to pacify the gods, whose wrath threatened the Greek's military success; Jeptha's killing of his daughter in fulfillment of a solemn vow made during battle (Judg. 11.30–40); and Brutus's command to execute his rebellious son. In Kierkegaard's terms, these three figures are "tragic heroes," who, to comply with some "higher expression of the ethical" such as the welfare of a state or of an entire people, must override a less pressing moral duty. Tragic heroes stay within the realm of the ethical even as they transgress some of its requirements. Their actions can be "mediated" or rationally justified, and, in principle at least, they can convey to others good reasons for their conduct.[12] But none of this, Kierkegaard insists, is true of Abraham. He is "at no time a tragic hero."[13] Rather than finding his telos, or supreme goal, in a higher expression of the ethical, he engages in a "teleological suspension of the ethical" and puts aside moral duty to obey God. As a result, Abraham "cannot talk" and must act in silence, not because he lacks an explanation for his conduct—clearly he is following God's command—but because this explanation does not constitute a valid moral reason. It makes sense only to those who accept at the outset the validity of such a command; who agree with Kierkegaard that "duty is simply the expression for God's will."[14]

I realize that some would take issue with this brief presentation of Kierkegaard's view, especially with my emphasis on the "unethical" nature of Abraham's conduct and, by implication, of the divine command that elicits it. *Fear and Trembling* is a hard book to understand. Its meaning is deeply rooted in the events of Kierkegaard's life, and this may suggest that there is a more complex aspect to Kierkegaard's use of the biblical episode than he makes clear.[15] Then, too, it may be unfair to regard the virtually uncompromising distinction he establishes between the divine command and rational ethical responsibility without taking into account the larger context of his religious thought. Gene

Outka, for example, has argued that Kierkegaard's firm belief that "God is love" must be recalled as we read this book.[16] In the next chapter, we shall return to these matters, as we locate *Fear and Trembling* within the tradition of Christian commentary on this text. But while these complexities are worth keeping in mind, they should not obscure the fact that Kierkegaard's surface argument amounts to a powerful non-rational and nonmoral reading of the biblical episode. It is this uncompromising, antirational interpretation of Genesis 22 that has shaped our modern approach to the biblical text itself. Indeed, this interpretation has even drawn support from some students of Judaism. Jacob Halevi, for example, maintains that in *Fear and Trembling,* Kierkegaard "re-created single-handedly the essential features of the Rabbinic interpretation of Abraham."[17]

In what follows, I propose to work with this 'Kierkegaardian' reading of Genesis 22 to challenge the claim that it has any relationship to the traditional Jewish interpretation. Further developing an argument begun by J. H. Gumbiner and Marvin Fox almost forty years ago, I want to show not only that Kierkegaard's rendition of Genesis 22 differs markedly from that found in the Jewish sources but that his interpretation from a Jewish point of view is "ethically and religiously impossible."[18]

Constructing a Midrash

The words *Jewish* and *Judaism* identify a tradition spanning more than two thousand years and comprising hundreds of texts and thinkers of widely different views. No statement concerning "Jewish" beliefs or teachings is absolute, and some degree of attention to internal differences and developments within the tradition is always called for. Nevertheless, where the understanding of Genesis 22 is concerned, one can easily be pardoned for adopting an approach that minimizes historical or source considerations, because, despite some small and nuanced differences in interpretation and some deepening of key themes, Jewish thinkers over the ages speak with almost one voice on the central religious and ethical meaning of this text. For this reason, I shall generally treat Jewish discussions as forming a single teaching, with all but the most important disputes relegated to footnotes. Following the approach so brilliantly elaborated by Louis Ginzberg in his multivolume *Legends of the Jews,*[19] I will try to present a single, coherent Jewish commentary, or midrash, on the episode, a synthetic rendition of the biblical passage as it was understood by the rabbis and other major Jewish commentators over the centuries. As I proceed through this commentary—really a compilation of traditional midrashim—I will point up the relationship of rabbinic teachings to the key elements of religious reasoning's deep structure.

Why Did God Try Abraham?

The time came when God put Abraham to the test. "Abraham," he called, and Abraham replied, "Here I am." God said, "Take your son Isaac, your only son, whom you love, and go to the land of Moriah. There you shall offer him as a sacrifice on one of the hills which I will show you."

Within the Jewish tradition, Genesis 22 is usually referred to as the-Akedah, or "binding," in reference to the central focus on the preparation of Isaac for sacrifice. With the Jewish consciousness thus riveted on this terrible image and with the approach to the passage shaped by the fearful import of the divine command, it is important to begin by asking how Jewish thinkers understood God's purpose in issuing this command. Specifically, why does God subject Abraham to trial and why does the trial take the dreadful form it does?

Jewish writers provide answers to both these questions. To the question of why God should impose demands or hardships on his faithful servants, the Jewish answer is almost unvarying: trials are not meant to break the will or spirit of those tested; nor are they even meant to prove to God the purity of the believer's devotion. Rather a central rabbinic teaching is that "God tries [only] the righteous."[20] Because of his foreknowledge and omniscience, God fully knows the outcome of a test and in his mercy and justice, he tries only those who can sustain the adversity. But if so, why does God test the righteous at all? An imaginative exchange between God and Abraham in one midrash provides an answer. Observing that God surely foresaw the outcome of this trial, Abraham asks why he was tested in the first place. God replies, "It was my wish that the world should become acquainted with thee, and should know that it is not without good reason that I have chosen thee from all the nations."[21] If we dwell on this comment a moment, we can see that it has the effect of converting a seemingly arbitrary and capricious act by God into proof of his equity and justice. Abraham is subjected to the ordeal to demonstrate that God does not play favorites. As Marvin Fox observes, this midrash is a "striking instance" of the Jewish conception of the "reasonability and comprehensibility" of the Akedah.[22] In typical fashion, the God who commands Abraham to sacrifice his son in Genesis 22 is made one by the rabbis with the God of whom Abraham, in Genesis 18.25, can ask, "Shall not the Judge of all the earth do right?"

Moralization of the episode continues as the Jewish sources seek to answer the question of why the trial takes the specific form of a command to sacrifice Isaac. The answers to this constitute some of the richest and most fanciful talmudic glosses on the event. In several key sources, for example, a Job-like prologue is added to the Akedah— Abraham and Job are frequently linked in rabbinic speculation[23]—and Satan is given an important role. In this connection, Satan is not an independent agent opposed to God, but instead is a servant in the divine court who has the responsibility of spying out, accusing, and prosecuting human wickedness. According to these sources, following a journey to earth, Satan reports back to God concerning the sad state of human beings, who no sooner receive a blessing than they forget God and abandon his commandments. Abraham is an example, says Satan. Before Isaac was born, Abraham beseeched God and worshipped him frequently, but following the birth, he ceased his offerings. Indeed, adds Satan, when Abraham prepared a great celebration for the birth, he failed to offer up a single lamb or goat—or even a turtledove—in gratitude. Satan concludes that Abraham has forsaken his creator and benefactor, but God replies that this is not true, that Abraham is an upright man who would not withhold even his son as a burnt offering if this were asked of him. To establish this point God permits the trial.[24]

The sources embroider this prologue and add different elements. Sometimes it is the angels who accuse.[25] Or it is said that Abraham himself takes note of his neglect of God.[26] In another variant, Abraham's apparent fault is differently described: to celebrate Isaac's birth, Abraham offers a feast especially for the magnates of the time and their wives. Satan appears at Abraham's door as a beggar asking alms and notes the absence of poor people at the party. Because Abraham and Sarah are so busy with the guests, they fail to pay due attention to the spurious beggar, and Satan, entirely omitting mention of Abraham's accustomed lavish hospitality to the poor, accuses him before God of a neglect of charity.[27]

Despite their different emphases, these stories share a common point. The source of the trial is the accusation that Abraham, having received a great blessing at the hands of God, has lapsed back into the state of "natural man."[28] Where formerly his supreme loyalty was to God *above* family or people, now, with the birth of a son, he has given himself up completely to love of the child and has forgotten his higher obligations both to God and to his fellow human beings. These accusations are false—as evidenced by the pains the rabbis take to show that the episode of the neglected beggar was trumped up. But they make it necessary for God to redemonstrate to all the grounds of his firm confidence in Abraham. Hence, the trial.

A contrast here with Kierkegaard's own midrash is in order. Repeatedly, Kierkegaard tells us that to appreciate the full dreadfulness of the divine command, we must understand that, ethically speaking, Abraham's primary responsibility is to the welfare of Isaac. "To the son the father has the highest and holiest" ethical obligation.[29] Presumably, then, any command running counter to this responsibility is morally wrong and can only be explained by a higher religious duty. But this is nonsense, as Kierkegaard himself recognizes when he introduces the idea of the "tragic hero." Certainly our moral responsibilities transcend family loyalties. If Kierkegaard were right, the vendetta code of inter-family violence would be a consummate illustration of moral responsibility instead of the outrage it is.

As this prologue material illustrates, the rabbis were keenly aware of this. In their view, the life of Abraham, including the trial, is an ongoing testimony to the moral limits of natural relationships. One midrash, for example, notes that in the first and last of God's revelations to Abraham—the command to depart from his country and kin (Gen. 12.1–3) and the command to take Isaac to Moriah—God uses the same words: "Get thee . . . ," evidence that the commands are somehow similar.[30] Commenting on this, Martin Buber observes that for the rabbis, these commands bracket the key events of Abraham's life. Together, they symbolize the transcendence of God's universal moral will over the most important natural relationships: the first severs Abraham's ties to the world of the fathers and the second to the world of the sons.[31]

This does not mean that the rabbis took these penultimate moral responsibilities lightly. They were particularly sensitive to the charge that in leaving his aged father, Terah, Abraham violated the very special duty of honoring one's parents. The rabbinic literature makes it clear that Terah, an unrepentant idolator, did not deserve unquestioning respect. One midrash even has God warn Abraham of his relatives' intention to kill him, but a still hesitant Abraham shares with God his anxiety about abandoning his father.[32] In response, God grants Abraham a special exemption from the duty of honoring one's parent. Interestingly, Jacob Halevi, a vehement defender of the compatibility of Kierkegaard's interpretation of the Akedah with Jewish teaching, holds this up as a further instance of the teleological suspension of the ethical in classical Jewish teaching.[33] But to accept Halevi's view would require us to believe that there can be no more lofty *moral* responsibility than to honor one's parents (even wicked parents). Against this, both our own moral sense and traditional Jewish teaching support the view that the divine command can correlate with our higher moral obligations.

Isaac's Role

So Abraham took the wood for the sacrifice and laid it on his son Isaac's shoulders; he himself carried the fire and the knife; and the two of them went on together.

The idea that God can have good reasons for calling Abraham forth in order to display the patriarch's excellence and his ability to transcend narrow family loyalties does not by itself fully justify God's actions. There still remains the problem posed by the content of the command itself. What conceivable justification can there be for God's ordering the murder of an innocent child? Why should Isaac be involved in a test of his father?

Before turning to the major rabbinic response to these questions, I want to offer a consideration that may reduce our perception of the seriousness of the problem. For Kierkegaard, Abraham's treatment of Isaac is essentially a moral issue: father and son are regarded as two independent persons with possibly conflicting interests that are subject to moral arbitration. There is a *moral* distance between the two, something evocatively displayed in Kierkegaard's "Exordium," where, to prevent Isaac from hating God, Abraham plays the villain by throwing the boy to the ground and allowing him to cry to God for help.[34] Now, while most of us share this conception of parent and child as two independent individuals, in some ways this is a modern idea, and it does not appear to be the view of either the biblical or the rabbinic writers. Traditionally, they conceive a young child legally as a possession of the parent, and morally as a physical-emotional part of the parent's person. Repeatedly in the biblical texts, for example, we see that divine threats and imprecations against wrongdoers include promises of destruction of their offspring.[35] These threats are often understood to involve a notion of collective responsibility, as though all the members of a household, a community, or even a nation are somehow primitively held to share in the guilt of the leader. But as David Daube points out in the context of a discussion of political leadership, these attitudes may sometimes be explained by a very different notion of "ruler responsibility," according to which punishment of a people is merely one further evil inflicted on the leader himself.[36] Similarly, punishment or threat of punishment of a child need not involve a presumption of the youngster's guilt so much as the view that the child is intimately a part of the parent's person. The child's suffering is merely an extension of the parent's suffering or punishment.

We may find this notion morally primitive (although it contains a powerful human truth), but if it forms part of the operative beliefs of a people, it has an important bearing on an episode like the Akedah. It suggests that, for those who hold this view, there is no essential moral distance between Abraham and Isaac. Isaac is merely an extension of Abraham. In this context, the divine command loses Kierkegaard's morally troubling dimension (no independent third party is involved) and, instead, becomes a call to consummate personal sacrifice for Abraham. In religious terms, Genesis 22 becomes a part of the theodicy problem, the question of why, in a world supposedly ruled by a just God, the righteous suffer. Now, while theodicy raises sharp moral questions, they are not the same as those posed by divine command morality. Because theodicy proceeds from the question of how a righteous god can permit suffering, it starts with an assumption of the essential morality and justness of the deity, something fully congruent with rationally founded religious belief.[37] From this starting point, it seeks humanly comprehensible reasons that morally justify God's conduct. Indeed, the issue of theodicy would hardly arise if it were believed, as some extreme proponents of divine command morality hold, that whatever God commands is morally right.

We can only speculate on whether this fusion of Isaac's interests with Abraham's underlies the biblical text itself, but there is some evidence for it in rabbinic discussions. For example, in the same series of exchanges where God explains that his aim was demonstrating to the world Abraham's righteousness, God says to the patriarch: "Before Me it is unveiled and known that even if I had asked thee for thy life, thou wouldst not have withheld it."[38] This is a strange remark. How can involvement in the murder of one's child be placed on a footing with, or even be seen as less demanding than, the voluntary sacrifice of one's own life? The answer to this, I think, is that the Akedah is not viewed here as having Kierkegaard's morally troubling dimension. The command to sacrifice and a possible command to yield up one's own life are primarily perceived in terms of the personal loss involved. In short, there are good reasons for assuming that the Hebrew and Jewish mind did not always presume Kierkegaard's perceived moral distance between father and son. God's command, though it might raise troubling questions concerning the reasons for the call to self-sacrifice, was not seen as involving a suspension of ordinary moral responsibility.[39]

This absence of moral distance between Abraham and Isaac was further suggested to rabbinic writers by the word *together* in the biblical account.[40] Speculating on the meaning of this, some commentators developed an understanding of the Akedah that eliminates any possible moral problem, not by diminishing Isaac's independent moral personality, but by magnifying it and making him a fully voluntary participant in the event. Nowhere do we find an illustration of the Jewish confidence that God cannot command wickedness, and nowhere do we see the rabbis' sense of interpretive freedom with respect to scripture more forcefully displayed than in the midrashic expansion of Isaac's role. Although the biblical text refers to him as a lad *(na'ar),* the rabbinic sources almost always describe him as a young adult. Reckoning by a chronology given elsewhere in the biblical text, they usually hold him to be thirty-seven years of age (a "lad," we might suppose, by biblical standards of longevity!).[41] Because of Isaac's age, some writers maintain that it is unthinkable that the elderly Abraham could coerce him to Moriah or bind him to the altar without his consent;[42] hence, in rabbinic teaching, Isaac is conceived as every bit as willing a participant as Abraham. Isaac is not distressed by his father's undertaking but accepts his fate;[43] he assists in the preparations, carrying the wood for the fire.[44] Throughout, he ignores the treacherous counsel of Satan to resist his father or God;[45] and, fearful that in a moment of uncontrollable panic he might cry out and curse Abraham or injure himself (thus becoming a blemished offering), he asks that he be bound securely.[46] But these fears are unwarranted and he cooperates to the end, stretching his neck beneath the knife.[47]

Isaac's free participation in the Akedah is further underscored by a series of midrashim that trace the trial itself to Isaac's initiative.

According to one of these, the young boy becomes involved in a dispute with his half brother, Ishmael, who argues that while Isaac had been circumcised involuntarily as an infant, he had himself freely undergone circumcision at the age of thirteen, and, as a result, his sacrifice was more beloved of God. To this Isaac retorts, "All that thou didst lend to the Holy one, blessed be He, was three drops of blood. But lo, I am now thirty-seven years old, yet if God desired of me that I be slaughtered, I would not refuse." At this, God intervenes, exclaims, "This is the moment!" and the trial of Abraham begins.[48]

What all these accounts make clear is that for traditional Jewish teaching, Isaac is not the terrified and unwilling victim Kierkegaard makes him out to be. Instead, as Davies and Chilton observe, he is the "exemplary martyr who, aware of his fate, is prepared to meet it with fortitude."[49] In fact, as my previous remarks suggest, whether the focus is on Abraham or Isaac, it is the lesson of self-sacrificial and willing martyrdom, not a commanded violation of the ethical, that Jewish sources derive from the Genesis episode. The historical setting of the rabbinic discussions partly helps explain this. Many of these sources arose during the long period of suffering framed by the Maccabean revolt and the later Roman war. Here, the choice of martyrdom to sanctify God's name (the concept of *kiddush ha-shem*) becomes the supreme religious act—and the Akedah its prototype. Small wonder, then, that when we turn to one of the most celebrated moments in the history of Jewish martyrdom, the case of the mother and her seven sons who die rather than prostrate themselves before a graven image, the episode concludes with a bold reference to the Akedah. Yielding her last son to slaughter, the mother bids him to convey to Abraham this message: "Thus, said my mother, 'Do not preen yourself [on your righteousness], saying I built an altar and offered up my son, Isaac.' Behold, our mother built seven altars and offered up seven sons in one day. Yours was only a test, but mine was in earnest."[50] Through texts like these, the Akedah became firmly rooted as a central event in the Jewish martyriological tradition. Martyrdom, of course, raises the deepest theological and ethical questions. But, once again, these belong to the domain of theodicy where God's humanly comprehensible justice is presupposed. That Jewish writers should interpret the Akedah in these terms, that they should connect it up with their other major efforts at theodicy, and that they should also try to provide morally justifying reasons for God's requiring Abraham and Isaac's self-sacrifice, shows how far we are from the world of Kierkegaard's antirational and antimoral interpretation of the text.[51]

Abraham's Silence

Isaac said to Abraham, "Father," and he answered, "What is it, son?" Isaac said, "Here are the fire and the wood, but where is the young beast for the sacrifice?" Abraham answered, "God will provide himself a young beast for a sacrifice, my son."

Abraham's evasive response to Isaac provides Kierkegaard with an extended opportunity to develop and comment on the theme of the patriarch's silence and concealment. Abraham, Kierkegaard remarks, *cannot* talk to anyone (not even Isaac), because he cannot offer the ethically or rationally intelligible word that explains anything. Agamemnon can speak to Iphigenia, says Kierkegaard, and she can understand because her father's undertaking "expresses the universal." But Abraham, for whom ethical responsibility is here a distraction from a higher religious duty, can only use irony and employ paradox.[52]

We have seen already that classical Jewish writers do not agree with Kierkegaard's assumption of silence and concealment between Abraham and Isaac—in the rabbinic accounts, there is no concealment, even though this makes Isaac's binding and his innocent question in the biblical text peculiar. Generally, however, these writers follow the biblical account and agree with Kierkegaard's assumption that Abraham does not publicize his undertaking. In an effort to spare Sarah anguish, for example, Abraham does not tell her of the command. (As it turns out this has unfortunate consequences since Satan's later false report of Isaac's death causes her to die of shock before Abraham returns.)[53] Nor is there mention of Abraham's conversing with others.

The rabbis themselves do not discuss or comment on the reasons for Abraham's silence. But one Jewish writer, Philo of Alexandria, deals with it at length, and his remarks provide a striking contrast to Kierkegaard's. The contrast is all the more important because in many ways Philo's discussion, one of the earliest Jewish commentaries, is similar to Kierkegaard's.[54] Philo, like Kierkegaard, is especially interested in demonstrating Abraham's uniqueness and in rebutting accusers who maintain that there is nothing singular about the patriarch's achievement. Like Kierkegaard, Philo contrasts Abraham with figures (including perhaps Agamemnon) who are well known for having sacrificed their offspring to deliver their country from the evils of war, drought, or pestilence. We might recall that in Kierkegaard's view what distinguishes Abraham from these figures is the fact that they remain "tragic heroes," who reside within the ethical and who in principle are able to talk about and morally justify their conduct. Abraham shares none of these qualities and must remain silent.

Philo, too emphasizes Abraham's silence. But despite the similarities between these discussions, Philo offers a quite different explanation for Abraham's unwillingness to speak. All these other figures, he says, have similar motives for their acts. They offer up their children either because they fear persons (or forces) more powerful than themselves or because they desire glory, honor, and renown. These figures, says Philo, do not merit praise. If moved by fear, their actions are not entirely voluntary and if motivated to kill their children by a desire for glory, they should be morally condemned rather than praised. But neither motive is attributable to Abraham. He could not be impelled by fear of others, Philo observes, because no one knew of his act, nor, clearly, was he involuntarily impelled by fear of an impending calamity, since Abraham was motivated by devotion to God, not fear of him.[55] Finally, there is no possibility that Abraham sought "praise from the multitude" for this deed:

> What praise could be obtained in the desert, when there was no one likely to be present . . . and when even his two servants were left at a distance on purpose that he might not seem to be hunting after praise, or to be making a display by bringing witnesses with him to see the greatness of his devotion?"[56]

Clearly, Philo does not present here an antimoral interpretation of Abraham's solitary silence. His point is not that Abraham is silent because of the ethically unjustifiable nature of his act, but rather that this silence proves the absolute purity of Abraham's intention. Depending on the final ethical judgment we render on the divine command, however, this is a point that any rigorous moral thinker could support. An act done out of fearful self-regard or for selfish motives is imperfect, and Philo's whole purpose is to find absolute purity of motive in Abraham alone. In many respects, Philo is a strange figure. With one foot planted in Hebraic thought and the other in the world of Greek philosophy, in some ways he represents neither viewpoint. But in this instance, the force of both Greek and Hebrew ethical wisdom comes through to support at least a potentially moral understanding of Abraham's conduct. Nowhere in this discussion do we see his Hebraic background—even in conjunction with the volatile contributions of Hellenistic speculation—supporting a nonmoral interpretation of the Genesis episode.

Death and Resurrection

> *There Abraham built an altar and arranged the wood. He bound*
> *his son Isaac and laid him on the altar on top of the wood. Then he*
> *stretched out his hand and took the knife to kill his son; but the*
> *angel of the Lord called to him from heaven, "Abraham, Abraham*
> *... Do not raise your hand against the boy; do not touch him. Now*
> *I know that you are a God-fearing man. You have not withheld*
> *from me your son, your only son."*

This dramatic moment in the episode occasioned a great deal of rabbinic commentary. The role of the angel, for example, was much
expanded. As Abraham himself had earlier intervened for the righteous
of Sodom and Gomorrah, the angels become intercessors on Abraham's
behalf. With the knife at Isaac's throat, according to one account, the
angels appear "weeping and lamenting" before the Lord. They make
appeal to Isaiah 33.8, "The highways lie waste ... " and remind God
of the patriarch's deserved reward for helping travelers by providing
them free bed and board: "It was through such help that Abraham made
Thee known to the world," they observe.[57] Another version has the
angels appeal directly on behalf of Isaac to God's mercy, compassion,
and righteousness.[58]

The prolongation of the moment with the knife at Isaac's throat,
the double repetition of Abraham's name, as though there were the real
possibility that Isaac might die, troubled the rabbis no less than the
modern reader and stimulated their imaginations. Some accounts have
the angels cry out asking God how much longer he will wait,[59] while
others venture into the most daring speculation: perhaps the command
to halt did not come in time? Perhaps Isaac perished? In one account
we find it said that the blade touched Isaac's neck and his soul departed.
Only after the command arrived did his soul return to his body. In this
way, we are told, "Isaac knew that ... the dead in the future will be
quickened."[60]

Thanks to Shalom Spiegel's *The Last Trial*,[61] we have become
aware of a vast undercurrent of later Jewish speculation on the possibility that Isaac died at Moriah. Spiegel and others ask the question of
whether this speculation precedes Christianity or is influenced by it (we
will see a similar understanding of the Akedah presented in Hebrews
11.17ff.).[62] But whichever is the case, for many Jewish writers clearly,
the Akedah receives its *central* significance as an instance of biblical
testimony to the doctrine of the resurrection of the dead. In this sense,

their focus is not on the beginning of the episode (the dreadful and perhaps ethically problematical divine command), but rather on its end and the lesson of God's unlimited capacity to redeem and reward the righteous. I have argued elsewhere that the doctrine of resurrection is one of the main pillars of the rational and moral edifice of religious thought constructed by Judaism and Christianity.[63] It represents a powerful effort to affirm that present earthly suffering is not the ultimate fate of the just. The association of the Akedah with this doctrine, therefore, is another illustration of how the commentary tradition uses the episode not to undermine but to affirm a moral conception of the deity.

Sacrifice

Abraham looked up, and there he saw a ram caught by its horns in a thicket. So he went and took the ram and offered it as a sacrifice instead of his son.

Among the more peculiar features of the commentary tradition is the amount of attention given the ram. This is partly explained by the animal's association with the temple cult. Very shortly we shall see the importance of this association of the Akedah with atonement. But for the moment, I want to point out some of the other ethically significant features of this emphasis on the ram, including some of its more whimsical aspects. According to most accounts, for example, the ram for this sacrifice was created at twilight on the eve of the first sabbath,[64] and was ordained as ownerless, so that Abraham would not be held guilty of the misappropriation of someone else's property.[65] The rabbis would spare Abraham even this minor wrong. One detailed discussion of the ram makes it a voluntary sacrifice. Running to offer itself, the animal is distracted by Satan and becomes caught in the thicket by its horns. To draw Abraham's attention, it puts forth its leg and tugs at his coat.[66] This is an example of rabbinic midrashic elaboration at its best, but it also conveys a sense of the rabbis' compassion and moral sensitivity: not even the ram shall be an unwilling victim. Reading passages like this, one is reminded of efforts in popular Hindu or Buddhist literature to qualify seeming wrongs done to animals (they are declared to be the recipients either of some deserved karmic punishment or some future reward). In these otherwise very different popular traditions, the aim is similar: to ensure that an ethically intentioned narrative not be blemished in any way.

On a deeper level, the substitution of the ram for the child—and hence of animal for human sacrifice—is treated by some Jewish commentators as the fundamental meaning of the Genesis episode. These sources repeatedly affirm, for example, that from the outset God had no intention of asking the sacrifice of Isaac and was always prepared to provide the ram in his place.[67] These statements are further linked to expressions of God's hatred of child sacrifice, as demonstrated by repeated scriptural condemnations of the practice.[68] We saw that biblical scholars have sometimes maintained that the Genesis text in its original historical setting was directed against the Canaanite cult of child sacrifice.[69] Whether this is true or not, such a meaning was clearly attributed to the episode by some later Jewish interpreters.

The Blessings of Redemption and Forgiveness

Then the angel of the Lord called from heaven a second time to Abraham, "This is the word of the Lord: By my own self I swear: inasmuch as you have done this and have not withheld your son, your only son, I will bless you abundantly and greatly multiply your descendants until they are as numerous as the stars in the skies and the grains of sand on the sea-shore."

It is not fair to say that the rabbis overlooked the terrible aspects of the Akedah. Anticipating Kierkegaard, they were sensitive to the divine command as it confronted Abraham, and although they tended to view this in terms of the anguish experienced by the martyr rather than the murderer, they did not omit the element of dread. Nevertheless, it is also true that far more than Kierkegaard, Jewish writers dwelled on the end of this episode, not just its beginning. In their view Genesis 22 was more an occasion for celebration than for anguish, and its principal lesson was not God's demand, but his ultimate compassion and mercy. This becomes partly understandable when we recall that in the commentary tradition, Abraham and Isaac are the prototypes of all later martyrs. It thus becomes entirely natural that during periods of pogrom and persecution, the Akedah should become a favorite text and a subject of popular piety. As Spiegel has shown, when, during the terrible persecutions of the eleventh and twelfth centuries, Jews called on God to remember the Akedah they were in effect asking him to spare their children from the flames as he had previously spared Isaac.[70] Here the

Akedah becomes an example of God's infinite solicitousness for his people and of his ability to intervene at the last desperate moment.

More than as an example of God's power and righteousness, however, the Akedah is also very often viewed as an express commitment made by God to his people. Repeatedly, God's promised blessing is alluded to, and the people's right to redemption is further grounded in a reserve of merit established by Abraham and Isaac's obedience. The two become a vicarious sacrifice for future generations. This conception is facilitated in rabbinic thought by the linking of the Akedah with the temple sacrificial cult.[71] For later piety and popular tradition, virtually all the elements of the Genesis episode assume a cultic significance. Moriah is said to be the site of the temple mount, the ashes of the sacrificial fire (Isaac's ashes in some accounts) underlie the altar,[72] and the various parts of the ram are identified with cultic objects, its horn becoming converted into the shofar blown on Rosh Hashanah, the Jewish New Year's Day, in anticipation of the season of atonement.[73]

Against this symbolic and conceptual background, certain rabbinic appeals to the Akedah make sense. One midrash, for example, expands on the meaning of Genesis 22.13, "after him caught in the thicket," by relating it to the future:

> The Holy One, blessed be He, meant: Behold what is to come! Thy children who will succeed thee will one day be entangled and caught in sins like the ram in the thicket. What use are they then to make of a ram's horns? They are to lift up the horns and blow them. Whereupon I will be reminded of the binding of Isaac and will acquit them in the judgment.[74]

Elsewhere, in a similar vein, the thicket is associated with the many foreign nations with whom the Israelite's sins will involve them, and the Akedah is appealed to as the sign and promise of redemption. Indeed, this explicit association of the Akedah with redemption from sin is the final motif I want to identify in the Jewish sources. And in many ways, it forms a fitting conclusion to this review, because we approach here a Jewish understanding of the Akedah that is at once similar to Kierkegaard's apparent reading of the text and yet—in the end—almost totally different. Briefly stated, in the Genesis episode, Jewish commentators did perceive something like a "teleological suspension of the ethical," but one whose implications were consummately moral.

Another version of the Akedah as an appeal to God's mercy, forming part of the Sephardic Rosh Hashanah liturgy, illuminates what I mean. In this text, the suppliant reminds God of the Genesis episode:

> And may there appear before Thee the Akedah to which Father Abraham subjected his son Isaac on the altar, suppressing his own feelings of pity in order to do Thy will with a perfect heart. So let Thy feelings of pity suppress Thine anger (and remove it) from us. . . . May Thy compassion suppress Thine anger, oh, may Thy compassion prevail over Thine (other) Attributes.[75]

In another version, it is Abraham who speaks and reminds God of how he resisted the impulse, on receiving the divine command, to recall to God the promise of offspring through Isaac. Abraham continues:

> Just as I had an answer to give Thee but I controlled my inclination and did not reply to Thee . . . , so when the children of Isaac give way to transgressions and evil deeds, do Thou recollect for them the binding of their Father Isaac and rise from the Throne of Judgment and betake Thee to the Throne of Mercy, and being filled with compassion for them. . . . change the Attribute of Justice into the Attribute of Mercy![76]

In both these passages, an analogy between the conduct of human beings and God is established. As Abraham did not permit himself to follow the normal and expected course of conduct, God ought not to do so. While it is not clear that Abraham's behavior in these instances is conceived as involving a suspension of the ethical—in the first passage it is parental affection that is suppressed, in the second the impulse to make a further moral appeal to God's promise—God is surely being asked to bend or abandon his firm standard of justice. The people fully merit punishment, but the hope is that God will remember the Akedah and allow his "attribute" of mercy to prevail over his "attribute" of justice.

The tempering of justice with mercy is one of the weightiest problems of the moral life. Within society it is the problem of establishing a fair, humane balance between punishment and forgiveness. On the religious plane, it is the problem of establishing the respective roles of God's justice and grace in the economy of redemption and of doing so in a way that compromises neither attribute. In general, Jewish thinkers explored this problem with boldness and honesty. Their moral sensitivity and experience told them that no human being or community could ever fully comply with God's uncompromising religious and moral demands.[77] They shared with Christian thinkers a keen sense of the evil that infects the human heart, and they repeatedly affirmed that if God were to rule by his strict standard of justice, the world could not endure.[78] As a result, they were fully cognizant of the need for God's mercy. Although they never qualified their insistence on renewed human ethical striving and repentance, they were prepared to give divine mercy primacy in the process of redemption. In rabbinic speculation, these tensions and their resolution are graphically illustrated by the association of justice and mercy respectively with God's left and right hands. Why is mercy the right hand? Because its greater strength is needed to suppress the left hand of justice.[79]

Against this background we can see that these appeals to the Akedah involve a "teleological suspension of the ethical," but one that occurs at the level of God's conduct and whose purpose *(telos)* is supremely moral. If God puts aside his strict standard of righteousness, it is not to kill but to prevent death, not to eliminate the ethical but to lift the burden of suffering, sin, and despair that impede human beings' religious and moral rededication. In terms of religious reasoning, the Akedah becomes a vehicle for affirming Judaism's response to the third element of reason's deep structure, God's ability to transcend his own retributive order to make possible human moral renewal. This employment of the Akedah vividly illustrates how at the furthest reaches of theological speculation, Jewish thinkers did not relinquish their insistence on God's righteousness or insist merely on the primacy of his will, as divine command theorists would have it, but rather pursued their understanding of God's will to a fully moral conclusion.

Judaism's Moral Faith

I have dwelt on the details of Jewish interpretations of Genesis 22 because I have wanted to provide the richest possible illustration of the ways rational and moral considerations mold a tradition ostensibly based on revelation and the divine command. Over the centuries, Jewish philosophers sometimes speculated about the role of reason and revelation in Jewish faith and ethics.[80] But when it came to actually filling out the content of the divine command and dealing with it in connection with a difficult text like Genesis 22, the rabbinic sources themselves present a portrait of God as righteous in all his ways. The treatment of this text reveals the spontaneous and most characteristic self-understanding of the tradition, a self-understanding marked from beginning to end by moral concerns. Within the Jewish sources, there is not a hint of Kierkegaard's interpretation, and within the Jewish tradition as a whole there is no thinker like Kierkegaard to raise the theoretical question of whether human moral reason and divine revelation can ultimately disagree: that they *cannot* is an implicit but defining tenet of the faith.

This means that in seeking to understand historical religious traditions in rational terms it is too simple to dwell on claims about the supremacy of revelation over human moral reason. Rather, we must always look to the *content* of revelation and to the nature of its *source* if we are to begin to appreciate the complex ways in which rational considerations underlie and shape religious thought. What Judaism's treatment of Genesis 22 shows is that an intensely moral intentionality can inspire and lie behind fervent emphases on God's will. The divine command and rational morality are fused together by an understanding of God's character that removes any possibility of his transgressing the dictates of informed human conscience. Perhaps the most astonishing piece of evidence for Judaism's commitment to reason and morality is the fact that although Genesis 22 was interpreted in many ways within this tradition, the text itself was never conceived to present a moral problem but was always regarded as one of the most important biblical illustrations of God's righteousness.

5

Revelation and Reason in Biblical Faith: Genesis 22 and Christianity

Over the centuries, Jewish thinking on the issue of morality and revelation displayed a tight, if internally tense, unity. While all ritual and moral norms were held to derive from God's will, this will was viewed as so unquestionably righteous that the prospect of an immoral or wicked divine command became unthinkable. In contrast, Christianity developed a tradition of thought that led to moral and religious possibilities largely unconsidered by the rabbis. For example, some Christian thinkers developed the idea of an ethic independent of revelation known to human beings on the basis of reason alone: the ethic of natural law. Others opposed this emphasis on human autonomy in ethics and set forth seemingly uncompromising defenses of a divine command morality that would equate morality with whatever God willed. Nevertheless, despite all this diversity of theological speculation, we can apply to Christianity essentially the same conclusion we arrived at for Judaism: in Christian thinking, the divine command was almost always interpreted to support the deepest requirements of human moral and religious reasoning.

As in Judaism, Genesis 22 remains our focal point for understanding Christian thinking about the relationship between religion and morality. Christian treatments of this episode largely carried over, and sometimes independently developed, interpretations set forth by the rabbis. Yet there was a subtle shift in emphasis in Christian thinking about the text. Whereas Jewish writers commonly defended God's justice in issuing the command to Abraham and were less inclined to develop the complex themes of vicarious atonement and divine mercy they also saw in the episode, Christian thinkers frequently made these themes the centerpiece of their discussions. This is understandable given the centrality of divine grace in the Christian message, but it becomes even more understandable when we recognize that in Christian thinking, the Akedah became the prototype of the Christ event. At Gethsemane, the act God commanded but did not require of Abraham is carried to completion: a father offers up his son for the salvation of the world.

One consequence of this reading of the Akedah in the light of the crucifixion is that in Christian thinking, the Genesis episode is always linked with God's forgiveness and with the apparent suspension of justice this involves. We saw this theme emerge in rabbinic treatments of the Akedah, but it was greatly expanded in Christian writings. This is why Christian discussions of reason and revelation in general, and of Genesis 22 in particular, sometimes take extreme forms; the suspension of strict justice required by forgiveness is the most complex element in the deep structure of religious reasoning. But I am running ahead of myself. Here it is enough to say that Christian interpretations of Genesis 22 often proceed on different levels. Frequently, surface discussions of the place of reason and revelation in the moral life conceal the faith's deepest theological involvement with the mysteries of divine forgiveness and grace.

New Testament Beginnings

In Judaism, the Akedah was a focus for imaginative glosses meant to flesh out the biblical narrative. Christianity also has its "midrashim" on this text, but among Christian writers, treatment of Genesis 22 more often occurs in the context of systematic theological treatises, where the Genesis episode is used to illustrate key themes of the writer. Christian treatments of Genesis 22, therefore, require a slightly different approach. Rather than gathering together separated references into a running gloss on the text, we have to locate and understand treatments of Genesis 22 within the context of the discussions where they occur.

Two brief New Testament passages that explicitly touch on Genesis 22 serve as the starting point for Christian thinking on this text.[1] The first reference, James 2.21–23, illustrates the tendency of Christian writers to use the Akedah as a vehicle for exploring other theological concerns:

> Was not Abraham our father justified by works, when he offered his son Isaac upon the altar? You see that faith was active along with his works, and faith was completed by works. And the scripture was fulfilled which says, "Abraham believed God, and it was reckoned to him as righteousness;" and he was called the friend of God.

Here, the specifically moral significance of the Akedah is eclipsed by the writer's theological interest in the question of whether faith or works are more important for salvation. Although the author of James, like Jewish writers before him, assumes that Abraham's conduct is praiseworthy, we are not told why this is so. Nor are we informed of the nature of the "belief" possessed by Abraham that served to ground his exemplary conduct. James leaves unanswered the moral questions raised by the episode, including why God should issue this command and whether Abraham was morally justified in obeying it.

Some of these gaps are filled by Heb. 11.17–19, the other New Testament text that explicitly deals with the Akedah. In fact, if we read Hebrews and James together we should be able to discern the general outlines of early Christian thinking about the moral questions raised by Genesis 22. As in some rabbinic midrashim, the sacrifice of Isaac is spoken of as having been completed, and the Genesis episode is held up as proof of the doctrine of resurrection:

> By faith, Abraham, when he was tested, offered up Isaac, and he who had received the promises was ready to offer up his only son, of whom it was said, "Through Isaac shall your descendants be named." He considered that God was able to raise men even from the dead; hence, figuratively speaking, he did receive him back.

Although very brief, this reference contains a partial moral justification of God's command and a clear justification of Abraham's obedience. These justifications were repeated over and over again in subsequent Christian discussions. To the question, "Would God command the destruction of a child?," Hebrews answers no. Although God appeared to require killing, his power renders death a transitory event soon followed by restoration to eternal life. Furthermore, in raising Isaac, God revealed his essential fidelity and trustworthiness. He did not make promises to break them. He was not motivated by caprice, nor is he a tyrant whose mere willing and power dictate required human conduct. Rather, he is a God who sustains the righteous and who remains true to his word.

This understanding also serves to define the faith of Abraham. This faith, which underlay Abraham's obedience and justifies his preeminence, did not consist merely of the volitional act of obedience to God's will. It had a cognitive component as well: Abraham obeyed *because* he believed God to be righteous and faithful to his promises. Faith, then, amounts to a *moral trust* in God. It is the conviction that, despite appearances, and in humanly understandable ways, God is just and shows himself to be so. To the extent that Hebrews represents an early Christian view of Genesis 22, therefore, it is very distant from the kind of divine command morality suggested by Kierkegaard's *Fear and Trembling*. God's will does not arbitrarily define morality, nor is it potentially opposed to morality; and faith does not consist of obedience to this will, regardless of the moral content of the divine command. As in Judaism, faith is obedience to God in the conviction that the divine will and human conscience cannot ultimately contradict one another.

The Early Church

Although Genesis 22 is touched on briefly by a number of early Christian writers,[2] the episode receives its next extensive treatment during the third century at the hands of Origen and, a century later, in the writings of St. Augustine. Each of these theologians contributed new elements to the treatment of the text. But each also carried over the essentially moral understanding established by the rabbis and by the New Testament.

Origen's treatment of Genesis 22 in his *Homilies on Genesis* is replete with the figurative and allegorical interpretations that characterize his approach to scripture generally. Every detail of the Genesis text, for example, is seen to bear christological meaning. The fact that Isaac carries the wood for his own sacrifice becomes a "figure" for Christ's carrying the cross;[3] the ram also represents Christ, as does Isaac in his role as both priest and victim.[4] Allegorically, Isaac signifies the "affections of the flesh" and the "joy" a believer must be prepared to offer up in sacrifice to God.[5]

Although seemingly remote from the moral issues raised by the text, these imaginative interpretations suggest that Origen, like the rabbis, conceived of the Genesis episode not as a divine command to kill an innocent victim but as a personal trial for Abraham. The emphasis in the allegorical reading is not on the patriarch's crisis of conscience but on the fact that he had to relinquish his joy and the object of his natural affections to obey the divine command. In addition, by assimilating the Akedah to the crucifixion, the figurative reading makes it, for both Abraham and Isaac, a matter of voluntary submission to God's will. Once again, therefore, we are on the terrain of martyrdom, not murder. Martyrdom was the fate of Origen and many of his Christian contemporaries, and they braced for it by looking back on the Genesis episode and Christ's sacrifice as illustrious precedents.

The moral framework of Origen's thought is further suggested by his handling of the specific moral issues he identified in the episode. One of these was the question of whether God's word could be relied on. In a colorful passage, Origen addresses himself directly to the patriarch:

> What do you say to these things, Abraham? What kind of thoughts are stirring in your heart? A word has been uttered by God which is such as to shatter and try your faith. What do you say to these things? What are you thinking? What are you reconsidering? Are you thinking, are you turning over in your heart that, if the promise has been given to me in Isaac, but I offer him for an holocaust, it remains that the promise holds no hope? Or rather do you think of those well-known words and say that it is impossible for him who promised to lie [Heb. 6.18], be that as it may, the promise shall remain?[6]

Declaring himself unable to examine the thoughts of such a great patriarch, Origen nevertheless calls on the teaching of "the apostle Paul," as found in Hebrews 11.17–19, to answer these questions. Abraham's confident trust in the resurrection, says Origen, allowed the patriarch to sustain the conviction that God did not deceive.

This concern with truthfulness also occupies Origen in another passage where he deals with Abraham's injunction to the servants to stay behind and his assurance to them that both he and the child will soon return. Again addressing the patriarch, Origen asks,

> Tell me, Abraham, are you saying to the servants in truth that you will worship and return with the child, or are you deceiving them? If you are telling the truth, then you will not make him a holocaust.

> If you are deceiving, it is not fitting for so great a patriarch to deceive. What disposition, therefore, does this statement indicate in you? I am speaking the truth, he says, and I offer the child as a holocaust. For this reason I both carry wood with me, and I return to you with him. For I believe, and this is my faith, that "God is able to raise him up even from the dead" [Heb. 11.19].[7]

If "so great a patriarch" as Abraham could not be thought of as telling a harmless lie to a pair of servants, what are we to think of the prospect of his murdering an innocent child at God's behest? Clearly, this is a possibility that did not even enter Origen's head. With him we are in a world of intensely moralized faith, and we are still far removed from any possibility of a Kierkegaardian "teleological suspension of the ethical."

Augustine's treatment of Genesis 22 in *The City of God* closely follows the lines set down by Hebrews and Origen. Abraham, Isaac, and the ram represented for Augustine, as they did for Origen, "types" and "figures" of Christ. Abraham's faith consisted, above all, in his belief in the resurrection. Although "God's thundering commands are to be obeyed, not questioned," says Augustine, "Abraham would never believe that God could take delight in sacrifices of man's flesh."[8] Abraham's merit consisted in resolving this dilemma through a "firm faith" that if Isaac were sacrificed, he would rise again.

The most novel feature of Augustine's account lies in his effort to provide a moral justification for God's conduct. According to Augustine, this was a temptation "without blame in itself" and one "to be taken thankfully." To the question, Why should God subject an innocent person to this severe trial?, Augustine answers that it was for Abraham's own good:

> [G]enerally man's mind can never know itself well, but by putting forth itself upon trials and experimental hazards; and by their events it learns its own state, wherein, if it acknowledges God's enabling it, it is godly, and confirmed in solidity of grace, against all the bladder-like humours of vainglory.[9]

The trial also served to confirm Abraham's reputation in the eyes of the world and, perhaps, to justify God's election and blessing of him. Augustine makes this point as an aside to his commentary on the phrase "Now I know" in the text. This is a peculiar remark, since it calls into question God's omniscience. Did not God necessarily know the outcome of this test in advance? Of course, Augustine replies. Hence, the phrase must be read, "Now I have made known." The trial was needed not to instruct God in Abraham's excellence but to display this both to Abraham and to the world.

These ideas, that God tries the righteous to reinforce their faith and that he tried Abraham to demonstrate the grounds of his just confidence in the patriarch, are already familiar to us from the rabbinic midrashim. Augustine' use of them shows that well into the most vigorous period of early Christian thinking about Genesis 22, the text continues to be regarded not as morally problematical but as a vivid exemplification of God's righteousness and justice.

Medieval Tensions

Nearly a millennium separates St. Augustine from St. Thomas Aquinas. Throughout this period, the few extant commentaries on Genesis 22 essentially repeat the interpretations handed down from the early Church.[10] But other intellectual forces at work during these years eventually had a major impact on the reading of this text. Stimulated by the rediscovery of classical Greek philosophy, especially the writings of Aristotle, Christian thinkers began to attempt to integrate philosophical rationalism with biblical faith. One fruit of this effort was the Christian doctrine of natural law, an ethic based not on revelation but on the exercise of human reason. As we might expect, the emergence of this ethic raised new questions about Genesis 22. Indeed, in the writings of Aquinas, where the ethic of natural law receives its most sophisticated development and treatment, we find evidence for the first time in the history of Western religious thought of moral discomfort over the Genesis episode. Nevertheless, this discomfort was very qualified. Although Aquinas was more sensitive than any previous Christian writer to the charge that the command of God appears to violate our ordinary human sense of right and wrong, like all his predecessors, he concluded that this was true in appearance only. In reality, no injustice or unrighteousness need be imputed to God in this episode.

Aquinas touches on Genesis 22 while replying to two "objections" raised by aspects of the theory of law he develops in a major section of his *Summa Theologiae*.[11] In the preceding discussion, Aquinas had defined law as "an ordinance of reason for the common good," made and decreed by the person who has care of the community. This simple definition contains a deeply important set of ideas.

Law, according to Aquinas, is not a matter of power and will. A law's validity and authority—its ability to command acceptance and to elicit obedience—rest on its being rationally ordained to the common good. This is true of any human law. The dictates of a tyrant, whatever their legal trappings, says Aquinas, are not properly thought of as law; they are a "perversion of law,"[12] and while practical considerations might recommend obedience, these corrupt dictates do not obligate anyone morally. If circumstances permit, they might be freely disobeyed. Because God is just, his normative enactments are always valid laws, not to be disobeyed. But they are valid precisely because they are rational ordinances for the common good and thus potentially accessible to human reason. This is true of the "eternal law" by which God created and rules the entire universe. We learn of God's order in the natural world, for example, by using our scientific and cognitive abilities. And it is also true of the "divine law," the special "revealed" normative requirements recorded in the Bible.

One implication of Aquinas's view is that we can partly understand God's moral nature and respond to his revealed moral requirements by calling on our innate human capacity for making moral judgments. A further implication is that the revealed divine law is not merely an act of will but is congruent with the lawful and just order that God has established in the world, an order of which our own moral capacity is a part.

Within our intellects, this moral capacity takes the form of the "natural law." This is our special mode of access as rational creatures to the eternal law of all creation. It comprises the fundamental code of morality and the basic procedure for moral reasoning known to all rational persons, and it consists, according to Aquinas, of a set of unchangeable principles that are applicable everywhere to all rational beings. No other normative standard may violate these principles, and one that does must be regarded as lacking the quality of moral law. Aquinas concedes that efforts to apply the natural law to complex specific cases may lead to conclusions seemingly different from the highest-order principles. For example, while it is a principle of the natural law that goods held in trust should be restored to their rightful owner, this principle might be suspended in time of war, if the owner were a citizen of an unjust enemy nation. But the basic precepts of the natural law always remain in force. No one, not even God, may appropriate what is rightfully another's property or intentionally kill an innocent person.

Because this theory gives such a central and commanding place to human moral reason, it appears to make even God hostage to the natural law. In fact, Aquinas does not shrink from this conclusion, but he sees it as no limitation of God's power or freedom. Since the natural law is one part of the eternal law, God's normative structure for the entire universe, in emphasizing and obeying its dictates, human beings are only heeding God's will in the special way to which they have been appointed. If the precepts of the natural law are binding even on God, this is because they express his eternal wisdom. God does not change his mind. His formation of the world and rational creatures are all part of his revealed relationship to creation.

This is a momentous series of ideas. It can be argued that modern efforts to emancipate human reason and conscience from the ties of tradition and authority find their charter in Aquinas's work. But where biblical revelation, at least, was concerned Aquinas was no revolutionary. Like all those who went before him, he was convinced that human moral reason and biblical faith were utterly consistent with one another, that the God who revealed himself in the "divine law" of the Bible was the same God who made himself known in the rational dictates of human conscience. Nevertheless, by its very structure, Aquinas's position posed a new problem for traditional piety. Reason and revelation were now identified as two potentially distinguishable sources of moral instruction, and the possible tensions between them were not hard to find.

These tensions are voiced in the two specific objections Aquinas replies to in the course of his treatment of the natural law in the *Summa*. One objection is directed against his view that the natural law is "unchangeable"; the second against his position that the Ten Commandments, which he regards as a revealed expression of the basic principles of morality, cannot be abolished. The objections dispute these claims by making appeal to God's conduct in Scripture, in particular, his apparent alteration or suspension of the moral law in three passages: God's command to Abraham in Genesis 22 "to slay his innocent son"; his order to the Jews (Exod. 22.35) to "purloin" the vessels of the Egyptians; and his command to Hosea (Hos. 1.2) to marry "a wife of fornications." Interestingly, the objections do not offer these passages as proof that Scripture is to be rejected or that God acts wrongly in issuing these commands. We are still too deeply immersed in the world of biblical faith for such a view to find expression. Rather, these passages are used to raise the question of whether the natural law and the standards of human reason have the stability and clarity Aquinas claims they do.

It is a sign of the novelty of this problem that Aquinas must strain so hard to come up with answers to these objections. He begins his response by reaffirming the integrity and unchangeability of God's will. Quoting 2 Timothy 2.13, God "continueth faithful, He cannot deny himself," Aquinas observes that God "would deny Himself if He were to do away with the very order of His own justice, since He is justice itself." This means that all the basic moral principles apply to all relations between God and human beings and among human beings themselves.

How, then, can we explain the seeming suspension of morality in the biblical episodes cited in these objections, for example, in God's command to Abraham to kill Isaac? Aquinas replies,

> The decalogue forbids the taking of human life in so far as it is undue; in this the precept embodies the very nature of justice. Nor can human law permit that a man be lawfully killed when he does not deserve it. But it is no infringement of justice to put to death criminals or the State's enemies. This does not contravene the commandment; nor is it the homicide which is forbidden.[13]

The same reasoning, Aquinas maintains, applies to the taking of property. This does not amount to theft or robbery if persons' possessions are not their own or if they are otherwise rightfully taken from them. These basic moral truths, Aquinas continues, apply to the three biblical episodes we are considering:

> Therefore when the children of Israel, by God's command, took the spoils of the Egyptians, this was not theft, because they were due to them by the sentence of God. Likewise Abraham in consenting to kill his son, did not consent to homicide, since it was right that his son should be put to death by the command of God, the Lord of life and death. For it is God who inflicts the punishment of death on all men, just as well as unjust, on account of the sin of our first parent; and if a man carries out this on the authority of God he is no murderer any more than God is.[14]

Aquinas's replies to these objections will certainly not satisfy the modern reader, who may be tempted to regard them as sophistry. After all, if God's power over life or property is so complete as to allow him to issue commands to kill an innocent child or to move material possessions from one group of persons to another, is anything forbidden him? Is Aquinas not saying here that God can do whatever he pleases and that his command will define right or wrong conduct? In other words, are we not essentially on the terrain of a divine command morality that defines right and wrong in terms of God's will alone?

I do not think so. Aquinas's handling of these episodes from Scripture is undoubtedly strained. After all, he is engaged in an almost unprecedented task, seeking to justify the ways of God to human beings in a context where these ways, however primitively recorded in the earliest texts, have always instinctively been regarded as just. But Aquinas's position does not amount to the view that God can do whatever he commands and that whatever he commands is right. There are firm standards of right and wrong: It is always unjust to kill an innocent person, and it is always wrong to take property rightfully belonging to another. But in each of these cases, Aquinas insists, God does not violate these norms. His deeds, even if performed by similarly situated human beings, would be morally justifiable. Do we not commonly recognize that it is morally permissible to take property from those who are not the legitimate owners and who have secured it, as did the Egyptians, by force? If so, then God's command to the Jews in Exodus is just. Do we not regard it as right for a sovereign to execute someone who has committed a capital offense? Aquinas believes so and argues that Genesis 22 involves nothing more. It follows that not even God can command the seizure of property legitimately appointed to someone's ownership, and, if a truly innocent human being were to be found (Jesus may be the only example), he could not be rightfully killed either by God or by human beings.

What is remarkable about Aquinas's brief discussion of Genesis 22 is that he makes no use of the implicit moral justifications of God's conduct found in the earlier commentary tradition. For example, he does not point to the belief in resurrection clearly signaled in Hebrews 11 to exonerate God, nor does he stick to the clear sense of Scripture and deny that God ever intended the sacrifice to be completed. It may be that Aquinas perceived that, within the framework of strict principles he had established, these lines of defense raised more questions than they answered. (For example, does the prospect of resurrection really render guiltless the killing of an innocent person? Would God's intention of forestalling the sacrifice exonerate Abraham from obedience to what seemed an unlawful command?) Or, it may be that Aquinas merely reached for an immediate and thorough solution to a perplexing series of problems. In any case, as the first explicit effort to harmonize revelation and moral reason, Aquinas's treatment evidences some of the difficulties of the task. Now that the problem was being directly addressed, confidences held for centuries were subject to more penetrating critical analysis and might be found wanting. Furthermore, the solutions inserted in their place might raise new questions, as Aquinas's efforts appear to do. Although these efforts stood firmly within the preceding tradition in asserting the essential and humanly understandable justice of God's ways, Aquinas's discussion in the *Summa* opened the door to ideas that would eventually tear apart the unexamined synthesis between moral reason and revelation that had prevailed during previous centuries. Small wonder that in the wake of his discussion and up through modernity, extremist views began to emerge. Some of these, taking a stand within human moral reason, would question the inherent justice of God's command and challenge the authority or integrity of revelation. Others, reacting against these "rationalist" criticisms and rising to the defense of revelation, would take the radical course of seeking to free God from any possible human moral constraints. Often lost in the fray was the naive confidence of the early tradition, still evident in Aquinas, that human moral reason and revealed morality are one.

The Emergence of Divine Command Ethics

This fracturing of Christianity's naive confidence in the unity of moral reason and revelation became apparent in the decades immediately following Aquinas's work, when a series of theologians undertook a criticism of the kind of rationalism represented by him and other Aristotelians. In the work of "nominalist" writers like Duns Scotus, William of Ockham, Pierre d'Ailly, Jean Gerson, and Gabriel Biel,[15] we encounter the first unabashed defense of divine command morality. Right is simply whatever God wills it to be. In his *Oxford Commentary* on Peter Lombard's Sentences, for example, John Duns Scotus explicitly makes this point and relates it to Genesis 22:

> No more is the object of speaking when all is believed to be false, improper, than is the object of murder—the death of a man who is innocent and useful to the State—illegitimate.... [I]t can become legitimate to kill such a man, namely, if God should revoke this precept, *Do not kill* ... and not only legitimate, but meritorious, namely, if God should give a command to kill, as He gave a command to Abraham concerning Isaac. Therefore, in the same way or even more so, it can become legitimate to utter a statement believed to be false, if the precept, which is considered

to be about not deceiving, should be revoked, just as if the precept concerning killing should be revoked.[16]

Clearly, we are in an altogether different world here from the one inhabited by Aquinas. It is not, as Aquinas argues, that God in Genesis 22 does not really violate the precept, "Do not kill" because of the special circumstances of his position or because of prior human wrongdoing; rather, God can revoke this precept whenever he wishes because, as Scotus puts it elsewhere, "The divine will . . . is the first principle of righteousness" and "whatever God may bring about, or may do, will be right and just."[17] Somewhat later, William of Ockham carried this point to its logical conclusion: if God so wished, he could blamelessly command any conduct: theft, adultery—even hatred of himself. While this last command could not morally be acted on by any human being (since the requirement of loving God and obeying his will was always the foremost human moral obligation), God, whose will constituted the only defining condition of moral rightness and who was under no obligation to himself, would not violate any moral requirement in issuing such a command.[18]

The idea that it is possible to think of God as morally commanding hatred of himself shows how eccentric this nominalist "divine command" position is. In fact, this view, with its reduction of God's nature and character to sheer willfulness, is deeply alien to the spirit of the tradition that preceded it, and in the years to follow it would be subjected to intense criticism. Within Catholic Christianity, at least, it was the rationalist natural-law position defended by Aquinas that became orthodoxy, while the voluntaristic position of the nominalists was rejected.[19] However, before dismissing this position as an aberration, although in many ways it was, we might ask why such a vocal subtradition should emerge in Christian thinking. Why, especially in the wake of rationalist efforts to defend God's humanly understandable justice, did some Christian thinkers feel impelled to insist on God's utter freedom from moral restraint?

One answer is that these writers were trying to defend God's omnipotence. But this only raises a question at a further remove, since it might then be asked why these writers were so eager to defend God's unlimited power, particularly his power over human standards of right and wrong. We can answer this question, I believe, if we look carefully at the religious framework within which the moral discussions of these nominalist advocates of divine command morality took place. There, we find a concern with one of the most difficult and important elements of the deep structure of religious rationality: the question of God's ability to suspend moral judgment in order to relieve moral despair and to make possible the forgiveness of sin. If these writers were willing to compromise God's moral character, and, with it, aspects of the first and second elements of religious reasoning, it is because they were seeking to preserve a unique Christian heritage of response to the third element of reason's deep structure.

This heritage goes back to St. Paul's doctrine of justification by faith through grace, which is found in a variety of his central epistles, especially the Letter to the Romans (chs. 1–7). This complex Pauline teaching sprang from an understanding of the persistent and inescapable fact of human wrongdoing and wrong willing.[20] A proudly righteous Pharisee himself, Paul was alert to the egoism that taints even the best moral efforts and makes the most sustained attempts to obey God's moral will an opportunity for prideful self-assertion. Paul's remedy for this complex moral and spiritual problem was to insist that there is no connection between human moral performance and spiritual reward (or punishment). If the conceptual ties between performance and reward had become an occasion for self-aggrandizement and pride, these ties had to be cut. Hence, the teaching of justification by faith. All are sinners, says Paul. No one merits reward. If some are saved, this is because God, in his gracious forgiveness, spares some the punishment all deserve. The appropriate response to this gift of salvation is not vanity and pride, but humble gratitude and, on a moral plane, similar displays of graciousness to those less fortunate than oneself.

But if salvation does not depend on works, on what basis does God bestow grace? Paul's efforts to answer this difficult question reveal the complexity of the problem with which he was wrestling. Clearly, he could not allow grace to be based on any new form of merit, since that would merely renew the "performance ethic" that leads to pride or moral despair in the first place. The only unchallengeable alternative was to affirm the essential arbitrariness or inscrutability of God's bestowal of grace, and this is what Paul did. God chooses and predestines his elect even before they are born (Romans 9.11). Since no one merits redemption and all deserve condemnation, no one may question why they either received or were denied grace. Like any act of philanthropy, Paul seems to say, the distribution of grace is not subject to claims of justice. Then, perhaps sensing that this reply raised as many moral questions as it answered (is it really morally true that a good vital for survival may be dispensed arbitrarily by someone possessing a surfeit, or that a supposedly righteous Creator may knowingly bring some persons into the world destined to salvation and others to perdition?), Paul terminates the discussion abruptly by stating that, in matters like this, it is not appropriate for the creature to question its creator: "Has not the potter power over the clay?" (Rom. 9.21).

Conceptually, Paul seems to have painted himself into a corner. In the effort to address one of the most serious problems of the moral life and one of the most difficult aspects of religious reasoning, he was forced into a seeming defense of God's moral arbitrariness. We can dispense here with an assessment of whether Paul's solution to this complex problem is adequate or is even morally sustainable. The point is that this apparent annulment of moral works and emphasis on God's free bestowal of grace reflect a profound engagement with a central problem of the moral life and have a deeply moral purpose. They are also among the most penetrating efforts ever developed to address the problems of moral egoism and moral self-condemnation. This partly explains why these ideas have persisted throughout the history of Christian thought.

The power of this view also explains why later Christian thinkers, seeking to reaffirm Paul's insights about human sin and its overcoming, also tended to pick up his assertion of God's essential freedom from human moral constraints and his immunity to human moral judgment. Usually, these claims are defended within a framework of recognizable moral concepts. For example, as with Paul, stress is placed on human beings deserving punishment and the inappropriateness of anyone demanding the gift of grace. Questions of why God should have ever created some beings destined for sin and perdition are handled in terms of God's generous bestowal of the gift of freedom and his right to abandon some who have forfeited it. Arguments like these are found in Aquinas's mature treatments of predestination and election.[21] But alongside these anguished rationalist efforts to justify God's freedom of election, we also expectedly find theorists joining Paul in asking whether the clay dares question the potter. Some of these thinkers merely reject human inquiry about these matters, while others, like the nominalists, ground their views in an account of morality that makes the very meaning of right and wrong depend utterly upon the divine will. This position has the advantage of clarity and simplicity, although they are purchased at an enormous price in terms of conflicts with human conscience and with equally deep religious claims concerning God's righteousness and justice.

This same concern with the issues of justification and predestination permeates nominalist discussions of divine command morality. The remarks by Scotus quoted above regarding the role of God's will in determining right and wrong and its relation to Genesis 22 are immediately prefaced by the question of whether God can damn a just person and save an unjust one. Scotus's sharp defense of God's moral prerogatives in this passage, including the justness of his behavior with respect to Abraham, thus aims at preserving God's freedom of election. More deeply, Scotus was defending the Christian understanding of human sin and the claim of our total dependence on God for redemption. Elsewhere in nominalist writings these various concerns are commonly linked. For example, in the course of a discussion of divine command morality, the later nominalist Gabriel Biel insists, "The divine will does not depend on our goodness, but rather, our goodness depends on the divine will; and something is good only because it is accepted by God."[22]

Reformation Views

Almost from the beginning of systematic discussion among medieval theologians about the role of reason and revelation in ethics, therefore, we find conflict. Tensions between the various rational convictions of Christian faith, its commitment to a belief in God's justice and to his power to suspend justice in the name of forgiveness, began to split the naive unity of earlier faith and stir disputes of the sort we have witnessed between Aquinas and his nominalist foes. In the next significant body of discussion of these matters, that found in the writings of the great Protestant Reformers Luther and Calvin, these tensions were not parceled out among opposing schools of thought but were reunited in a single religious viewpoint. Like the nominalists to whom they were indebted, Luther and Calvin stressed the primacy of God's grace in the process of salvation, and they also insisted on God's essential immunity to human moral judgments. But the Reformers were not theological eccentrics with a single ax to grind. In almost all respects, they stood firmly in the mainstream of the tradition on matters of faith and morals. When they turned from abstract theological discussions about God and morality to concrete portrayals of his conduct in a passage of Scripture like Genesis 22, therefore, their treatments followed the orthodox tradition in emphasizing the understandable justice and righteousness of all God's ways.

Discussing the role of grace and election in the economy of salvation, both Reformers characteristically stressed the primacy of God's will in determining right or wrong. Luther, for example, in his treatise *The Bondage of the Will,* states emphatically that "God is He for Whose will no cause or ground may be laid down as its rule and standard; for nothing is on a level with it or above it, but it is itself the rule for all things." And he adds, "What God wills is not right because He ought, or was bound, so to will; on the contrary, what takes place must be right, because He so wills it." But these assertions occur within a context where Luther is seeking to establish the pervasiveness of human sin and God's corresponding power, through grace, to save those he elects.[23] Similarly, Calvin, in a discussion in the *Institutes of the Christian Religion,* where he seeks to rebut charges that God acts like a tyrant in predestining some to salvation and others to damnation, dismisses these objections with the flat statement, "God's will is so much the highest rule of righteousness that whatever he wills, by the very fact that he wills it, must be considered righteous."[24]

Anyone working with these passages alone would naturally conclude that Luther and Calvin espouse an unqualified divine voluntarism, a view of morality that makes everything depend on God's will. But nowhere do we see more clearly the importance of looking at a tradition in its entirety, with an understanding of the deeper rational considerations at work beneath isolated surface claims and doctrines. For when we turn to Luther and Calvin's treatment of Genesis 22, all the traditional assumptions about God's character and nature reappear. The God actually described in the Reformers' commentaries is not the arbitrary despot who can do whatever he wishes without excuse—the deity advanced to forestall questions about election and predestination—but the just ruler and creator of the universe.

Of the two Reformers, Luther gives the most attention to the text, devoting a long section of his *Lectures on Genesis* to an interpretation of the episode,[25] while Calvin deals with it more briefly in his *Commentaries on the Book of Genesis.*[26] As we might expect, both writers use the passage as a proof text for important Reformation themes. For example, both offer the fact that Abraham was elected by God before he underwent the trial as evidence for their claim that God's grace precedes good works in the process of redemption and is not dependent on them.[27] Luther also uses the text to support his doctrine of *sola scriptura* and to criticize the "invented" piety and religious practices of the Papists. Abraham's conduct teaches us that we are to obey the Word of God, says Luther, not human commandments. Religious "works" conjured up by the Pope do not please God, but only those works he has expressly enjoined in Scripture.[28]

When we turn from these matters directly to the moral questions raised by the text, all the themes we encountered in the previous tradition reappear. Both reformers even appear to draw on rabbinic midrashim now available to them in Bible commentaries.[29] Thus, we read that God had a full knowledge of Abraham's ability to withstand the trial and that he permitted it only to display to the patriarch and others the firmness of Abraham's faith.[30] For both Reformers, Isaac was a mature individual (twenty-five years old according to Luther; of "middle age" according to Calvin) and it was unthinkable that he should be forced to his death. He acquiesced in the sacrifice with full understanding of the divine command and consented to be bound only to prevent some unseemly occurrence.[31]

Above all, there is the theme of God's faithfulness to his promises. For Luther, this is a matter whose importance transcends the Genesis episode, since faith is the ability to rely on the fact that God keeps the promise of redemption he has made in Jesus Christ. In this respect, Abraham was truly the father of faith. He was confronted with a seeming contradiction in God's words. On the one hand, God had promised descendants from Isaac. On the other hand, there was the command to sacrifice his son. "Fleshly" human understanding would be prone to conclude either that God was lying—and this, says Luther is blasphemy—or that the promise had been withdrawn and the patriarch had perhaps been rejected by God for some sin he had committed. Christian believers frequently experience such a contradiction in their own lives between the promise of salvation and the sense that it has been withdrawn because of some sin of their own, says Luther, and when they do, they sink into despair. Not Abraham. He relied entirely on the promises he was given and obeyed God's command in the certainty that he would have descendants through Isaac.

How was Abraham able to maintain this reliance in the face of God's command? The Reformers agree: through his belief in the resurrection of the dead. "Just as he saw that Isaac was born of a worn-out womb and of a sterile mother," says Luther, "so he also believed that he was to be raised after being buried and reduced to ashes."[32] In this belief, faith transcends reason. For when death occurs, reason says, "the flesh turns to dust and the worms consume it." But faith, says Luther, believes that it is always within God's power to mold dust and ashes

into life. Calvin's words are similar. Abraham, he says, clings tena-
ciously to the promise and perceives in the "quickening power of God"
the assurance of a blessing out of the ashes of his son. In doing so, he
points the way for all Christians. "We act unjustly towards God," Calvin says, "when we hope for nothing from him but what our senses can
perceive." Instead, Christians should follow Abraham in trusting
entirely in the divine providence.[33]

Once again, we see how sharp the contrast is between this traditional understanding of Abraham's faith and the view of faith suggested
in Kierkegaard's *Fear and Trembling.* Faith, for Luther, Calvin, and the
whole tradition that precedes them, was not just a matter of unflinching
obedience to God's command. It also involved the beliefs needed to
ground this obedience and make it reasonable: the belief that God is
faithful, that he is just, and that he possesses the power needed to sustain his will. Furthermore, the conflict between faith and reason outlined here is wholly different from that suggested by *Fear and Trembling.* In Kierkegaard's treatment, reason stands on the side of ethics
and judges the killing of Isaac to be murder, whereas faith dictates
unquestioning obedience to the divine command, regardless of its
moral content. But for Luther and Calvin, "reason" was a shortsighted
worldly "wisdom," that confined itself to observable facts and that
doubted the possibility of resurrection, whereas faith was a tenacious
adherence to God's promise combined with the confidence that he was
able to keep it. The conflict between faith and reason for these two
thinkers, in other words, was not a conflict between obedience to God's
will and obedience to our moral reason. Rather, it pitted a religious confidence in the ability of God's moral will to prevail over the worldly
forces that oppose it against human doubt in that ability. If we recall
that the key element of religious rationality is a belief that righteousness
will prevail despite the bitter facts of experience, then we can say that
the faith the Reformers defended was consummately rational and
moral.

Rereading *Fear and Trembling*

The writings of the Protestant Reformers are representative of the scattered treatments of Genesis 22 found after them in the premodern
period.[34] Not until Kierkegaard do we find a thinker offering a genuinely
novel reading of the text. Indeed, we are now in a position to see that

Kierkegaard's interpretation of Genesis 22 is enormously eccentric. Apart from a few brief references to the passage by nominalist thinkers seeking to emphasize God's absolute moral prerogatives, Kierkegaard stands alone in his reading of Genesis 22 as a command to murder.

This raises an important question. How are we to understand, in the writings of a passionate apologist for Christian orthodoxy like Kierkegaard, the emergence of an interpretation that seems so markedly out of character with the entire tradition? Why, in the mid-nineteenth century, do we suddenly find the Genesis episode held up, in its seemingly most antirational and antimoral form, as the epitome of faith? In the course of these two chapters I have tried to show that, in reality, the contrast between human moral reason and God's revealed will is nowhere as sharp, within either Judaism or Christianity, as Kierkegaard makes it out to be. Indeed, I have suggested that for the mainstream of this tradition there is really no conflict at all between human moral reason and revelation. Thus, it is tempting simply to dismiss *Fear and Trembling* as an aberration. Nevertheless, Kierkegaard's discussion has been extremely influential. It shapes modern access to the Genesis text, and has come to be regarded as one of the most powerful defenses of the claim that biblical ethics derive solely from the revealed divine command. This makes it important to understand what prompted Kierkegaard to present the text this way. If we can gain some insight into why Kierkegaard takes the extreme and seemingly aberrant position he does, perhaps we can better understand the recurrent impulse within Christianity to view religious morality as sharply opposed to ordinary moral reasoning.

Kierkegaard's extremist view has several explanations. Kierkegaard was an imaginative religious polemicist interested in troubling the complacency of his contemporaries, many of whom had come to believe, as he put it, that to be a Christian one only had to be born in a Christian country.[35] What better way to remind them of the distress and suffering that characterize genuine Christian existence than to recall the trial of Abraham? And what better way to convey the hardship of the patriarch's ordeal than to depict it as a command to murder that makes the patriarch not a "saint," but a "criminal" in the eyes of his contemporaries? In other words, *Fear and Trembling* presents Genesis 22 in a poetically enhanced way to convey the challenge of Christian faith, and Kierkegaard's emphasis on the moral scandal of the command is part of this enhancement.

On another level, *Fear and Trembling* was directed against a view prevalent in the nineteenth century that would reduce Christianity to a series of "lofty" moral teachings. Although this view was widely held in Kierkegaard's day (and perhaps still is), it found its most vehement defenders among followers of the philosopher Kant. In his *Foundations of the Metaphysics of Morals* and *Religion within the Limits of Reason Alone,* Kant had argued for the excellence and "purity" of Christian moral teachings, but at the same time he rejected most orthodox Christian theological doctrines as superstitions or the work of immoral "priestcraft."[36] In the *Religion,* Kant also discussed Genesis 22, and offered a criticism of Abraham's conduct. No one should place alleged revelations and voices from heaven on a par with the clear inner voice of moral duty, said Kant.[37] While Kant did not openly condemn Abraham, the implications of his view were clear: people who act as Abraham did are dangerous religious fanatics. In coming to the defense of "father Abraham," therefore, Kierkegaard was resisting a Kantian perspective that would condemn the patriarch and subject all Christian religious teachings to the censorship of ethics and philosophy.

Nothing I have said so far contradicts the established view that in *Fear and Trembling* Kierkegaard was essentially espousing a suprarational, supramoral understanding of Christian ethics, a view that makes the revealed divine command, not conscience, the supreme guide for Christian life. If rational morality brands Abraham a criminal and if Abraham really is the father of faith, then rational morality must be rejected or at least subordinated to the higher norm of revelation. But I want to go beyond this now to suggest that, at its deepest level, this was not at all Kierkegaard's main point in *Fear and Trembling,* nor was it his most fundamental view of Christian ethics. *Fear and Trembling,* I believe, does not deal with normative moral questions concerning which rules or principles should guide the conduct of our lives. Instead, its focus is on the very different "transnormative" or "transmoral" religious question of whether we can count on God's grace and forgiveness to help us fulfill our moral destiny. If I am right about this, *Fear and Trembling* is not the idiosyncratic moral treatise it seems to be but, despite its misleading surface argument, a very traditional work of Pauline-Lutheran theology.[38]

There are a number of different but interrelated reasons for reading *Fear and Trembling* this way. One is the observation, already familiar to us and reiterated by Louis Mackey in his book, *Kierkegaard: A Kind of Poet,* that when Abraham and Isaac appear in Christian theological discourses, they frequently serve as figures, or "types," of the relationship between God and Christ. Mackey himself believes that *Fear and Trembling* is primarily a theological treatise about the issue of sin and grace, with Abraham and Isaac used in this figurative way to hint at Kierkegaard's deeper meaning.[39]

Related to this is the fact that the problem of sin and its overcoming was one of Kierkegaard's major intellectual and personal preoccupations. Most of the writings that bracket *Fear and Trembling* in Kierkegaard's authorship deal with this issue,[40] making *Fear and Trembling,* with its apparent concern with divine command morality, seem an anomaly. On a personal level, in a pervasive and crippling sense, sin was the omnipresent reality of Kierkegaard's life. Biographers report that this preoccupation with sin could be traced back to Michael Pedersen Kierkegaard, Søren's brilliant and moody father. The elder Kierkegaard was a self-made man, who, in a moment of loneliness and abandonment while tending sheep on the Jutland heath as a young boy, cried out in anger against God. This and later deeds, including an out-of-wedlock sexual relationship with his housekeeper Anna Lund, Søren's mother, while he was still in mourning for his first wife, led the elder Kierkegaard to believe that he and his entire line lay under a curse of God. Søren apparently picked up this belief.[41] It was a source of what he called "the eternal night brooding within me,"[42] and it was a major factor in his life. For example, the conviction that he was too encumbered with sin and melancholy to inflict himself on a lighthearted young woman led Søren to break off his engagement with Regine Olson, the event that is commonly believed to be the immediate stimulus for Kierkegaard's writing *Fear and Trembling.*[43]

Interestingly, this episode of a broken engagement has real bearing on the question of what lies behind Kierkegaard's writing of this book. It has long been known that *Fear and Trembling* contains a hidden meaning, a "secret message" directed at a special reader. This is suggested by the book's epigraph, which alludes to an event in the life of the Roman general, Tarquinius Superbus.[44] The general's son had seized control of a city and sent a messenger to his more experienced father to learn how he might best secure his tenuous hold on power. Suspecting that the messenger might be a spy, the father said nothing, but took him for a walk in the garden. As they strolled, Superbus periodically removed his sword from its scabbard and cut off the tops of the highest poppies. When later told of this strange behavior by the uncomprehending messenger, the son understood that he was to execute the city's indigenous leadership.

This epigraph, with its suggestion of a hidden message and special recipient, has led generations of readers and scholars familiar with Kierkegaard's biography to the conclusion that *Fear and Trembling* was secretly addressed to Regine Olson.[45] It was Kierkegaard's way of explaining to her why, at the last moment, he was compelled to break off their engagement. Just as Abraham, in a fearful teleological suspension of the ethical, had been summoned by God to place his religious duty above ordinary moral responsibility, so Kierkegaard had been called to put off personal happiness and moral duty, including his pledge of marriage to Regine, in order to assume his vocation as a Christian writer. Understood this way, the "hidden" message of *Fear and Trembling* squares exactly with its seeming religious and moral content. The central theme appears to be whether there is a religious calling higher than moral duty and Kierkegaard's answer, both for Abraham and himself, seems to be yes.

But what if Regine was not the special recipient of this "hidden" message? What if, instead, it was directed to the spirit of Kierkegaard's father, Michael Pedersen Kierkegaard, who had died three years before the writing of the book? There are important indications in Kierkegaard's journals and papers that this may be so.[46] Furthermore, the whole theme of *Fear and Trembling* concerns the relationship between a father and a son, indeed, a father whose conduct physically imperils his son's life, just as the elder Kierkegaard's conduct had spiritually imperiled Søren's. And there is the fact that the book's epigraph deals with a message sent by a silent father to his son. The pseudonymous author of *Fear and Trembling* is named Johannes de Silentio. Is *Fear and Trembling* possibly a message from a silent son to his father?

If the elder Kierkegaard is, in fact, the secret recipient of *Fear and Trembling*'s hidden message, what, then, is the message? In this context, it no longer makes sense, I think, to see it as having to do with the superiority of God's commands over moral duty, since that issue is pertinent to Kierkegaard's relationship with Regine but not to the relationship with his father. Instead, I believe, the major theme of this book, its "secret" message, is that sin can be overcome, that what had been the weightiest personal problem in the life of both Søren and his father, was conquerable within the grace of God.

If we reflect back briefly on Kierkegaard's argument, we can see how this message is conveyed within the surface text of the book. The ostensible object of Kierkegaard's inquiry is Abraham and how we are to understand his conduct as depicted in Genesis 22. The problem is that if moral duty is the highest sphere to which human beings can aspire, then "judgment has fallen upon Abraham."[47] He stands condemned as the murderer of his own child. But if moral duty is not the highest sphere, if there is in fact the possibility of a religious "teleological suspension of the ethical," then Abraham is saved. No longer a murderer, he becomes the "father of faith."

Now, Kierkegaard seems to say, if God is able to do this in the case of Abraham, to convert him from being a condemnable sinner, in ethical terms, to a favored saint, then he can also do this for you and me. It is true that we are not like Abraham. Abraham "did not become the single individual by way of sin," Kierkegaard tells us, "on the contrary, he was a righteous man."[48] In comparison, our failings are at once both less serious and more serious. We do not commonly attempt to murder our children, but neither are our sins akin to the stalwart, selfless response to God of "righteous" Abraham. Instead, they are usually craven and lustful acts of selfishness. Nevertheless, whatever the character of our sins, God has shown in Genesis 22 that his judgment is not his last word on them. There is the possibility of a teleological suspension of the ethical. Beyond the realm of ethics lies the sphere of faith; beyond moral self-condemnation lie mercy and forgiveness. If God is able to draw Abraham to himself, if the lesson of Genesis 22 is that, in God's eyes, "the single individual is higher than the (ethical) universal,"[49] then God is also able to forgive and redeem each one of us. Understood this way, *Fear and Trembling*'s surface argument corresponds exactly to the secret message we would expect Kierkegaard, in a renewed and enthusiastic phase of his life and authorship, to wish to send to the spirit of his father: the message that God's ability to forgive and redeem can triumph over his and our need to condemn.[50]

There are a number of other reasons for believing this is the essential meaning of *Fear and Trembling*. Well into the book, for example, Kierkegaard introduces a long "comment" on the themes of sin, guilt, and repentance, and he signals this as saying "more than has been said at any point previously."[51] This comment may be read as a response to Kant's own treatment of these issues in his *Religion within the Limits of Reason Alone*. As I indicated in chapter 1, in this important work on the philosophy of religion, Kant had developed an understanding of the pervasive and "radical" nature of human sin. He had also tried to solve the moral problem this entails by stressing the possibility of self-initiated repentance as a cure for moral self-condemnation and moral despair.[52]

But in *Fear and Trembling,* Kierkegaard will have none of this. "Repentance," he says, "is the highest ethical expression, but precisely as such it is the deepest ethical self-contradiction."[53] Elsewhere, he clarifies this point: "Repentance cannot cancel sin, it can only sorrow over it."[54] In other words, Kierkegaard believed that human beings cannot lift themselves out of the quicksand of moral self-condemnation and sin. Only divine grace, the "teleological suspension of the ethical" for which *Fear and Trembling* argues, satisfactorily points the way out of the problem identified by Kant. If we bear in mind the fact that in the *Religion,* Kant, alone (then) among philosophers, had the audacity to scold Abraham and suggest that the patriarch should have placed moral duty above God's command, I think we can understand that in embarking on the defense of "father Abraham" in *Fear and Trembling,* Kierkegaard was criticizing the kind of moral rationalism that would either forget the problem of sin or would believe it soluble apart from the deepest resources of divine grace.

This has been a long digression through what may seem a special matter in Kierkegaard studies. But its value, I think, becomes apparent if we reflect back on the long commentary tradition on Genesis 22 we have surveyed in both Judaism and Christianity. We know that with few exceptions, this text was not viewed as a justification of an unqualified divine command ethic, but rather as proof of the unerring justice and righteousness of God's ways. Occasionally, however, Christian writers have spoken out in defense of the absoluteness of God's will and the priority of his command above any human moral considerations. Kierkegaard is one of these writers. Indeed, he is probably the most important, for his reading of the Genesis text has given voice to modern perceptions of the conflict between moral reason and revelation and has helped convert Genesis 22 into a proof text for champions of "divine command" morality.

What we have seen, however, is that those few Christian thinkers who have espoused this extremist view, and Kierkegaard is certainly among them, have almost always done so for reasons related to the deepest moral concerns of this faith. They have not really been interested in the question of normative ethics at all, the question of how we derive the moral principles by which we live our lives, but with the important trans-normative question of how we can escape from the guilt and self-condemnation that accompanies all conscientious moral striving. To address this question, they have emphasized their tradition's teachings about God's unlimited capacity to forgive and redeem, and this, in turn, has led them, almost as an afterthought, into the complex matter of God's relationship to human morality. If these thinkers have sometimes ended by portraying God as totally unfettered by human moral constraints, they have paradoxically done so to preserve God's most lofty moral attributes of mercy and grace.

Divine Command in Retrospect

I began these two chapters by observing the challenge posed by revealed morality to the claim that religious belief has a rational and moral foundation. We saw that, however understandable it may be in rational terms to want to trace all of morality to a supreme power like God, doing so can threaten the necessary role human reason must play in determining the norms that govern moral conduct. This threat can be avoided only if a religious tradition basing itself on God's will also interprets this will so thoroughly in moral terms that it becomes unimaginable in reality that God should ever command what violates human conscience. By tracing the course of Jewish and Christian commentary on Genesis 22 we have been able to perceive the spontaneous instincts of these two religious traditions, and we have seen that these instincts conformed in every way to the program of religious rationality and its deep structure. Even the few thinkers who seemed to depart from this program did so only to preserve and defend their tradition's important effort to comply with the third element in the deep structure, the suspension of moral judgment and retribution in the name of forgiveness.

This inquiry has importance in both theoretical and practical terms. For students of religion and religious ethics, it points up the value of understanding religion's essential moral foundation as we trace the tortuous and often confusing surface course of theological and religious debate. The claims and counterclaims that mark Jewish and Christian discussions of revelation and morality will confuse and mislead anyone trying to comprehend them without an understanding of the deeper, more fundamental issues at work. A theory of religious rationality seeks to provide this understanding.

Practically speaking, this discussion affords some critical insight into current debates over moral reason and revelation. Contemporary defenders of divine command morality and of the specific norms they draw from it in the areas of sexuality, race, and interreligious relations, are certainly correct that the Jewish and Christian traditions have always emphasized obedience to the revealed divine command. But they are mistaken if they juxtapose this command, in any of its interpretations, to the conclusions of informed and impartial human moral reasoning. For centuries, the possibility of such a conflict was not even conceived by our religious forebears. Their faith was that God's moral will as revealed in Scripture and rational human conscience are two identical aspects of divine revelation. In view of this, today's contemporary defenders of forms of revelation that defy reason and common sense are challenged to ask whether they have not, in some essential way, departed from this faith tradition.

II

RELIGIONS AS
MORAL TEACHERS

6

Religious Ritual and the "Pedagogics of Liminality"

Conceptions of moral retribution and forgiveness are among the most fascinating aspects of religious rationality. They represent sophisticated exercises of the human mind, and they provide an uncharted realm for comparative study. But religions' service to the moral life does not end with the development and communication of these key retributive and transmoral ideas. Religions also play a more familiar role as moral teachers, instructing their adherents in normative issues of right and wrong. A familiar expression of this role is seen in the great codes of conduct set forth by many of the historic religious traditions, ranging from the Ten Commandments of the Bible to the Five Precepts of Buddhism. The fact that the codes or teachings of widely separated traditions contain so many similar rules—what C. S. Lewis called the "First Principles of Practical Reason"[1]—testifies to the underlying moral rationality of human religiousness.

Imparting specific rules of conduct is only one part of religions' teaching role. Behind and beneath any concrete set of rules of conduct lies the "moral point of view." This standpoint of impartial moral choice is the center and touchstone of all moral reasoning. The moral rules and principles arise from it as an abiding result of the "legislative" activity of impartial rational persons. And because these rules often conflict in practice, they continually require contextual application under the guidance of impartial reasoning. It is thus not surprising that religious traditions devote great energy to conveying an appreciation of impartiality (or "omnipartiality") to their adherents. Through instruments that range from religious narrative to the example of "saintly" or sacred personalities, religions seek to illustrate, validate, and encourage the adoption of an approach to life that sets the interests of one's fellow human beings on a par with one's own.

In this chapter, I hope to show that religious ritual is one of religion's most important instruments in this task of moral instruction. Ritual is a powerful means by which human communities convey to their members an understanding of the bases and logic of moral reasoning. This claim is meant to be controversial, since the specific role of ritual in the rational moral life has been largely ignored. True, a long tradition in anthropology and the sociology of religion has viewed ritual as having social importance, but this was usually held to be so only in the most general sense, and the relation between ritual performance and the universal process of moral reasoning was never directly explored. For example, Emil Durkheim, a founder of this tradition in religious sociology and anthropology, viewed ritual occasions as reinforcers of social solidarity, but he attributed this integrative effect to the emotional experience of intense fellowship provided by ritual moments, and he never identified any specifically cognitive or moral implications of ritual performance. For Durkheim, the religious idea is born of "effervescent social environments and out of this effervescence itself."[2] Durkheim's tendency to view religion and ritual in emotional terms was accentuated by his rejection of the then-prevailing positivist explanation of ritual as a kind of primitive science that sought control over external reality. Durkheim shared the positivists' narrow definition of rationality as concerned with adequate empirical prediction and control, but since, for him, religious rites had no discernible rational purpose, their persistence could only be explained in terms of their impact on participants' emotions and, through these, on society.[3]

This view remained popular even among those who went beyond Durkheim's general stress on the integrative role of rituals to emphasize ritual's role in upholding specific group values or social structures. For anthropologists like Radcliffe-Brown, Nadel, Firth, and others, ritual events tended to mirror social judgments of right and wrong or to uphold existing social and political authority.[4] But the source of ritual's power in this respect lay in its ability to fuse these values or structures together with the intense emotion of group experience. A further implication of this position is that ritual has a morally conservative effect, since it does not appeal to the critical intellect but contributes to the emotional reinforcement of existing group values.[5]

More recently, this view of ritual has been challenged by the anthropologist Victor Turner. In a series of writings including *The Ritual Process,* Turner tries to develop a view of ritual that stresses its morally instructional aspects and that sees it as playing a catalytic moral role in reforming human communities.[6] Nevertheless, because Turner has only an inchoate notion of the moral-reasoning process, he is unable to locate ritual within a larger context of human rationality. At moments, he even mimics his functionalist predecessors in relegating ritual to the affective or emotional sphere of life (although for him this sphere is more creative and transformative than it is for most functionalists). Turner's account thus has to be supplemented by a more thorough understanding of religious rationality, but it is a useful starting place for understanding ritual's moral significance.

Liminality and *Communitas*

At the heart of Turner's view is the conception of rituals as "liminal" moments in human community. This idea is borrowed from the work of the French folklorist Arnold van Gennep, who identified liminality as one of three universally present stages in the rites of passage that mark major changes in life or social position for individuals or communities the world over. The first phase of these rites, *separation,* is marked by symbolic behavior detaching the individual or group from a previous state of life. In the typical rite of passage of coming of age at puberty in preliterate societies, for example, initiands may be physically removed from the larger group and required to stay, either singly or as a group, in a separated area or dwelling. Following separation, the ritual actors enter the liminal phase proper. Here, they assume a special status that takes them beyond the sphere of ordinary group norms and values. In Turner's phrase, they are "betwixt and between." Outside the prevailing classifications of the social structure, they find that usually important matters of kinship ties or differences in family background and social status are ignored. (In some rites involving older persons, even sexual distinctions and the prevailing gender hierarchy may be set aside.) Those in the liminal state are also freed from norms ordinarily governing life in community. Foods usually regarded as taboo may be eaten; strict celibacy may be required or forbidden sexual practices may be allowed. During this period initiands often assume a special dress or, in an even more dramatic repudiation of culture, go naked. As elders impart the sacred knowledge needed to bring them to adulthood, initiands are often subjected to ritual afflictions and trials. Symbolic or real humiliations are thrust upon them. This phase concludes with a rite of *aggregation* or *reincorporation* that marks initiands' transition to their new status as adult members of society. Because of the shared hardships and common experience of intense comradeship and equality in the liminal phase, an experience often described in terms of metaphors of death and rebirth, the liminal period remains a permanent feature in the lives of the ritual cohort.

Turner goes beyond van Gennep to argue that liminality is not simply one phase in a rite of passage, but a concept that has application to the entire sphere of human social life. For Turner, liminality constitutes the essential quality of a universally present mode of human association he calls *communitas.* Although religious rituals provide the preeminent occasions for the experience of *communitas,* it may be found in secularized forms as well. In Turner's view, *communitas* is omnipresent because it serves as a necessary counterpoint to life within the "status system" of ordinary society. Where the status system is characterized by social heterogeneity and often proudly maintained differences in rank or authority, *communitas* is characterized by homogeneity, social equality, and humility; where ordinary society stresses the physical accoutrements of ordered existence, such as distinctions of clothing and private property, *communitas* effaces these distinctions and stresses common sharing of simple necessities; where the status system places a premium on the avoidance of pain and suffering and the provision of creature comforts to some, *communitas* involves the voluntary acceptance of hardship and suffering by all.[7]

Turner further maintains that these two, the status system and *communitas* are not just contraries, but stand, as structure and anti-structure, in a dialectical relationship to one another. "It is," he says, "as though there are here two major 'models' for human interrelatedness, juxtaposed and alternating."[8] Sometimes he presents this dialectical relationship primarily in social-psychological terms, with *communitas* seen as furnishing members of structured society an emotionally cathartic experience that allows the discharge of instinctual energies. Occasionally, he even speaks of a basic human emotional need for the *communitas* experience, a need that, if frustrated, can result in individual or social disturbance:

> The basic and perennial human social problem is to discover what is the right relation between these modalities at a specific time and place. Since communitas has a strong affectual component, it appeals more directly to men; but since structure is the arena in which they pursue their material interests, communitas perhaps even more importantly than sex tends to get repressed into the unconscious, there to become either a source of individual pathological symptoms or to be released in violent cultural forms in periods of social crisis. People can go crazy because of communitas-repression; sometimes people become obsessively structural as a defense mechanism against their urgent need of communitas.[9]

This seems to impute to *communitas* an antirational or antimoral quality, as though structured status society represents the sphere of reason and morality, and *communitas* a domain of primal impulses, bonds, and nonrational affections. But this is not Turner's only view of the matter. Elsewhere, he attributes to experiences of *communitas* important cognitive and moral dimensions, among which is the instructional capability he calls the "pedagogics of liminality."[10] In part, this derives from the psychological effects of *communitas,* the suspension of ordinary activities, the heightened attention and receptivity of participants in ritual moments. Following Lévi-Strauss, Turner suggests that rituals furnish an occasion for society to inscribe on participants the generative rules, codes, and media that form the stuff of culture:

> In order to implant this instructional structure firmly in the minds of neophytes it seems necessary that they should be stripped of structural attributes in the social, legalistic, or political sense of the term. Simpler societies seem to feel that only a person temporarily without status, property, rank, or office is fit to receive the tribal gnosis or occult wisdom which is in effect knowledge of what the tribespeople regard as the deep structure of culture and indeed of the universe.[11]

This psychological readying of participants for the reception of new information is not the only aspect of the instructional power of *communitas.* Turner believes that the experience of *communitas* also has specific cognitive content: it mediates a series of ideas and insights that

are central to life in community. Above all, these include an understanding of the basic humanity one shares with others, the recognition,
as Turner puts it, of "an essential and generic human bond, without
which there could be *no* society."[12] Structured human society presumes
this generic bond as the most important basis of its cohesion. Within
status society, the primacy of this bond is obscured, as human beings
are led to value one another and themselves in terms of the various
attributes and ranks associated with complex social existence. But in the
ritual moment of *communitas* this obscured foundation of social existence once again comes to the fore. Describing pilgrimage experiences,
which he believes to be neglected but important instances of *communitas,* Turner states, "[P]ilgrimage liberates the individual from the
obligatory everyday constraints of status and role, defines him as an
integral human being with a capacity for free choice, and within the
limits of his religious orthodoxy presents for him a living model of
brotherhood and sisterhood."[13]

The primacy of this generic human bond is mediated to participants, in Turner's view, not only by the positive experiences of human
interrelatedness and comradeship ritual provides. It also results from
the discipline of the ritual moment. In this sense, *communitas* and liminality are a kind of negative ascesis that purges the individual of the
pride and vanity of social existence. Turner identifies this dynamic in
some African ceremonies of status elevation that precede the installation of a tribe's new chief or headsman. As in all rites of passage, the
ritual subject is expected to live apart, to endure a spartan existence and
undergo ritual afflictions. A special feature of this ceremony, however,
is a rite in which the chief-elect is admonished and even reviled by his
future subjects. He is told to give up selfish ways, to put aside haughti-
ness and be prepared to eat and live with his subjects. He is also
instructed to subordinate the claims of his own ego in order to judge
and serve his neighbors in an evenhanded fashion. Through this experience of voluntarily accepted suffering and abasement, the chief-elect
is placed momentarily on a level of interdependency and equality with
his subjects, and the lesson of this experience is designed to affect the
quality of his rule when he assumes leadership. Generalizing from this
experience to rituals as a whole, Turner points up the social significance
of the complex lesson mediated by this ritual moment:

> After his immersion in the depths of liminality—very frequently
> symbolized in ritual and myth as a grave that is also a womb—
> after this profound experience of humiliation and humility, a man

who at the end of the ritual becomes the incumbent of a senior
political status or even merely of a higher position in some particularistic segment of the social structure can surely never again be
quite so parochial, so particularistic, in his social loyalties.[14]

We have here a specific and powerful moral implication of the ritual event and *communitas,* but Turner himself seems not to appreciate
the full rational significance of the experiences he describes so well.
Though he senses the importance of the generic human bond experienced in *communitas* and though he perceives the social importance of
ritual humiliation, he sees no connection between these experiences and
the requirements of the human moral-reasoning process. For him, these
rites have the primarily emotional significance of reinforcing bonds of
affection and of releasing the immediate feelings of human fellowship
obscured by ordinary social life. On one occasion, it is true, he suggests
a link between experiences of *communitas* and human reason:

> Instinctual energies are surely liberated by these processes, but I
> am now inclined to think that communitas is not solely the prod-
> uct of biologically inherited drives released from cultural con-
> straints. Rather it is the product of peculiarly human faculties,
> which include rationality, volition, and memory, and which
> develop with experience of life in society.[15]

But despite this suggestion, Turner nowhere traces the ways that ritual
experiences of *communitas* reflect the exercise of human reason or contribute in specific and precise ways to the rational governance of social
relations. Nor is this omission surprising, since it takes a more precise
understanding of the logic of moral discourse and of the nature of the
moral reasoning process to establish these links between rationality and
communitas.

Communitas and Moral Equality

We can begin to forge these links if we consider that human equality
and the primacy of a generic human identity, as these are experienced
in moments of *communitas,* have a complex but central place in the
moral reasoning process. They do not reflect mere emotional preferences, nor do they even express a basic *moral* ideal that might be chosen
over more hierarchical principles of justice or right. It is sometimes
alleged that a moral ideal of this sort underlies the equality with which

John Rawls endows the parties in the "original position" of his contract theory of justice.[16] A similar nonrational and premoral preference for equality is also sometimes found in Kant's formulation of the categorical imperative as requiring respect for persons as 'ends' rather than 'means' or in his other formulation of the moral law as deriving from the free legislation all rational persons as members of a 'kingdom of ends.'[17] The theories of both Kant and Rawls, it is said, are not morally neutral, but begin with a deep, nonrational, possibly even "religious" commitment to human dignity and equality, and the theories themselves are little more than workings out of this initial moral preference.[18]

But all these interpretations miss the point that human equality is not one value among others. It is the precondition of moral discourse and the necessary first assumption of any moral system, whatever its resultant values. If we regard morality in minimal terms as a rational means of arbitrating social disputes, a means whose principal alternative is coercion or force, then it is axiomatic that an equal role in the choice of moral principles must be accorded to all parties capable of this means of settlement, that is, to all rational beings. To deny any rational people equal say in the determination of principles is to foreclose the possibility of a reasoned settlement of disputes with them. Those excluded must conclude that they may legitimately defend their interests by force. The result is the kind of Hobbesian "war of all with all" in which animal strength is vastly amplified by the power of rational agency. The alternative to this is to invite all beings capable of governing their conduct by principles to participate in the formulation of these principles. In that case, a "one-person-one-vote" rule is the unavoidable conclusion if each person is allowed a say in this process consistent with a like say for all others.

Equality of persons in the determination of moral principles may be thought of as the unique rational solution to the problem of establishing a reasoned social order, one based on the free consent of its members. Equality is not in the first place a moral preference, therefore, but a logically necessary assumption of anything that calls itself a moral system. The equal empowerment of persons in the selection of principles will also ordinarily yield roughly egalitarian moral principles for the governance of society. But this is not necessarily the case. In the face of clear social needs or in times of emergency, equally placed free persons might rationally agree to principles of hierarchy or to forms of coercion. (In classical moral literature the effort was made—not always successfully—to justify slavery in this way as a necessary resort under extreme conditions.) But whatever concrete principles are arrived at, they are only definably moral to the extent that they can be thought of as eliciting the free consent of all those equally placed rational persons who come under their jurisdiction. Equality in this sense is at the heart of morality and the process of moral justification. This is why we must consider the impact of our conduct on *all* rational persons when we assume "the moral point of view."

A further logical consequence of this stress on equality is the primacy of a generic human nature in the determination of moral principles. If we conceptualize moral principles as being arrived at in a quasi-legislative process in which all rational persons have a vote, then merely private human ends and interests must take a subordinate place in this process. However much individuals may urge their particular values, these are not likely to be enshrined as high-order common objectives. Instead, where universal assent to principles is required, it may be supposed that the values able to muster support will have the following qualities: they will be widely shared, have a special urgency in the lives of most persons, or be instrumentally useful for the pursuit of a wide variety of specific ends. Where human beings are concerned, the values meeting these criteria are easily identified. They include life, physical security, liberty, the freedom to pursue one's happiness (to the extent that this is compatible with others also doing so), the minimum of material goods needed to sustain well-being. Other values might be added, including opportunity for intellectual, emotional, sexual, and aesthetic self-expression. The point, however, is that these basic values are shared by almost all human beings; they are the values of our generic human nature. While it is possible that no single human being esteems all these values—some of us do not value life, some are ascetic or celibate—we may assume that such idiosyncratic preferences will not be those adopted by any community of equally placed human beings seeking to protect their most vital objectives (although, to the extent possible, this community will probably try to protect the pursuit of such idiosyncratic ends). Rather, it is the generic values that become a reasonable priority under the necessarily constrained circumstances of moral choice.

No less than equality, therefore, a generic human nature is a logical entailment of the concept of moral choice. To put this another way, the concept of morality has both a formal and a material side. The formal side, which identifies the procedural dimension of moral choice, is the insistence that moral principles be such as could be adopted as public rules by equally placed rational persons. The material side comprises those substantive ends that might reasonably be selected in and for this procedure of moral choice. But these ends are precisely those of our generic human nature. I might point out that this understanding was clearly expressed by Kant when he set forth both a "formal" and a "material" formulation of the categorical imperative.[19] The formal expression is the rule requiring our maxims to be chosen "as if they had to hold as universal laws of nature," one expression of Kant's requirement that intended acts be capable of universal applicability and assent. The material formulation requires us to treat every rational being "always as an end in himself" and "as a condition limiting all merely relative and arbitrary ends." This is no place to debate fully the meaning of this formulation. It is sometimes taken as a principle of respect for all the ends and wishes of real persons, although this interpretation fails to consider that is is impossible always to respect persons' actual wishes. Indeed, Kant himself, by insisting that the categorical imperative should not be construed so as to rule out the punishment of criminal offenders, strongly suggests that "respect for rational nature" does not mean acquiescence to whatever any real person happens to want.[20] By "respect for rational nature," I believe, he had in mind a willingness to place the generic ends of all human beings at the top of our list of priorities and before any particular desires or objectives we might have as individuals. Someone following this imperative, for example, might willingly subordinate his desire for extravagant luxury to other persons' vital needs for sustenance. A person with idiosyncratic sexual desires that would involve the coercion of others would be required to subordinate these desires to the more important and more general human need for freedom from coercion.

Against this conceptual background, we are now better able to understand and appreciate the moral significance of the liminal *communitas* experience which, as Turner shows, is the recurrent feature of religious rituals. Succinctly stated, *communitas* represents an experiential vivification of the moral point of view. In these special ritual moments, religious participants are made to relinquish the social distinctions and advantages that distinguish them and are led to perceive the essential equality of persons that must be respected by any social order that makes an appeal to moral principles. Momentarily forced into comradeship and made to cooperate out of necessity, social unequals are able to perceive the hidden bonds of mutual restraint and cooperation that undergird the social order, including its structure of tolerated inequalities. They are thus forcibly reminded that the peace of society rests on the tacit consent of all its members and will only endure so long as society's basic principles and structures are able to elicit this consent.

In this process of moral tutelage, the ritual humiliations and ascesis of liminal moments play an important part. Voluntarily undertaken, they symbolize and enact the essential relinquishment of possession, comfort, or advantage that marks adoption of the moral point of view. For the privileged "winners" in society's unavoidable process of social differentiation, respecting the moral principles that underlie a cooperative order—thinking or acting morally—is always to some extent a sacrifice. It may also, at any moment, require accepting a new and immediate vulnerability to hardship or suffering. In ritual humiliations, this negative dimension of moral commitment is displayed, even as it is immediately fused with the positive solidarity of *communitas*. Ritual thus communicates the easily forgotten lesson that self-renunciation on everyone's part through moral commitment is the necessary precondition of collective flourishing. In addition, the experience of suffering has direct pedagogical value. As the quest for luxury and ostentation gives way to an appreciation of simple necessities, as finely wrought pleasures are replaced by a welcomed relief from induced hardship, ritual participants are afforded a clearer apprehension of the genuine order of human priorities. They are made, above all, to see and value those generic human goods whose protection must be the first task of any just human society.

Ritual moments are thus a pedagogy in ethics. They embody and reflect the key elements of the moral point of view, and they impart the information and skills needed for its successful application. I have no wish to deny the importance of the emotional dimensions of *communitas*. They, too, play a role in vivifying moral awareness and lend a human affective dimension to rational structures. But *communitas* is not only an emotional experience; it embodies, reflects, and sustains key aspects of moral rationality. Nor do I wish to argue that ritual always produces moral renewal. *Communitas* can become an anodyne for social injustice. The intense fellowship of ritual moments can be used to forestall or replace genuine moral reinvigoration. The exuberance and equality of Mardi Gras or the intense fellowship of a sectarian communion service can help perpetuate the daily injustices of class society. But these abuses should not be allowed to obscure the authentic moral power of the ritual process from which they derive their strength.

Up to this point, I have spoken only in general terms. None of this can convey the full moral significance of any particular ritual occasion, because every ritual has its own instructional content and mediates more general moral ideas through symbols or concepts that may be specific to the tradition or the society from which it emerges. Like religions themselves, rituals are individual cultural creations that accomplish universal tasks in unique and novel ways. To illustrate this combination of specificity and universality in ritual moments, I want to look briefly at three ritual events drawn from different religious contexts. The first is a rainmaking ritual among the Taita people of southeastern Kenya, a ritual which involves animal sacrifice and the sharing of a sacrificial meal. The second is the Jewish Passover ritual, the Seder, and the third is the classical Christian baptism service. Although the last two of these are probably in strict cultural dependence on one another—we will see that Christian baptism at least indirectly draws on symbols from the Passover rite—the Taita ritual belongs to an entirely separate cultural tradition. These three ritual events, therefore, enable us at once to appreciate the uniqueness of specific ritual occasions, allow us to discern some of the moral properties common to all rituals, and afford us a glimpse into the creative process whereby ritual meanings are both passed on and transformed within a single cultural tradition.

Taita Rainmaking Ritual

As described by Grace Gredys Harris in her book, *Casting Out Anger,* Taita religion shares many of the traits we encountered in our earlier treatment of African traditional religion.[21] One of these is belief in a high God (here known as Mlungu) who is regarded as the suprapersonal creator of humankind and distant sustainer of the natural and moral order. Apart from sending the great misfortunes of drought or famine as punishment for widespread moral corruption in society, Mlungu is usually regarded as removed from the affairs of daily life. Closer to home are a variety of mystical entities. They include righteous ancestor spirits, who superintend the moral affairs of lineages by sending illness or disease as a punishment for quarreling or selfishness among descendants. And they include purely malevolent agents, sorcerers, whose motivations of greed and envy, manifested in secret and angry malevolence, are regarded as the cause of the great mass of individual suffering.

According to Harris, Taita ritual is characterized by three principal features.[22] First and most central is *kutasa,* the spraying out of mouthfuls of liquid—usually cane beer, juice, or water—as a means of invoking the blessings of mystical entities and of "cooling" one's heart of the anger or malice that are regarded as causing sickness and misfortune either directly or through the agency of angered spirits. Since *kutasa* is believed to be effective only when accompanied by the most sincere inward renunciation of anger, its performance exerts a powerful effect toward stilling resentments and righting any wrongs that may have caused resentment in the first place. A second feature of Taita ritual, *kizongona,* or ritual sacrifice, involves the slaughter of a sheep or goat and the use of its entrails for purposes of divination to determine whether the rite has been effective. The final feature is commensalism, the sharing of portions of the sacrificial animal among all participants following an offering of the best or choicest pieces to the ancestral or other spirits.

Rainmaking among the Taita is one of several rites that transcend specific ancestor rituals and involve not lineages but neighborhoods or entire local communities.[23] Similar rites are employed for crop-further-ance rituals and for the communal preparation of defensive "medicine" against sorcerers and enemy tribesmen. The rainmaking ritual normally takes place in the season before the rains are expected. It transpires in a small separated grove reserved for this purpose. All members of the community participate, although women do not enter the grove itself except at the beginning of the rite to add their portion of beer to the common pot.

Under the direction of the community rainmaker, the ritual begins with the preparation of a "medicine" made from twigs of trees growing on the highest local mountain, a place where the first rains are believed to fall. This medicine is administered to a sheep whose slaughter con-stitutes a central event of the rite. *Kutasa* is then performed by the elders over the animal's carcass, prayers for rain are directed at Mlungu, and the entrails are read to determine whether the rite will prove effec-tive. A *kioro* mixture of water and the stomach contents of the sheep is then prepared. Some of this is added to the beer pot, and the beer-*kioro* drink is used by the assembled men to perform *kutasa.* Some is sprin-kled on a special ritual horn that is blown in the grove and surrounding area by the individual who has provided the sheep for the rite. Some is set aside to be sipped by everyone during the feast to come. The balance of the *kioro* mixture is taken by two men and sprinkled on surrounding fields. A final blowing of the ritual horn marks the beginning of a seven-day *mdumba* period during which agricultural work and sexual activity are banned. It also begins the more festive part of the rite, including a common meal of the roasted meat and a dance involving married per-sons that may last until dawn. This dance, known as *mbeka,* is generally chaste and dignified, although pelvic movements and the systematic exchange of dance partners lend it an erotic air.[24]

It is not hard to discern in this ritual important aspects of the universal structures discussed by van Gennep and Turner. The rainmaking rite itself is a liminal moment: out of time, in a place apart, the entire community is "betwixt and between." Special conduct is required—all quarreling and fractiousness are prohibited, ordinary agricultural work comes to a halt, and the norms of sexual life are suspended either by imposed abstinence or by the constrained orgiasticism of the *mbeka* dance. *Communitas* is exhibited in the special emphasis on equality of status and sharing that mark the rite. Although not all status distinctions are effaced—women are kept apart from the central events and differences in economic position are acknowledged by the fact that the individual who provides the offering is allowed the special honor of blowing the ritual horn—there is a sense in which the entire community stands as one in this rite before Mlungu. Part of this equality stems from a destructive power: ritual or moral infractions by any member of the group, including women and children, might endanger the rite's efficacy. More positively, all are empowered to contribute actively to the rite, whether by distributing the *kioro* mixture or by performing *kutasa*. Everyone shares in the sacrificial offering.

The rainmaking ritual thus is a special moment when matters that normally divide a Taita community are put aside and the ultimate moral and religious equality of members is acknowledged. Harris herself points out these implications. The rainmaking and crop-furtherance rites, she observes,

> stressed things and activities which were not the focus of economic differentiation. They aimed at securing things which human beings everywhere want: long life, health, the perpetuation of their kind, prosperity. Taita wanted certain of these goods in a particular form: they desired many children, but particularly sons to carry on the agnatic line; they wanted prosperity not only in the form of an abundant food supply, but also in the form of numerous cattle, sheep and goats. It was by means of these specific good things that Taita were differentiated from one another as members of different great lineages and also as rich men or poor. Nevertheless, it was neither for the continuation of any particular lineage nor for the wealth of any individual that the rites were held. Just as all the fields of the "country" benefited, so well-being was sought for all its inhabitants. The prayers asked for the fecundity of all the herds.

In order to realize the common welfare which the rites sought, a common effort had to be made. This included on the one hand, participation: attendance, contributions of beer to the common pot, the sharing of food and drink, participation in *mbeka* or other dancing and observance of the *mdumba* period of restrictions on garden work and sexual activity. It included also the common effort to maintain peace, to avoid raising or pursuing matters which might initiate quarreling. True, it was a feature of all Taita rites that quarreling, or even shouting which sounded like quarreling, was supposed to ruin the performance. On most other occasions, however, only the welfare of an individual or small group of individuals was affected. Here it was the welfare of an entire community that had to be protected. There had to be peace in communities as in families and within individual persons.[25]

Drawing on this description, we can see that the Taita rainmaking ritual has broad moral significance in at least two different directions. On the one hand, the ritual experience adumbrates and models the state of society toward which moral striving aims: a state marked by peace and harmony between human beings and a pacified, productive relationship between human beings and nature. On the other hand, this experience also symbolizes the moral point of view needed to bring this state about. It effects a dramatic, if momentary, equality of power and privilege among persons and, in various ways, requires voluntary renunciation of private advantage in the name of the common good.

This renunciation is effected and symbolized in the abstentions and acts of generosity during the ritual period, and it receives special symbolization in the sacrificial offering that is an integral part of the rite. Voluntary renunciation most characterizes the individual who provides the sheep for the offering. He willingly gives up part of his wealth to exhibit his dependence on the community and to make a contribution to its common good. The rest of the community follows him in this by contributing beer or not eating the slaughtered animal until it has first been presented as an offering to the high god or other benevolent spirits. Taita rainmaking does not involve the harsh suffering or abasement found in some other rituals. But the acts of giving or offering that precede the common meal convey essential moral attitudes of self-restraint, voluntary self-renunciation, and generosity to others.

This aspect of Taita ritual incidentally affords us insight into the moral significance of the sacrificial rites of many different religious cultures. A great deal has been written about sacrifice, and various distinctions among sacrificial forms and motives for sacrifice have been advanced.[26] A major distinction is made between sacrifices that aim at stimulating or reciprocating the generosity of spiritual agents and sacrifices that seek to expiate sin or effect atonement. Sacrifice among the Nuer, we saw, may be of the latter type, with the sacrificial animal regarded as a substitute for guilty or sinful human beings.[27] Taita ritual perhaps more closely approximates the former type of sacrifice, since, as Harris maintains, the Taita appear to lack any substitutionary notions and regard *kizongona* merely as an "offering" that reciprocates the generosity of the spirits.[28] This distinction may be less sharp than it appears, of course. Even in the Taita case, though no substitutionary ideas are present, "offerings" are frequently made as part of rites meant to avert the moral wrath of mystical beings, and they thus play an "expiatory" role within the larger framework of Taita religion. In any case, these different forms of sacrifice—the freely bestowed offering and the means of expiation—display some common moral qualities. In sacrifice, individuals demonstrate their acceptance of a moral order larger than themselves and their willingness to renounce things of value to maintain it. Repentance or contrition is an advanced form of moral self-renunciation. In repentance, one renounces not only material or social claims, but also the moral pretensions of the self. Whereas simple acts of offering and generosity can be thought of as responding to the first element of religious reason's deep structure (adoption of the moral point of view), repentance and contrition respond to the third element of this structure (the awareness of moral failure and the effort to suspend justified condemnation). Nevertheless these distinctions are artificial, because self-renunciation is the defining feature of moral reasoning and of sacrifice in all their phases.[29]

Taita rainmaking thus performs a variety of morally important roles in the life of its participants. It reinforces appreciation of the essential equality of respect owed to each member of the social order. It highlights those generic human values whose protection is an essential responsibility of the community. And through ritual abstention and sacrifice, it furnishes opportunities for exemplary displays of self-renunciation. Of course, the Taita probably do not view the conveyance of moral insight as the major point of this rite. They are, as Harris puts it, "sacramental realists" who perform the rainmaking ritual primarily in order to move the spirits to provide rain.[30] But to acknowledge this external objective does not require us to deny the existence of moral purposes that give shape to the rite and explain its continuing appeal.

The Passover Seder

When we turn from Taita rainmaking to the Jewish Passover Seder, we are initially struck by the surface differences between these rites. The role played by oral tradition in the Taita rite is assumed in the Seder by a complex written liturgy, the Passover Haggadah. The immediate external and practical focus of the rainmaking ritual is replaced by a nonutilitarian celebration of sacred events thousands of years in the past. But despite these differences there are important similarities between these rites that point to their common moral significance. Both include preparatory abstentions, a focus on real or symbolic sacrifice, a suspension of ordinary communal norms and hierarchies, and the celebration of a common meal. Above all, both rituals display the qualities of "liminality" and *communitas* identified by van Gennep and Turner.

The Passover Seder, performed today as a home ceremony taking place on the first night of the eight-day Passover period,[31] is the outcome of a long process of ritual evolution. While formally based on the biblical Passover rite, a mandated commemoration of the Exodus event that draws on pre-Exodus spring-ritual traditions, the Seder is very much the creation of rabbinic Judaism. It replaced a pilgrimage rite centered on the Temple cultus with a home service available to Jews wherever they might be and thus contributed to the survival of Judaism under conditions of dispersion and exile.[32]

The Seder comes at the end of a busy period of ritual preparation. In obedience to the prohibition of the consumption of leavened bread, homes must be emptied in the preceding days of any leaven or leavened products. The special Passover foods must be prepared and the ritual objects for the Seder table arranged. The last meal of leavened bread is usually eaten at breakfast, and amidst the hurriedness of preparations, only a light lunch is taken. Because the Seder may not begin until after sunset, the hours before the ceremony are a semi-fast.[33] This work and partial fasting is felt in the tradition to fall particularly hard on the women and children. As Ruth Fredman observes, while Passover is frequently called the "Festival of Joy" or "Festival of Freedom" by the men, it is sometimes termed a "joyous ordeal" by the women and children.[34]

But if women and children are considered to bear a special burden during the preparatory period, they also assume a special role during the Seder rite. Indeed, an important feature of the Seder is the way it displaces and even inverts the usual order of Jewish social and ritual hierarchy. Women are ordinarily excluded from Judaism's male-centered worship service—an exclusion physically represented by the separate women's section in orthodox synagogues. At the Seder, however, they are active participants in the rite. Children also assume an extraordinary role, since the rationale for the Seder is that it is a forum for teaching the Exodus story to each child. Their significance is symbolized by the tradition that the children be allowed to "steal" the *afikoman,* a small portion of "dessert" matzo reserved for the end of the service. This practice has the practical effect of sustaining the children's interest to the end of the service, when the sequestered matzo is searched for, but it also begins the process of social leveling that characterizes the rite.

In Mishnah Pesaḥim, the classical rabbinic source on which the Haggadah depends,[35] this leveling is most pronounced with respect to class and income differences. For example, the Mishnah states that on the Passover night, all are to "recline" during the meal. This requirement, symbolized in the medieval and modern Seder service by placing a small pillow at the side of each participant's (or the Seder leader's) chair, reflects the freeman's position at the Hellenistic banquet. By insisting that "even a poor person in Israel should not eat until [he] reclines,"[36] and by stipulating that, if necessary, the required four cups of wine for the meal be furnished for the poor out of charity funds,[37] the Mishnah deliberately sought to efface status distinctions. This emphasis carried into the practice in medieval Jewish communities of providing places for the poor and for students at the tables of affluent families.

The process of leveling was also symbolically suggested by the custom of the Seder leader's wearing a white garment, the *kitel.* This is otherwise worn by all men during the services of the Rosh Hashanah and Yom Kippur holidays, the latter being the solemn "Day of Atonement," when each Jew stands before God as penitent and as subject to judgment. The *kitel* also serves as the individual's burial shroud. Thus, although in one sense the *kitel* is a mark of distinction as a sign of leadership during the Seder, in another sense it subverts distinctions by conveying the message that all persons, no matter what their status, are equally subject to sin, judgment, and death.

This lesson is most fully expressed in the Seder's commemoration of the Exodus. During the service, those present are removed from daily existence and carried back to the events of enslavement, suffering, and miraculous redemption that mark the Exodus event. Within the Seder, the Exodus is first symbolically called to mind by the main ritual objects on the table and by their employment during the service. Tradition requires that the Seder table be set with three cakes of matzo placed one on top of the other; a roasted egg and shankbone or other bone; a dish of salt water; *karpas,* or greens for dipping (ordinarily parsley or celery are used); *maror,* the "bitter herbs" for which endive, lettuce, or horseradish are employed; and a small dish of *haroset* (clay), a paste commonly made from nuts, apples, wine, and cinnamon. Later in the service, after a prolonged recitation of the Exodus narrative, the meaning of these symbols is formally expounded. The matzo is said to represent the unleavened bread on which the Israelites were forced to rely for nourishment following their hurried flight from Egypt. The shankbone and egg take the place of the Temple sacrifices, one of which itself symbolized the paschal lamb whose blood, spread on the doorposts and lintels of the Israelites, protected their children during God's slaying of the firstborn of the Egyptians. The bitter herbs are consumed, says the Haggadah, "Because the Egyptians made the lives of our forefathers bitter in Egypt."[38] Although the meanings of the salt water and *haroset,* in which the greens are dipped, are not formally expounded in the Haggadah, they too are assumed to have an Exodus significance. The salt water symbolizes the tears shed by the Israelities while in bondage; the *haroset,* the mortar used by the Hebrew slaves to construct Pharaoh's cities.[39]

This focus on the Exodus is the principal feature of the liturgy of the rite. Following some brief ritual preliminaries—including a blessing and drinking of the first cup of wine and the dipping of the greens in salt water—the head of the household removes the middle piece of matzo, breaks it in half, raises it up for all to see, and recites the Seder introduction: "This is the bread of poverty which our forefathers ate in the land of Egypt. Let all who are hungry enter and eat; let all who are needy come to our Passover feast. This year we are here; next year may we be in the Land of Israel. This year we are slaves; next year may we be free men."[40]

Attention then turns to the youngest child who asks the "four questions." Mentioning, in order, each special feature of the Seder meal—the presence of unleavened bread, the bitter herbs, the dipping of these herbs twice (once in the salt water, once in the *haroset*), and the reclining position of the guests—the child asks, "Why does this night differ from all other nights?" The other participants recite the response,

We were Pharaoh's slaves in Egypt, and the Lord our God brought
us forth from there with a mighty hand and an outstretched arm.
And if the Holy One, blessed be He, had not brought our forefa-

thers forth from Egypt, then we, our children, and our children's children would still be Pharaoh's slaves in Egypt.

So even though all of us were wise, all of us full of understanding, all of us elders, all of us knowing in the Torah, we should still be under the commandment to tell the story of the departure from Egypt. And the more one tells the story of the departure from Egypt, the more praiseworthy he is.[41]

This response may be regarded as the pivotal event of the service. In establishing the order of the Seder, Mishnah Pesaḥim stipulates that this introduction be one which "begins with the humiliation and ends with the glory."[42] Although the long exposition on Deuteronomy 26.5–8 that follows recounts the Exodus events in much greater detail, this brief introduction conveys the essential *kerygma,* or proclamation, of the Deuteronomic passage. In the words of Brevard Childs, "This response is not simply a report, but above all a confession to the ongoing participation of Israel in the decisive act of redemption from Egypt."[43] Through it, Seder participants return momentarily to the events three millennia before and become one with the community of Israel as it suffers enslavement, unjust oppression, and the sudden miraculous events of flight and redemption.[44]

It is important to note that this identification with the historic Exodus community is not just an implication of the Seder service, but a mandated requirement. Following the response, the Haggadah makes reference to "four sons," one intelligent, a second wicked, a third simple, and a fourth who does not yet know how to ask the questions. Three of these sons require teaching suited to their abilities. The "wicked" son, however, is incapable of instruction. His question, "What is this service to you?" shows that he has removed himself from the community. The Haggadah remarks that this son deserves rebuke. The father is instructed to repeat to him, "It is because of that which the Lord did for me when I came forth from Egypt," and the son should be told that had he been present in Egypt he would not have been redeemed.[45] Later in the ritual, following the exposition of Deuteronomy, this same point is made in one of the most forceful statements of the liturgy: "In every generation let each man look on himself as if *he* came forth out of Egypt."[46]

At its center, in its symbols and its liturgy, therefore, the Seder is designed to convey an experiential participation in the Exodus event. More precisely it aims at providing a direct encounter with the major polarities of that event, the experiences of humiliation and triumph, oppression and liberation. In the words of Jacob Neusner, what the Seder service conveys, above all, is the lesson that "to be a Jew means to be a slave liberated by God."[47] In trying to understand the moral significance of the Seder ritual, it is important, I think, to keep both sides of this polarity in mind. It is easy to view the Seder primarily as a celebratory event, as the "Festival of Freedom" simply. In that case, the emphasis on suffering and oppression merely serves as a contrast to or preparation for the dramatic redemptive "conclusion" of the ritual moment. Darkness must be emphasized so that salvation appears even brighter. But this interpretation overlooks the enormous stress placed by the Seder rite on these negative experiences. The Seder is as much a celebration of oppression, if this idea be allowed, as it is a celebration of freedom. But how are we to understand this? How can we make sense of the central place given in this rite to the bitter and humiliating features of the Exodus event?

Part of the answer, I believe, may be found in Turner's conception of *communitas* and our own moral elaboration of it. *Communitas,* we saw, is a morally salutary wiping away of human social distinctions, a return to the "essential and generic human bond," to the "moral point of view" without which there can be no human society. In its positive dimensions, *communitas* is the joyful experience of human fellowship. Negatively, it is the stripping away of all those signs of social difference and status that cloud moral judgment and obscure the more basic priorities underlying individual human existence and life in community. Through the ascesis of the *communitas* experience, individuals are abruptly made to perceive their dependence on the community. Subjected to physical suffering and affliction, they better appreciate the most basic values of life, ranging from simple nourishment and freedom from pain through the solace and comfort of their fellows. As a result, it is only after having passed through this ordeal experience that they are really able to make enduring moral choices, choices likely over time to elicit the free consent and support of *all* members of the community.

Clearly, the Seder, and the earlier Passover rite on which it draws, are meant to convey an ordeal of this sort. Recognizing the threat to group cohesion and morally founded cooperation posed by the status distinctions of ordinary social life, the Hebrew and Jewish tradition sought from the earliest date to provide for a periodic reliving, in both its positive and negative aspects, of the *communitas* experience represented by the Exodus event. Furthermore, within the Bible the connections between this experience and the actual moral life of the community are repeatedly expressed. Nahum Glatzer observes that "Classical Hebrew writings lay stress on the fact that the external liberation was not an end in itself, but the necessary precondition for receiving the law on Mount Sinai."[48] Indeed, the Deuteronomic *kerygma* that celebrates the Exodus precedes a stern reminder to uphold the covenant and to obey its stipulations, especially those requiring just treatment of the poor, the weak, or the bondsman in Israel's midst. Within this tradition, as Franz Rosenzweig observes, the moral entitlements of those within the community are inseparably connected to the whole community's redemption from bondage: "In every command to respect the freedom of even the man-servant, of even the alien among the people, the law of God renews the awareness of the connection holding between the freedom within the people, a freedom decreed by God, and the freeing of the people from Egyptian servitude, a liberation enacted by God."[49] It should be stressed, however, that this connection between national liberation and the freedoms of those within the community is not only a consequence of the fact that these are joined in the biblical under- standing of God's will. At a deeper moral level, emancipation from bondage or poverty and concern for the plight of those who continue to experience them are conceptually and experientially linked. Personal suffering and respect for others go together because those who have been humiliated or oppressed are most alert to the evils a society must avoid.

These links between Exodus *communitas* and devotion to the moral norms governing life in community are perhaps less explicit in the Seder liturgy than they are in the biblical sources on which it draws. But these norms form the context of the rite. They are assumed in the special attention given humble guests at the Seder table, and they endure in the great emphasis on communal solidarity and support of the poor that characterized traditional Jewish communities during the Passover season.[50] The links between communal suffering and moral rededication also play an important role in the repeated expressions of hope for redemption from exile that mark the Seder rite. For much of its existence, the survival of the Jewish people was in question. In the face of constant religious persecution, both the maintenance of Jewish identity and the lives of individual Jews depended in large part on the degree of internal cohesion and mutual support maintained by the com- munity. Remembering the Exodus, therefore, was not just a way of voicing a hope for a similar liberation in the future. It contributed to that liberation. By providing a vivid reminder of the moral priorities and attitudes needed to preserve life and identity in a community under seige, the Seder rite helped sustain the ongoing Jewish struggle against death and oppression.

In an effort to understand the Seder in anthropological terms, Ruth Fredman takes note of the strong play of opposites that mark the symbol system of the rite. Frequently, as when the bitter herbs are dipped in the sweet *haroset* or when the humble bread of poverty is raised on high, polar opposites are brought together in the closest proximity. This, says Fredman, is an especially important, even deliberate feature of the Seder. The ritual, she says,

> tries to relax the tensions generated by the necessary ordering of experience through dichotomy by introducing ambiguities or compromises that are acceptable, and they are acceptable because they are related to a sacred, unknowable, but rational source. The symbolic actions of the ritual engage the community in a game of intellectual *trompe-l'oeil* as they present contradictory experiences of bitter and sweet as divinely ordained and so somehow not mutually exclusive. The symbols can appear to present harmony because they can be the place where disharmonies meet: the matzah can represent both election and affliction, the egg both life and death."[51]

Undoubtedly, the Seder, like much religious ritual, offers its participants the intimation that life's most seemingly contrasting oppositions are somehow related within a rational structure. But Fredman and structuralist anthropologists who share this view often miss the specifically moral dimensions of the conceptual and ritual systems they study. For the fact is that some of the most important polarities of human life and their resolution occur within the structure of reasoned morality. Again and again, we have seen this to be true. Thus, self-denial and personal well-being often seem tensely opposed to one another. But within the context of moral reasoning, they are deeply related since the first is the precondition of the second: self-denial is the key to the communal flourishing on which the welfare of everyone depends. It follows that a person prepared to give his or her life—through a commitment to conduct needed to sustain community—is most likely to protect it. Similarly, if our understanding of the Seder rite is correct, experiences of suffering and oppression paradoxically prepare the ground for triumph and liberation. A ritual like the Seder can express these truths in symbolic form—through acts of abasement that are also an exalta-

tion, through symbols of death that also promise life—not just by forcing these opposites into conjunction, but because this conjunction
already exists within the deepest structures of human moral reasoning.

Baptism in the Early Church

This ability of a religious ritual to draw into closest proximity the contrasting realities of the moral life, and by doing this to reveal their inti-
mate connection, is nowhere better illustrated than in the rite of baptism as it was practiced in the early Christian church. We also find in
this ritual an intense compacting and interplay of symbols. Some of
these are drawn from the Hebrew tradition, including the Passover
rite,[52] while others are new to Christianity. Many of these symbols or
symbolic acts are morally "multivocal." They not only comprise within
themselves specific moral and religious polarities, but they are simul-
taneously able to address very different aspects of the structure of religious reason. For example, within this rite, a single symbolic act suggests a vivid experience of suffering, reduces the individual to the most
basic elements of the human condition, and conveys the possibility of
atonement for sin. In the Passover rite, we saw some of this multivo-
cality in the symbolic garment or *kitel* worn by the Seder leader. But
perhaps because Christianity begins from the already complex Jewish
ritual tradition, it is able in the baptismal ritual to carry this multivo-
cality to new levels.

Over the centuries, Christian baptism underwent considerable
change, evolving, in time, into the routinized rite of infant baptism
widely practiced by Christian communities today. But for at least the
first two centuries of the Christian era, it had a more vigorous form.[53]
From the earliest days, for example, baptism was conceived as the
unique Christian rite of initiation and the defining mark of membership
in the Christian community. It was understood to involve the voluntary
assumption of Christian faith and was preferably (though not exclusively) performed on adults. Departures from the practice of adult baptism were usually made to accommodate the lingering Jewish notion of
corporate responsibility, according to which heads of households
involved their offspring in their religious choices.[54]

The actual structure of the early rite displays the familiar tripartite
progression of a rite of passage. Preliminary to the ceremony, the catechumens underwent an extensive phase of separation from their former
lives. It is noteworthy that this separation, although it received physical

expression during the rite, was primarily conceived in ethical terms. The catechumens had to repent past sins and abandon conduct or professions contrary to Christian faith and morals: procurers, prostitutes, gladiators, charioteers, the makers of idols, actors, and soothsayers were all excluded from Christian fellowship and participation in baptism.[55] As the rite proceeded, this separation intensified and the group of catechumens was not only isolated from the outside world, but was remanded to a portion of the church cut off from the rest of the congregation. Commentators are agreed that the ceremony featured ethical instruction and exhortation, possibly a reading from that portion of the *Teachings of the Twelve Apostles,* or *Didache,* where the Christian way of life is contrasted with the pagan way of death.[56] In an act of public renunciation of evil that reminds us of the Taita *kutasa* practice, the catechumens solemnly foreswore the Devil by "blowing-out" air against him and made a vow to live in obedience to Christ and by the rules of the Christian religion. The renunciatory portion of the rite was made facing west, the symbolic domain of death and evil, while the vow to righteousness was made facing east, the realm of light and purity.[57]

After these exhortations and vows, the catechumens disrobed, and then in a steady line, men preceding the women, entered a well of consecrated water. Except for the aged and infirm, each catechumen was totally immersed so that the head was repeatedly held below the surface or in the flow of water from the spigots. An effort was apparently made to have the catechumen undergo, however briefly, the experience of drowning and asphyxiation. Only then was the catechumen raised from the well, dried, given a new white gown and a lighted candle (both symbols of purity and life), ending what might be considered the liminal phase of the rite. At this point, a separate rite of laying on of hands for the reception of the Holy Spirit was practiced, and the ceremony ended as the group of catechumens, in the final phase of aggregation or reincorporation, was ushered into the presence of the body of worshippers for a celebration of the Eucharist.

It is not hard to discern the important elements of *communitas* implicit in this ritual. The separation of the initiands from the concerns of the daily world, their reduction to a generic human status through nakedness followed by the donning of a simple garment, the symbolic common meal and sharing of humble fare (here a wafer identified with the Passover matzo)—all this is by now familiar. But if we wish to understand the special contribution of baptism as a morally instructional *communitas* experience, we should focus on its central event, the ritual immersion of participants. Although probably borrowed from

various Jewish practices of ritual immersion and cleansing,[58] in its symbolism and conceptualization, baptism is really a novel Christian creation and a unique exercise in the mediation of moral learning through
symbolic experience.

It helps to keep in mind here some of the rudimentary baptismal
theology presented in the New Testament, especially the writings of
Paul, that was developed in later, extended, patristic treatises on baptism. Throughout this literature, several major themes predominate.
Above all, baptism is regarded as an act of spiritual regeneration and
redemption from sin. On the one hand, it is held to symbolize the death
and resurrection of Christ so that, as Paul says, in baptism the Christian
believer dies with Christ, is buried and raised to newness of life (Rom.
6.4; Col. 2.12). Apparently the reference is to the thrice repeated practice of submersion and lifting from the water. On the other hand, baptism is also likened to rebirth, and emphasis is placed in this respect on
the symbolism of water and nakedness (John 3.3–5).[59] In either case,
the efficacy of the rite was held to lie in its moral and experiential meaning, not in a magical direct cleansing from sin. Indeed, early Christian
writers sought to emphasize the psychological dimension of the rite and
to resist the natural, but in their view corrupt, tendency to attribute efficacy to elements of the rite apart from the experience of the
participant.[60]

Some of these theological interpretations of baptism can be understood in a direct, if superficial, way. Thus, to the extent that baptism
symbolizes dying and rebirth, it can be simply said that in this act the
Christian "dies to" sin and is raised to a state of innocence. Or, if the
issue of sin is taken in a narrow, juridical sense, then it is reasonable to
view the semi-death of baptism as a kind of "punishment" and "satisfaction" for wrongs done. Interpretations of this sort rely on purely
symbolic equations, however, and neglect the moral and experiential
dimension of the rite to which even the early commentators attributed
its efficacy. An important question, therefore, is how we can make sense
of the claims that baptism furnished an occasion for the real experience
of moral renewal and rebirth. To answer this question I think we must
look again at the basic logic of the moral life.

The principal obstacles to moral commitment are the variety of
personal and selfish claims that might be summed up dramatically in
each individual's desperate clinging to life. Because we are finite beings,
with one seemingly limited chance to pursue our happiness, every
important moral choice poses the either/or of obedience or disobedience. Do we act in the name of a larger good and perhaps sacrifice our

happiness? Or do we put concern with our happiness aside and possibly risk losing it forever? This problem would be eased, of course, if human beings did not die. In that case, the long-term benefits of moral obedience would eventually accrue to each of us. In the long run, morality is advantageous for everyone. But, of course, as the popular witticism has it, in the long run we are all dead. Hence, as individuals, we are sorely tempted to moral transgression. This is the central problem of religious reason, and it is addressed by religious systems through the various retributive ideas—from resurrection to karma—that seek to remove the obstacle death poses for moral commitment. Paul's insistence that Christ's resurrection *proves* the truth of resurrection for all (1 Cor. 15), and his linking of this teaching to baptism, suggest another way the ritual serves on a purely symbolic level to address this problem of sin and death.

But we can also see that the baptismal rite, though it certainly presupposes and draws on the doctrine of resurrection, dramatically enhances it in many ways. Ritual immersion, being forcibly held below water, is a frightening experience. Like the moments of terror we sometimes face today in a bad plane landing or in a near accident on the highway, it converted death from a remote possibility to an immediate reality. As in the moments following a near accident, release from this brush with death must have been emotionally powerful. To be pulled up from the well after three ritual immersions was to physically experience the joy of resurrection. More, it was an abrupt opportunity to reexamine and reorder the priorities that shape our lives. Individuals who have suffered a serious, life-threatening illness commonly emerge from this experience with their values fundamentally changed. Serious illness often makes the goods we normally pursue—wealth, power, or status—seem irrelevant or trivial. In their place, physical suffering and impending death bring to the fore values ordinarily taken for granted: basic human fellowship, mutual care, love. Not only do these values prove themselves immune to hardship, they grow in meaning as suffering increases.[61]

We can think of baptism as seeking to provide a dramatic opportunity for just this kind of reordering of vital priorities. By forcing the initiand to face death, the rite illuminated our shared human destiny. It exposed the hidden vulnerability of our lives and the relative insignificance of our outer "achievements," and it graphically portrayed the extent of our dependence on others. Psychologically, it forced the initiand to confront the unacknowledged vital fears and anxieties that subtly prompt the selfish quest for power or security, and it dramatically rendered irrelevant the frantic quest for wealth or prestige, a point frequently emphasized by baptismal theologians.[62] Finally, at the culmination of the rite, the initiands were dramatically returned to the warmth and light of human fellowship. Hands that moments before had threatened death pulled the initiand up to safety. In the immediate gathering of the group of catechumens, in the donning of simple, dry clothing and in the eucharistic meal that followed, as the initiands were welcomed into the Christian community, the reassessment of values begun with the formal disavowals of evil assumed definite shape. Narrow self-regard and the pursuit of private ends were naturally replaced by the joy taken in fellowship and by a sense of solidarity with one's fellows no matter what their outer social status or condition.

Like all *communitas* experiences, therefore, the early baptism rite was an effort to convey the fundamentality of the generic human condition as a standpoint for personal and social moral choice. It was the effort to present those facts of the human condition, including its vulnerabilities, that are easily overlooked in the pell-mell rush for advantage in status society and to make apparent the genuine priorities that sustain and nourish human life. It accomplished this by a symbolic mediation of the most extreme sort, the act of total affliction and self-negation represented by violent death. In this connection, we can now perhaps better understand the claims made by early Christians for the rite's regenerative efficacy and power. Not only did baptism provide a powerful set of encouragements to moral dedication, it afforded a direct change of heart and transformation of priorities, a *metanoia,* that distanced the individual from previous tendencies toward selfishness. This is the deepest inner moral sense of the Christian understanding of baptism as an "efficacious symbol" of Christ's redemptive passion and resurrection.[63]

Ritual and Rationality

For more than a century, a major tradition of social-science research has interpreted religious myth and ritual as involving nonrational, emotional, or "expressive" activity. More recently, in the work of structuralists like Lévi-Strauss, this view has been opposed by the claim that ritual and myth both have important cognitive and conceptual dimensions. Myth and ritual, it is argued, are culturally specific ways of working out universal laws governing thought itself and they necessarily involve the exercise of human rational faculties.[64]

The interpretation of ritual I am offering probably stands closer to the structuralist position in that I view rituals not primarily as occasions for emotional release but as articulations of universal conceptual categories and as complex vehicles for the conveyance of essential information. In contrast to the structuralist understanding, however, this universality does not derive from the formal logical conditions of thought, such as the binary organization of experience emphasized by Lévi-Strauss. Instead—or in addition—rituals have an important practical-rational or moral dimension. They convey an understanding of the logic of moral reasoning, of the conditions of social cooperation and of the order of human priorities needed to make possible voluntary social life. They convey, in other words, the series of concepts that underlies the moral point of view and that justifies its adoption. This lesson is mediated through experiential presentations of this viewpoint and may be enhanced and driven home through the powerful emotions associated with *communitas*. But both experience and emotions are here in the service of imparting cognitive insight.

Do all religious rituals have this morally instructional effect? And is the meaning of ritual limited to this moral significance? The answer to both questions, I suspect, is no. To answer the first question properly would require an extensive review of the myriad forms and expressions of ritual.[65] Within this mass of data, some rituals can certainly be found that appear nonmoral or even antimoral. All these instances require careful study, with the rituals themselves considered not in isolation, but as parts of total ritual-religious systems. In any case, this kind of investigation is beyond the scope of my discussion. My point has been that some central types of ritual, possibly all those involving a *communitas* experience, can be understood in moral terms.

Similarly, I would not argue that the impartation of moral instruction constitutes the sole meaning or explanation of religious ritual. Religion itself is a domain where numerous human capabilities, from the exercise of cognitive skills through the display of aesthetic creativity, find expression. This is perhaps even truer where ritual is concerned, since so many essential human activities come together in the ritual moment. Nevertheless, just as I have argued that religion is primarily animated by moral concerns, so I contend that ritual has an important moral dimension. This understanding may help us perceive aspects of specific ritual traditions that are otherwise missed. Finally, it may lead us to a deeper appreciation of the important, possibly irreplaceable, role religions have played in encouraging commitment to the moral life.

7

Religions and Social Justice

Questions of social justice are probably not the first thing that comes to mind when one thinks about human religiousness. We ordinarily assume that religions deal primarily with matters of personal destiny and ultimate meaning. While these preoccupations may involve ethical issues, mundane questions of fair economic distribution hardly seem central to religions' spiritual concerns.

This view is not just wrong, it is seriously wrong. Next to urgent matters of sexuality, questions of social justice are among the most central concerns of religious traditions in their role as moral teachers. This is partly because these questions are unavoidable. Every society faces a scarcity of material resources. Disagreements about access to them can become a source of bitter conflict, and religions, in their essential moral role, are naturally drawn to the task of developing and promoting fair norms of distribution.

The urgency of this task is matched by its difficulty. Few issues place more stress on moral agents than this one. In matters of economic distribution, the tensions between self and society, between particularity and impartiality, that surround all instances of moral choice are heightened because moral reasoning about economic distribution is itself tension ridden. In determining the distribution of scarce social resources, even impartial persons face conflicts among the goals they seek to promote, and these conflicts are magnified by full knowledge of one's social position. As a result, movement from the purely hypothetical moral standpoint of impartiality to real social life imposes serious strains on any norms of social justice. One of religion's most important teaching tasks is to minimize these strains and to promote acceptance of the difficult set of commitments that it is rational to adopt under complete impartiality.

To illustrate this point, I want to examine how four different religious traditions respect the universal structure of moral reasoning and uphold a set of basic norms of justice that bear on economic life. Three of these traditions, Judaism, Christianity, and Islam, are historically related to one another. The fourth, Buddhism, is so far removed and so outwardly different in much of its moral teaching that it is sometimes held up as an example of a religion unconcerned with issues of social justice. Nevertheless, we will see that even Buddhism conforms to the basic norms rational, impartial persons would advocate to govern economic life.

Reason and Economic Life

Given the diversity of moral views about social justice in Western culture, it seems reckless to claim that there is a universal structure to human moral thinking about economic distribution. If socialist, libertarian, and welfare-state views seem sharply opposed even within our society, how can I say there is a basis of moral agreement across distant cultural boundaries? In fact, I believe that recent work in political philosophy has pointed the way to resolving some major disputes about the principles of social justice.[1] From this theorizing, a broad set of norms have emerged that reflect the major concerns of impartial, rational persons in this area. This does not mean that everyone can be persuaded that there is a single just way of organizing economic life. For one thing, even where there is moral agreement on norms, factual disagreements can lead to different policy recommendations. Democratic socialists and welfare-state capitalists, for example, agree that society should protect its weakest members, but they disagree about the best ways of meeting this objective. Only careful research and accumulated social experience can help determine which strategies are best. Another difficulty is that moral reasoning in this area does not permit mathematical precision. While impartial rational persons may arrive at some parameters for the fair division of economic resources, these parameters

leave considerable room for the expression of particular values and for
the process of selecting among these by just political means. This means
that there is a broad "gray" area in our thinking about economic distribution. Nevertheless, the presence of this gray area should not cause
us to overlook the realms of black and white, those matters on which
there is clear agreement about what is just or unjust.

The boundaries of this realm of universal agreement are shaped by
two tensely related considerations governing the thinking of impartial,
rational persons. One is a concern to ensure equality of access for all
persons to society's vital material resources. The other is the desire to
allow some naturally occurring inequalities free play in the determination of social shares. In reasoning about economic justice, impartial,
rational persons find themselves called on to measure each of these concerns both in general terms and in relationship to different social circumstances. What results are some broad guidelines that can expectedly
vary for different cultural settings. On the religious level, the relative
indeterminacy of these matters is reflected in the specific normative differences religions display within a broad framework of moral
agreement.

Rational persons' concern with economic equality is easily understood. It follows from the essential equality created by the moral point
of view. Although material goods like food, shelter, and money are not
equally needed or desired by all persons, they play an important role in
a variety of life plans. This is why Rawls places them among the key
"primary goods" distributed by contract parties in his "original position
of equality" and why a thinker like Alan Gewirth includes them among
the "generic goods" closely tied to rational agency.[2] Since an insufficiency of these goods can impede one's most important pursuits, it is
rational within the circumstances of uncertainty created by the moral
point of view to opt for as large a share as possible. Given the lack of
self-knowledge created by impartiality, this results in an insistence on
equal shares. An illustration of this logic is found in a familiar device
for putting an end to childrens' squabbling over shares of a birthday
cake: have the child who cuts the cake take the last piece. While each
child may want a larger than equal share or may even feel "entitled" to
it, the strict impartiality created by this procedure makes it difficult to
enforce such claims and naturally leads the child who does the cutting
to the "least worst" outcome of equality. Of course, access to scarce
material resources is a far more important matter than shares of a birthday cake. But the more valued resources are, and the less able any party

is to force others to reduce their shares, the more we might expect equal access to be a major pole in impartial, rational agents' thinking.

However, other considerations weigh against equal distribution and have to be taken into account by impartial persons. For one thing, not all persons equally require material resources and "need" may sometimes form a just basis for distribution. Of course, matters of need are notoriously difficult to ascertain and this argues against giving them any weight. It is not clear where "needs" cross the line to become less urgent "wants." We might presume that whenever scarce vital goods are involved, differing wants alone will not persuade impartial persons to depart from equality. After all, why should I relinquish a share in something I desperately need merely because another person (whom I must also consider myself to be) merely wants more? But while need is often a doubtful basis of distribution, in extraordinary situations it can become a compelling distributive precept. At one extreme are situations of great affluence, where the distinction between wants and needs becomes unimportant and where all may take as much as they desire from the common stock. This logic has governed access to air and water where they have been abundant, and it may contribute to the Marxist vision of distribution "to each according to his need" under the conditions of vastly enhanced productivity envisioned for "communist" society.[3] At the other extreme are conditions of extreme hardship where a strictly equal distribution might result in excess vital goods for some and desperate insufficiency for others. This has sometimes been true in situations of drought or famine, when it has been natural to distribute food and water on the basis of body size or the number of persons in families. Of course, even here there may be sharp disagreements about what constitutes need or what is a legitimate basis for measuring it. When this occurs, it is common for communities to revert to the more basic criterion of equal distribution as a fair means of settlement. Equality, in other words, whether as equal distribution or as equal consent to departures from it in urgent situations, is a fixed pole of moral reasoning about vexing questions of distribution.

A second consideration militating against equality is more commonly encountered. It constitutes the other major pole of thinking about just distribution. For simplicity's sake, we can call this the consideration of "productivity." It stems from the fact that social resources rarely exist "out there" as a fixed sum of goods awaiting distribution. Instead, most resources are produced by individuals whose willingness to contribute is a function of many factors, not least of which are the public moral rules governing possession and distribution. It is commonly maintained, for example, that individuals' willingness to create or produce valued goods partly depends on society's allowing them to retain the fruits of their effort. To the extent that this is true, it favors a precept of distribution according to one's productivity and it argues against egalitarian redistribution which, in this light, becomes self-defeating.

As compelling as this conclusion may seem, it is offset by several considerations that are important in the eyes of impartial, rational persons. First, there is the fact that some highly valued resources do exist "out there" unproduced by human effort. Where these resources are concerned, the logic of equal access becomes more compelling. This is why even those who strongly support distribution according to productivity usually accept a principle of equal "initial" access to virgin resources and why societies faced with the task of distributing such resources commonly employ some egalitarian formula or procedure. (Where it is impossible to control the entire process of appropriation, the impulse to equality in these cases usually takes the form of the crude rule of "first come, first serve"; where tighter control of holdings is feasible, stricter equality may be imposed through a rule of "equal shares." The early period of American colonization provides examples of the first kind of distribution, the U.S. Homestead Act of the second.)

Remarkably, this circumstance of nonproduced, naturally occurring, and highly valued goods obtains with respect to some of the basic traits that underlie human productivity itself. Many of these traits—health, intelligence, and bodily strength, for example—result from natural factors having little to do with human effort, and other traits, like fortitude and stamina, are a complex result of both effort and natural endowment. Given their value, we might expect impartial, rational persons to want these traits to be equally distributed.[4] While this recourse has usually not been available, the fact that these traits are *not* equally distributed counsels great caution in adopting the productivity principle as the sole basis for economic distribution. We can see that this principle takes a series of qualities that are not distributed as fairly as rational persons would like and proceeds to make them the basis of a further distribution of vitally needed material goods.[5] Of course, if it were true that productive effort is unavoidably and directly linked to the degree to which individuals are allowed to keep the fruits of their effort, this would be a powerful argument against redistribution. But experience shows that for several reasons individuals are willing to exert effort even in a redistributive context. People often work and produce for reasons other than the material rewards. They may also perceive the unfairness of nature's "lottery" and be willing to share some of the fruits of their own more fortunate endowment. Whatever the case, because productivity is not inseparably linked to reward, impartial, rational persons have a reason for qualifying distribution according to productivity and yielding to their understandable impulse to equal distribution.

We can see therefore, that impartial reasoning about economic life moves between these two poles of equality and productivity. As a result, in the actual adoption of moral principles, we might expect a compromise to be effected between these competing values. We can discern the broad outlines of this compromise in the rules commonly adopted by human communities to govern this area. Out of respect for the productivity principle, people are usually permitted to retain the fruits of their effort. This is especially true in traditional societies where productivity is low, where it involves strenuous personal labor and where redistribution is difficult to enforce. Legal concepts of private property are also frequently developed by communities as a way of establishing rights in goods so produced. But the constant pull of equality and the vital interest all persons have in access to necessary goods reveal themselves in the fact that these rights are usually not regarded as absolute. They are often limited in duration or extent, with concentrations of wealth subject to periodic redistribution. They are also usually balanced by emphasis on corresponding obligations to those less well-off. These may involve only expected acts of generosity, or as social institutions develop, they can extend to the imposition of redistributive taxes. Finally, these obligations are usually held to grow in importance where the most vital goods are concerned. Indeed, during periods of severe hardship, when strict adherence to property rights may involve excess for some and absolute deprivation for others, the primitive situation of equal access is commonly thought to obtain, and a "right" of every person to these vital goods may be asserted.

The Role of Religion

When we look at specific religious traditions, we will find this broad structure of norms very much present. Though traditions differ on specific details—on the precise extent to which sharing should be required or left to individual discretion, for example—all stress social responsibility and make special provision for sharing where serious hardship is involved. In relationship to this body of basic normative reflection, religions also have a multifaceted role. Beyond establishing norms for economic life and embodying these in their structures of religious law or moral teaching, they also seek to justify these teachings by means of their other most basic beliefs. Most important, they try in various ways to encourage their adherents to abide by these norms and to give them a central place in their religious lives.

The task of encouraging the adoption of these norms is especially difficult. Although it makes sense under conditions of impartiality to care about those less fortunate than oneself, this concern is easily eroded by real life in society. One reason is the simple absence of impartiality. Individuals have powerful incentives to want to hold onto larger shares of valued goods, and they may find it rational to seek security in their possessions rather than by cooperating with norms designed to protect those who face hardship. These selfish tendencies are also accentuated by the complexity of moral reasoning about economic life. The legitimate place given productivity in impartial reasoning and the difficulty of determining in any real-life situation of material accomplishment the exact role played by effort, natural endowment, or plain good luck make it very natural for persons to see their larger shares as morally justified. Where real persons are concerned, therefore, just redistributive efforts not only run counter to powerful forces of ordinary human selfishness, they may also appear to violate individuals' sense of what is fair or right.

Responding to these problems, religions apply all the tools at their disposal, including the reiteration of norms of justice and sharing, expressions of praise for those who abide by them, and threats of punishment—whether in this life or the next—for those who fail to do so. Religions also commonly establish opportunities for sharing and generosity. In our discussions of African traditional religions and religious ritual we saw many of these approaches at work. African religions, for example, may regard stinginess and excessive wealth either as signs of sorcery or as possible objects of sorcerers' malice. Either way, there exists the strongest encouragement to share. This usually takes place in special festive or ritual occasions furnished by the religion, like the *ngbaya* ceremony or Taita rainmaking rituals we discussed. In Judaism, the Passover Seder, with its emphasis on the openness of the table to the poor or needy, is a distant relative of this kind of ritual occasion. It also exemplifies use of a *communitas* experience to summon individuals back to a moment of radical equality and shared deprivation as a means of reinvigorating their concern for the disadvantaged.

But perhaps the most intriguing ways in which religious traditions encourage adherence to these norms are the series of beliefs they develop to subvert the natural but distorted moral reasoning that supports selfishness and excessive acquisitiveness. We just saw this selfish reasoning to work by overestimating the role of effort in one's material accomplishments and by viewing economic success or failure too simply in terms of moral desert. Religions' most interesting instructional efforts do not resist these modes of reasoning so much as turn them to advantage. For example, powerful intuitions of legitimate possession and desert may be employed to shift rights and entitlements away from apparent owners to the disadvantaged. Or, accumulation may be actively encouraged, and wealth may be entirely attributed to moral desert, but these ideas may be fused with complex notions of religious merit that make giving the final purpose of getting, with the consequence that the most materially deserving individuals dare not cling to their wealth. In these respects, religions operate in a way best understood through an analogy drawn from sailing. Although a vessel cannot move directly into the wind, it can sail obliquely to it and capture its force to make headway upwind. Religions do much the same thing by capturing the force of a selfishly employed moral logic and using it to restore movement in the direction suggested by impartial rationality.

Historical religious traditions employ all these strategies, although certain approaches are usually more pronounced in one tradition than another. As we turn from the abstract to the concrete, from the theory that lies behind religious teaching about social justice to the teachings themselves, it is helpful to remember that religions are systematic conceptual structures.[6] Adoption of one retributive or pedagogical strategy early in the life of a tradition represents an intellectual commitment not easily abandoned. Once a basic line of thought is selected, subsequent developments usually take the form of variations on it rather than entirely new departures. Among the biblically related traditions,[7] this means that strategies adopted by Hebraic thought have importance for later Jewish, Christian, and Islamic thinking as well.

Biblical Foundations

It is hardly necessary, I think, to develop the profound themes of social justice and concern for the poor that run through the Hebrew Bible, whether in the law codes or the impassioned discourses of the prophets. Some have regarded this teaching as an anticipation of modern radical social theory, with the prophets viewed as forerunners of contemporary

socialists or Marxists,[8] while others have stressed their essential conservatism and the appeal of their teaching to "reactionary," religious
notions of divine authority.[9] In fact, both interpretations are true. The
hallmark of biblical and prophetic social teaching is a conservative rad-
icalism: a call for ongoing redistribution and reform based on the most
past-oriented and religiously grounded property considerations.

A strong but very special concept of property rights underlies the
many obligations to the poor and disadvantaged specified in versions
of the Covenant code. First, the effort is made to suggest that at the
beginning of the national life, entitlements in land were established on
an equal basis for all Israelites. This is the meaning of the description
recorded in Numbers 25.53–57 of an initial distribution of the promised
land by lot and in proportion to the size of families. On the basis of this
initial idea of fair distribution, the impulse toward equality in Hebrew
thinking about social justice subsequently takes a peculiar and fascinating form: henceforth those who defend the poor do so in terms of an
Israelite's primordial property rights, his or her stake in an inalienable
patrimony. Inalienability is a crucial feature of this appeal. Through
various additional provisions in the covenantal code, such as the Sabbatical year of release (Deut. 15; Exod. 21.2; Lev. 25.1–7), during which
debts were cancelled and Hebrew slaves emancipated, and the Jubilee
requirement that all property sold or mortgaged to meet urgent needs
be returned to the original owners every fifty years (Lev.25.8ff), Israelites were guaranteed a perpetual title to productive land. Vast differences in holdings—social injustice brought on by the slow accumulation of property in a few hands (the "joining of house to house . . . field
to field" denounced in Isa. 5.8)—far from being justifiable as a result of
freely acquired possession, assumed the character of theft and violation
of covenantal obligations.

Behind this employment of property conceptions lies a more
important and more powerful notion of legitimate possession: God is
the land's basic "owner" (Lev. 25.23). The narratives of the Exodus and
confederation period all emphasize that the Israelites have received the
land from God as a free gift to which they have no initial claim or entitlement. In the strictest sense, Israelites are not truly "owners" of the
land they live on, but are better described as God's tenants. Efforts to
alienate property thus violate the terms of God's original lease. This is
true whether the intention to alienate originates on the side of the poor
farmer compelled to sell or borrow against his patrimony to survive, or
whether it originates among the more fortunate, who would exploit his

vulnerability to acquire additional holdings. However voluntary these transactions may be, they violate God's property rights.

The notion of God as property owner also explains the ongoing provisions for the poor and the religious leadership established in the covenant. As Roger Brooks points out, these two classes of people are deprived of access to land—the first temporarily by misfortune, the second perpetually by covenantal design. In compensation, they receive support from the landed citizen. The latter, God's "tenant farmer,"

> works God's land and enjoys its yield, with the result that a portion of all he produces belongs to God. In order to pay this obligation, Israelites render to the priests grain as heave offering, tithes, and other priestly rations. Similarly, a specific portion of the Land's yield is set aside, by chance alone, for the poor. So underlying the designation of both priestly rations and poor-offerings is a single theory: God owns the entire Land of Israel and, because of this ownership, a portion of each crop must be paid to him as a sort of sacred tax.[10]

The use of chance as an allocative method, for example in connection with the law of the forgotten sheaf (Deut 24.19), is particularly interesting. We know that in much early religious thought, randomizing procedures are used in divination or ordeals as a way of discerning the intent of supernatural beings. Here, the application of this habit of mind not only guarantees the poor a small share of each harvest but is a sign of God's presence and his involvement in the use of his property.

We can see, therefore, that Hebrew property conceptions work in their entirety to uproot some of the most powerful and corrupt "justifications" of excessive wealth and unjust accumulation. Claims to entitlement and ownership based on long-standing possession, so often used to legitimate inherited wealth and entrenched class systems, are inverted and made to serve an egalitarian purpose. Chance occurrences like a series of good harvests or the possession of an especially productive tract of land, so easily traced to divine "favor," are religiously ignored, while random occurrences that benefit the poor are viewed as signs of God's will. The process of "free" exchange, so commonly used to justify proliferating inequities, is also severely constrained and subordinated to more pressing covenantal obligations.

In pointing to how these biblical strategies are used to subvert intuitive ideas, I do not want to imply that these strategies are merely clever ruses designed to upset sound moral intuitions. Rather these intuitions are themselves misleading and incomplete versions of a larger moral reasoning process. Taken out of context, they are used to defend unjust shares or practices. The aim of biblical thinking is to make this more comprehensive reasoning process apparent. For example, the stress on God's bestowal of land as a free gift reflects the insight that all initial productive endowments, whether personal or social, are "unearned." This fact is usually missed by those who interpret present ownership as an unqualified right of possession. Similarly, stress on the inalienability of one's patrimony and the ongoing redistribution of inheritances that it implies reflect the deeper moral understanding that inherited inequalities have only a tenuous moral justification. While the right to bequeath wealth may be modestly justified to encourage productivity in the parental generation, it can erode incentive or lead to misallocation of resources in the childrens' generation. Concerns of both equality and productivity, therefore, counsel the kind of periodic redistribution of inherited property reflected in biblical teaching on this matter. Finally, while the limitations on exchange wrought by this same body of legislation may appear to run counter to freedom, they really manifest the larger understanding that not every act entered into without coercion is free. Freedom involves not only the absence of coercion by other human beings, but also possession of enough power and means to allow one to express one's will.[11] While a small farmer driven by a sustained drought to surrender his land or to sell himself into slavery may be free from coercion by others, we would hardly regard him as a "free" person in the fullest sense of this term. The effort to impede such desperate acts or to make them unnecessary, therefore, reflects a fuller understanding of freedom than is possessed by those who interpret it narrowly in terms of an uncontrolled right of exchange.

I have chosen to dwell on the approach to economic distribution taken by the Hebrew Bible both because it provides an excellent illustration of the way religions, as moral teachers, lead adherents to a deeper appreciation of the demands of moral reasoning and because it provides the ground plan for later variations on these themes we meet in rabbinic Judaism, Christianity, and Islam. Each daughter tradition introduces novel features to this social teaching, but whatever they add, all employ the basic strategies we have seen: the turning of normal assumptions about property rights and merit against themselves to expose our ultimate lack of moral entitlement; stress on the merely contingent nature of ownership and material advantage; and, as a consequence, the insistence that those better-off have strict obligations to the less fortunate.

Jewish 'Welfare' Institutions

The rabbinic tradition offers many illustrations of this carrying forward of biblical ideas. While Jewish thinking about property offers little that is conceptually new, the institutional embodiment of these ideas is richly developed. It might seem that the events of the first century of the common era would have changed Jewish thinking about these matters, since many of the redistributive provisions of the law that dealt with land were rendered inapplicable by the destruction of Jewish nationhood and the movement of Jewish life into the Diaspora. In reality, during the biblical era, the requirements of the Sabbatical and Jubilee years were already found to be impractical and the principal burden of social welfare had shifted to the tithes and other measures of direct aid to the needy. With the development of village or urban civilization in the Diaspora, this transformation accelerated. Now the biblically and Talmudically mandated requirements of aid to the poor, comprised under the two headings of *gemiluth hasadim* (voluntary acts of charity) and *zedakah* (enforceable obligations of justice), became the responsibility of special communal institutions.[12] As Isadore Twersky observes, each autonomous community assumed the form of a "modified welfare city-state, with its special functionaries who collect the compulsory levy and act as trustees for the poor and needy."[13] Each city, town, or village was required to set up two basic funds for poor relief, one the Tamchui, or "Plate," for emergency relief of transients and local poor, the other the Kuppah, or "Chest," for the ongoing support of the community's poor.[14] Moses Maimonides' comment that he had "never seen or heard of an Israelite community that [did] not have an alms fund"[15] suggests the prevalence of these institutions during the medieval period. Their importance is signaled by the rules governing their administration, including the provision that whoever refused to pay their legally stipulated minimum obligation of *zedakah* might be compelled to do so by the rabbinic court (Bet Din), and their goods might be seized for this purpose.[16]

Behind this extensive structure of social-welfare legislation lay the series of ingenious theological and ethical conceptions we saw in the Hebrew Bible. Foremost among these was the idea—now rooted in

Psalm 24.1 "The earth is the Lord's and the fulness thereof" —that material resources are not the exclusive possession of any human owner but are goods bestowed by God and held in trust for him. For the rabbis, this supported the conviction that needy persons who call on the community's assistance do so as a matter of right, not charity. This belief is evidenced in a Talmudic story concerning a poor man who had visited Raba. The sage inquired what his guest usually had for dinner and the poor man replied, "Fatted chicken and old wine." Surprised, Raba asked, "But do you not feel worried that you are a burden to the community?" To which the man replied, "Do I eat what is theirs? I eat what is God's."[17] Although this story certainly exaggerates the reality of Jewish charitable practices, it captures their underlying rationale. In rabbinic thinking, *zedakah* was not a favor that might be withheld but an obligation of justice stemming from God's ownership and from his conditional bestowal of his property. In the words of Maimonides, "Gifts to the poor are not benevolence but debts."[18] Some commentators also drew from this the idea that wealth is bestowed by God *in order that* it might be given away. In keeping with this idea, the poor exist partly to assist the spiritual advancement of the rich, so that if the poor need the support of the rich, even more do the rich need the poor to gain religious merit.[19] With this idea we are on the threshold of a complex new way religious beliefs may be used to subvert ordinary notions of material entitlement. However deserved they may be, riches exist only to be transmuted into the higher religious merit of giving. Although this approach is sometimes found in Christianity and Islam, we will see it most fully developed in Buddhism.

Christianity's Vision of Equality

To a large extent, Christian thinking about economic life continues the normative teachings and theology of the Hebrew Bible. As a part of this tradition, it elaborates a powerful ethic of almsgiving rooted in the familiar idea that property is a trust bestowed by God on the condition that it serve the needs of the poor.[20] By equating the poor and outcast with Christ (Matt. 25.31–46), the Gospels also greatly accentuate and lend new symbolic depth to the Exodus theme's identification of Israelites with the poor and oppressed.[21] Christian thinking also contains two new ideas not present in Hebraic thought. One is a theme of asceticism, the devaluation of wealth not merely because it provides an occasion for injustice but because it "attaches" believers to worldly things and jeopardizes their pursuit of higher "spiritual"values. With this theme, the disavowal of material possessions, in whole or part, becomes a form of spiritual discipline.[22] We will also see this as a major motif in Buddhism, which, through the Gnostic tradition, may actually have influenced Christian thinking on this matter.[23]

A second relatively new theme in this tradition stresses the primordial equality of human access to material resources and calls for the restoration, by one means or the other, of this ideal primitive state. This theme is important because it "humanizes" thinking about economic life and brings to the surface some of the deep-structural rational considerations that underlay biblical social ethics but were previously expressed through more immediately religious and theistic conceptions (such as the idea that God bestows property). While it is not right to say that this new theme "demythologizes" Jewish-Christian thinking about economics—we will see, in fact, that it draws on a cosmological myth of its own—it does effect a significant "rationalization" of earlier teaching.

For social and intellectual reasons, Christian teaching about economic life tends toward a greater extremism in thought and practice than Jewish views: it is at once more radical and more conservative than the broad position worked out by the rabbbis. The radical tendency is shown in the special place given the poor and outcast in the New Testament and early Christian writings, in the sharp denunciations of wealth found in many of these texts, and in the repeated efforts—whether in monastic or sectarian groups—to replace private property with communistic forms of economic organization. The conservative tendency is found in the early Church's reluctance to challenge or replace unjust social institutions, in the eventual acceptance of vast economic differences in the Christian community, and in the persistent tendency to reduce obligations to the poor to a matter of personal charity.

Among the social and historical factors contributing to these opposing tendencies in Christian social ethics, the urgent apocalyptic expectations of the early community are certainly important. They played a dual role, on the one hand sharpening the call to disinvolvement with worldly goods and emphasizing the importance of sharing in the brief time before God's Kingdom but on the other hand making the task of institutionally embodying these values seem unimportant. This apocalyptic "quietism" is perhaps most evident in the writings of Paul, where the strong emphasis on economic injustice found in the Gospels and in Acts is replaced by exhortations to Christians to love one another within the framework of existing, but soon to vanish, social structures.[24] The transplantation of the early community from Israel to the Hellenistic world contributed to this relative conservatism by sundering the connection with established Jewish institutional forms and accentuating the development of interpersonal charitable practices more appropriate to a voluntary religious fellowship than an autonomous legal community. Finally, the vast and constantly changing influx of converts was significant, as the earliest converts among the working poor and, less frequently, slaves were replaced by an increasing number of new Christians from the upper strata of society. This had the effect of softening the contours of worldly Christian ethics, while driving many idealists into the radical alternative of monasticism.[25]

This extremism of attitudes also stemmed from ways that the church interpreted and transformed its legacy of biblical thought. The theme of stewardship, for example, though potentially radical, worked along with the growing worldliness of the Church to create an attitude increasingly more favorable to wealth and less prone to go beyond interpersonal charity as a corrective for severe economic inequality. If, as Ernst Troeltsch observed, the "wine" of Christian social teaching was soon diluted with the "water" of social inequality,[26] this positive esteem for wealth and the diminished emphasis on stewardship's more rigorous demands were largely responsible.

In contrast, the idea of the primordial common ownership of property was potentially far more radical and transformative in its implications. Even when this idea was domesticated by the medieval Church by being relegated to a time before history no longer relevant to life in society, it tended to reappear in the "absolute natural law" of sectarian protest groups.[27] In fact, this conception of primordial common ownership has been one of the most creative and influential Christian responses to the task of justifying economic sharing and redistribution.

Various strands of thought contributed to the emergence of this idea. Speculation on the nature of economic life "before society" was already present in Greco-Roman thinking. Plato and Aristotle's writings debate the merits of common possession. Stoic philosophers like Cicero and Seneca connect this tradition with speculation about humankind's original condition, and Virgil's *Georgics* even depicts a happy original state before the existence of private property.[28] Communistic religious groups in Judaism during the intertestamental period, such as the Therapeutae or the Essenes, and early Christian monastic experiments may have provoked thinking about the original, uncorrupted form of economic life.[29] An important stimulus is the Book of Acts, where the fervor of the early Jerusalem community is reported to have taken the form of holding "all things in common" (2.44, 4.32). Since Acts depicted the presumed "eschatological" state of the Christian community where sin was being overcome, it was also natural to regard it as providing insight into the condition of humanity before the Fall. As a result of all these strands of thought, we begin to see, during the patristic period, theologians discussing the primordial and divinely intended shape of human economic life. In the writings of church fathers like Basil of Caesarea, Gregory Nazianzen, Ambrose of Milan, and St. John Chrysostom, depictions are offered of the Edenic state before the emergence of "mine" or "thine." For these writers, private property is not a feature of the pristine human condition but is related to the subsequent appearance of sin in history.[30]

Of the several Christian contributions to earlier biblical thinking about economic life, this one has special interest from the point of view of religious rationality. By speculating on the primordial state of economic life, Christian thinkers were able to make explicit and actually trace some of the reasoning about economic distribution that might be expected of a community of impartial, rational agents. Because the Edenic vision embodies the elements of full equality and freedom assumed for the moral point of view, it becomes a convenient base from which to reconstruct the reasoning of equally placed persons as they confront the choice of economic arrangements under varying conditions and different assumptions about human nature. Before the Fall, for example, impartial, rational persons faced with at least a modest sufficiency of resources are presumed to accept open access to needed goods and commodities, and there is no need to regulate conduct by constraint or coercion. But this relaxed distributive approach makes sense only so long as each person is ungrudgingly willing to do his or her part for the common good and has no wish to take more from the common stock than is needed for a modest living; in other words, so long as individuals are not subject to sloth or greed. With the appearance of sin in its root form as narrow self-interest, these ideal arrangements become self-defeating. People now make individually rational decisions that lead to what the modern writer Garret Hardin has termed the "tragedy of the commons."[31] Hoping for a "free ride," individuals typically undercontribute effort (the sin of sloth) or else, believing that whatever damage they do to the common good is offset by their own immediate gains, excessively appropriate shared resources (the sin of greed). The result of these individually "rational" decisions, of course, is a ravaged commons and an insufficiency of basic goods. To control these evils, rational persons now find it necessary to impose constraints on one another, some form of what Hardin terms "mutual coercion mutually agreed on."[32] This can involve ongoing administrative measures to control utilization of the commons, or more simply, it can take the form of private property: by dividing up the commons among themselves and limiting access to one another's parcels, the costs and benefits of individual conduct are internalized for each actor, and the discrepancy between rational individual action and what is good for everyone is eliminated.

Although Christian thinkers rarely spell them out, all the details of this mythical account are implicit in depictions of the beginning and the Fall that are found in various moral discourses on wealth and charity. Some early thinkers, it is true, identify the impulse to private possession as itself sinful. [33] But most Christian thinking, especially the later Thomist tradition, with its great debt to Aristotle's defense of private ownership, tends to view property as a legitimate effort to control in all its forms the chaos created by prior human selfishness.

In this account of beginnings, theologians and homilists possessed a powerful tool for justifying the ethic of sharing and generosity to which they wished to summon Christian believers. Since Christians were called on to reflect in their actions their salvation from sin, the Edenic model became a ground plan for social change that was actually carried out in the monastic movement. For those within propertied society, this mythical account served in new ways to qualify the right of private possession. For one thing, in all its interpretations, even those allowing a legitimate role for property, private ownership was regarded not as a happy part of God's original plan for the world but rather as an unfortunate by-product of human sin. It was at best a lamentable necessity, no more to be celebrated than the executioner's ax. In this respect, classical Christian thinking makes a far more concerted intellectual attack on intuitive perceptions of property than does the Hebrew or Jewish notion of primordial divine ownership. It calls into question not just any single individual's entitlement, but the whole institution of property itself. Small wonder that Christianity has always inspired a vigorous tradition of sectarian protest against class society.

By suggesting the logic of the transition from a primordial "commons" to private possession, Christian thinking also exposed more clearly, and in more transparently rational terms than ever before, the limitations that attach to any moral justification of a right to property. If private possession was ever allowed at all, this was presumably because everyone consented to arrangements needed to secure each person's access to vital goods. Aware of the dangers posed by their individual exercise of self-interest, rational persons took steps to protect themselves against themselves and against one another. But in accepting the self-limitation represented by a right of private property, individuals surely did not rationally relinquish all the advantages of the commons and they presumably placed severe constraints on the exercise of the right of property. For example, it would be foolish to allow absolute ownership by some beyond what is needed for survival when others' survival is threatened by forces beyond their control, such as during periods of sustained drought. To protect themselves against this contingency, rational persons would reasonably insist on some degree of "recommonization" of excess property in these times. In addition, since it is never entirely clear to what extent economic failure is the consequence of one's preventable failures or of bad luck or injustice, it was also rational to ensure some degree of ongoing support for those in need and hence some permanent duties of sharing and generosity.

In fact, Christian thinkers drew all these conclusions from this teaching of primordial common possession. In the writings of the great classical theologians, from Ambrose and Augustine to Aquinas, the original common right of all was frequently appealed to in connection with exhortations to care for the less fortunate. The later Scholastic tradition also insisted that failures of support were violations not of charity but of justice, and this tradition taught that in times of desperate need, one might, without injustice and without being regarded as a thief, openly or surreptitiously take goods from those with a surplus they refused to share.[34]

A remarkable feature of this entire approach is how little it relies on any specifically theistic premises. Apart from the more or less explicit appeal to the Genesis cosmogony, religious beliefs play a small role in this account. Whereas Hebrew efforts to counter illegitimate human claims to entitlement rely on strong beliefs about God's activity, the argument from common possession has a human focus. Its strongest premises are not theological but have to do with the facts of human prehistory and human nature. The humanistic and rationalistic emphasis of this tradition of thought becomes apparent during the medieval and early modern period, when Christian teachings about property came to be viewed as part of a "law of nature" available to all rational beings regardless of their religious beliefs. The assertion by Grotius in the sixteenth century that the law of nature exists independently of God's will and is "unalterable. . . even by God himself"[35] expresses in forceful terms the virtual absence of appeal to divine authority within this tradition of thinking about justice. It is not surprising that this same tradition of speculation, inherited by "contract" theorists like Hobbes and Locke, should eventually lead in the West to the emancipation of social philosophy from religion.

Christian thinking on this issue provides an impressive illustration of how this tradition was often able to weave together rational strands from Greek philosophy and Hebrew ethics. From the Hebrew side, Christian thinkers drew a strong commitment to social justice that, although deeply rational, initially assumed a strongly theistic and revelational form. From the side of Greek and Roman philosophy it borrowed a more apparently rational tradition of speculation about justice, but one whose conclusions, especially in the works of Plato, Aristotle and some Stoic thinkers, were often skewed by deep class prejudices and faulty factual assumptions.[36] By fusing biblical norms with Greek and Roman philosophical method, Christian theology was able to develop a structure of thought rational in both method and conclusion. This is not to say, of course, that this approach was always effective in achieving its ends. For some of the social and intellectual reasons I mentioned, Christianity more than once came to accept vast class differences. With Islam, we return to a revelational tradition that utterly eschewed the philosophical course taken by Christian thinking on economic life but that sometimes gained in vigor what it lost in reasonability.

Justice in Islam

The relationship between reason and faith has been a bitterly contested issue in Islam. Overall, probably no major theistic tradition has been more insistently revelational than this one, with important rationalist forays like the Mu[c]tazilite movement of the eighth through tenth centuries ending in sharp repudiation by the dominant tradition that became Islamic orthodoxy. By now we have some idea, of course, that religious diatribes against reason are not necessarily irrational; they can be part of a strategy designed to ground the authority of an otherwise ethically rational tradition. Although this is not the place for the thorough exploration of law, theology, and ethics that would be needed to determine whether this is true in Islam, when we look at the limited domain of Islamic economic ethics, we see just what we might expect of a religiously rational tradition: the forceful use of revealed religious authority to ground a thoroughly rational and comprehensible set of moral norms.

Islamic teaching in this area proceeds from God's commands recorded by Muḥammad in the Qur'ān. These are supplemented by traditions about the custom of the Prophet during his lifetime (Sunna), and by an extensive body of subsequent legal interpretation on which the community reached a consensus *(ijmā')*. The central norms in this area, roughly corresponding to the requirements of *gemiluth hasadim* and *zedakah* in Judaism, are voluntary acts of charity *(sadaqah)* and compulsory almsgiving *(zakāt)*. Along with denunciations of those who "hoard" gold and wealth, both forms of giving are mentioned in the Qur'ān.[37] We also find there (sura 9.58–60) a specification of charity recipients: the poor (later defined as those who are utterly destitute), the needy (those in less desperate circumstances), slaves (who may, with assistance, buy their freedom), travelers, recent converts to Islam, and those appointed to the task of collection. Although the Qur'ān is imprecise about where the line is to be drawn between *sadaqah* and *zakāt* and never specifies many details for implementing the compulsory alms tax, these texts furnished a basis for the extensive structure of religious "social-welfare" legislation worked out by later jurists and legal scholars. In Islamic states, the collection and disbursement of *zakāt* was a responsibility of the public treasury. Minimum qualifications for liability to the tax were specified and rates of taxation of wealth were established, ranging from 10 percent for rain-fed land (5 percent for irrigated terrains) to 2.5 percent for gold, silver, money, or merchandise.[38]

The many details of Islamic poor laws are less important to us than *zakāt*'s religious significance. In the course of history, the proliferation of additional, non-Qur'ānic taxes under later Muslim regimes often made the full payment of *zakāt* impossible. But even when this was so, *zakāt* was always considered a central component of the "submission" to God that Islam represented. Along with obligatory prayer *(ṣalāh)*, fasting during month of Ramadan, pilgrimage to the sacred mosque at Mecca (hajj), and the profession of faith *(shahāda)*, it was regarded as a defining feature of membership in the Muslim community, one of the "five pillars of the faith." This made *zakāt* an expression of religious orthodoxy on a par with creedal confession in Christianity. Almsgiving in general was also thoroughly woven into Islamic ritual. For example, it became a customary part of the celebration of two major Muslim festivals, the ᶜ*Īd al-Fiṭr,* marking the end of the month-long daily fasting of Ramadan, and ᶜ*Īd al-Aḍha,* the culminating event of the Meccan pilgrimage.[39] A full treatment of each of these important annual observances properly belongs with our previous discussion of religious ritual, since each occasion bears many of the marks of *communitas,* especially the stress on equality and shared suffering by the entire community of believers. But it is not hard to see that the importance of almsgiving on these occasions both reinforces our understanding of the moral dimensions of ritual and helps illustrate *zakāt*'s place in Islamic piety.

Behind this structure of norms and religious legislation lies the familiar idea that God is the absolute owner of property, who bestows it on individuals so that they might administer it productively for the good of all. This stress on the social appointment of property explains not only the emphasis on support of the poor and the needy, but also the whole pattern of Islamic thinking on ownership, inheritance, and public taxation.[40] All the provisions in this area of *sharīᶜah,* religious law, conform to the general Qur'ānic principle that wealth should circulate widely and not be something "taken in turn among the rich of you."[41] This teaching underlies Islamic law's insistence that certain essential goods of nature like air and water may never be privately owned, and it explains the provision that ownership of virgin land is obtained only by one who puts it to productive use for a period of at least three years.[42] The idea of God's bestowal for productive purposes also accounts for the especially strong Islamic opposition to usury, which, as in most traditional economic contexts, was considered to be an exploitive source of income. Although these prohibitions are found in Jewish and Christian teaching,[43] their continuing importance in Islamic law is a measure of how seriously this tradition connects the right of ownership to social productivity. Finally, this idea of the social appointment of property underlies the special effort made in Islamic inheritance law to ensure than an amassed fortune be widely distributed at an individual's death. Thus, the law limits to one third the amount of an estate one may freely will, with the remainder distributed among kin on the basis of a formula determining shares in proportion to each recipient's religious obligations to support others.[44]

This basic theme of God's bestowal of possessions is an important feature of Hebrew, Jewish, and Christian thinking about economic life. But it assumes a new dimension in Islam by being linked to the stress on God's unlimited sovereignty and to the insistence, itself a reflection of Islam's unsparing monotheism, on his absolute freedom from necessitation by lesser powers, including the constraints of human moral standards. Repeatedly in the Qur'ān the point is made that whatever blessing humans have received flow from God's unfettered compassion. Everything good in the universe, including our being itself, derives not from our intrinsic worth or attractiveness but is a sign *(āyah)* of God's absolute generosity. The moral norms incumbent on humankind reflect this fact. One must be generous because God has been generous: "Give them of the wealth of God that He has given you," the Qur'ān admonishes.[45] Refusal to do this—stinginess and injustice in all their forms— is thus not only a moral failure but a form of unbelief *(kufr)*, literally "ingratitude" to God for his works of compassion:

> God is All-knowing, All-powerful.
> And God has preferred some of you over others
> in provision; but those that were preferred
> shall not give over their provision
> to [their slaves], so that
> they may be equal therein.
> What, and do they deny God's blessing?[46]

We have seen that a major obstacle to the acceptance of rational norms of economic distribution are the fragmentary and misplaced intuitions of merit or entitlement that people use to rationalize and justify existing inequalities. Islam combats these prideful and misleading notions precisely by denying that human beings "merit" what they have received or that their deeds or excellences in any way compel God. Far above human standards of right and wrong, God does what he wills and each act can only be regarded as a display of utter mercy to human beings who, strictly speaking, deserve nothing.

Within Islamic theology this tendency to exalt God's sovereignty is so pronounced that it sometimes appears that God can do whatever he pleases even if this violates human moral sensibilities. While some orthodox theologians were driven in the course of debate to defend God's sovereignty in these radical terms,[47] within the Qur'ān and in the normative teachings of subsequent Islamic law and ethics, God was viewed as just in humanly understandable terms, and he correspondingly expected just conduct of human beings. By focusing on Islam's economic teachings, we can see why this overwhelming stress on God's sovereignty correlates so thoroughly with a rational structure of moral norms. For here, at least, the emphasis on God's power is not antirational or antimoral but is meant to encourage acceptance of a profoundly rational set of requirements. Much like the important predestinarian tradition in Christianity we explored in chapter 5, Islam's elevation of God's power forms part of a larger effort to combat human pride and to ground important features of reason's total program. Islamic social teaching, therefore, provides another illustration of how important it is to place individual religious teachings within their full context and to interpret them in terms of the deep structure of religious reason.

Buddhism's Social Vision

When we turn from biblically influenced religious teachings on economic life to Buddhism, we seem at first to be in an alien world. None of the familiar themes of regard for the poor appear, none of the strategies designed to reduce false human claims to entitlement have a place, and economic issues in general seem almost entirely eclipsed by flight from wordly involvement. The temptation is very strong, therefore, to conclude that the matter of fair economic distribution is a peculiarly Western concern, something limited to the traditions stemming from the Hebrew Bible. One may also be led to conclude that religions differ fundamentally in their preoccupations. After all, if Buddhism can neglect an issue as morally important as this, how can it be said that all religions are animated by common moral concerns?

I believe that none of these conclusions is correct. Like the other traditions we have looked at, classical Buddhist teaching contains a comprehensive vision of a just social order, one that emphasizes sharing and wide human access to the basic goods of the earth. Although this vision permits private ownership as an unfortunate concession to greed, it condemns selfish material acquisition and hoarding. Moreover, this vision is a central feature of Buddhist thought. It underlies Buddhist social theory, informs the specific norms governing the employment of wealth, and receives vigorous expression in the Aggañña suttanta, a key cosmogonic myth sometimes called the "Buddhist Book of Genesis." Before looking at this myth as a representation of Buddhist social and economic teaching, I want briefly to consider why Western interpreters have tended to overlook the existence of this powerful tradition of economic justice in Buddhism. In each case, we find another instance of religious conceptions being taken out of context, with little sensitivity to the ways they fit into complex rational systems of religious and moral teaching.

Since the work of the great sociologist of religion, Max Weber, it has been commonplace for Western scholars to assert that because of its fundamental teachings, Buddhism cannot really have an economic or social ethic. At least four different reasons have been offered for this claim. First, it is argued that Buddhism's key doctrine of "no self" *(anattā)* undermines concern with the welfare of one's neighbor or one's community. As Weber put it, a social ethic predicated on the value of individual persons "must be as remote as possible from a salvation doctrine which, in any value emphasis upon the 'soul,' could discern only the grand and pernicious basic illusion."[48] Second, it is claimed that Buddhism's emphasis on the goal of nirvana and on monastic withdrawal from the world can at best produce only an attenuated social ethic. Thus Weber, again, regarded Buddhism's entire lay ethic as an afterthought, an "insufficiency ethic of the weak" altogether lacking in normative specificity about economic life.[49] Third, it is claimed that the karma doctrine of moral retribution erodes any possible critical perspective on economic life. Since individuals' material circumstances— whether they are rich or poor—can be traced to their moral conduct in some previous life, all social and economic status becomes "deserved" and immune to criticism. Related to this is the observation that in Buddhist lay morality, karmic aspirations frequently take the form of hope for improved material conditions and wealth.[50] Finally, there is the powerful observation that economic generosity in Buddhism, *dana,* is almost always purely *religious* in nature. Not only is the motive self-regarding and oriented toward one's own spiritual advancement rather than the good of the recipient, but even the recipients are religiously defined. The aim is to support not the weak and needy but the monastic community of religious virtuosi. *Dana*'s primarily religious quality is epitomized in the teaching that the worth of giving is a function of the spiritual attainments of the recipient, not his economic need. This makes the monastic community (the *sangha*), rather than the poor, the primary "field of merit" for charitable donations.[51]

None of these alleged difficulties, I think, need dissuade us from looking for a Buddhist social and economic ethic. In contrast to the common Western perception of the doctrine of "no self" as undermining moral concern, for example, Buddhist scholars and a growing number of Western interpreters have pointed out that *anattā* has rarely been understood among Buddhists as eroding altruism. Rather, is has been used to encourage purely "selfless" compassion for the suffering of others. "No self" does not mean that "others" do not exist or may be neglected but that one's own ego may be set aside. Economically, this teaching has the powerful effect of countering the selfishness that stimulates greed.[52]

The second contention, that Buddhist ethics focuses principally on the monastic community with lay conduct an afterthought, has likewise been brought under sharp criticism by recent interpreters. The work of Stanley Tambiah, for example, makes clear that Buddhist social ethics are badly misunderstood if the ethics for the monastic community is severed from the important body of teaching regarding the ideal political order and the duties of the righteous Buddhist monarch, or *cakkavatti*.[53] The fact that the Buddha himself was predicted to become either a great world renouncer or a great world ruler suggests that the idea of individual spiritual salvation *and* the hope for political and economic renewal may have been part of the earliest Buddhist vision. We will see just this interweaving of political and religious aspirations when we turn to the Aggañña suttanta.

The claim that Buddhism's teaching of karma implies acceptance of the economic status quo seriously confuses the question of how individuals have arrived at their present circumstances with the question of how they or others should properly respond to these circumstances. Within this framework, less advantaged persons surely deserve their lowly place on the economic ladder, but this no more justifies others' keeping them there through greed or injustice than the karmic fact that murder victims "deserve" their fate justifies anyone's committing homicide. Karma certainly ensures that wrongful behavior is punished, but it has no bearing on the question of what constitutes such behavior or what Buddhism's norms are for the proper use of wealth.

It may be argued that Buddhism's reliance on karma, by making suffering the result of one's past deeds and volitions, tends to reinforce the pernicious human tendency to see all possessions, however arbitrarily come by, as deserved. We saw that the biblically influenced traditions strive to combat this habit of mind. But the absence of this effort in Buddhism is not a concession to injustice so much as a sign that, in approaching the difficult task of detaching persons from their advantages, Buddhism adopts a different strategy from that found in Judaism, Christianity, and Islam. In these traditions, enormous effort is made to weaken human claims to entitlement by making God the sole owner of property. But in Buddhism this approach is not available. Possessions do not derive from God's bestowal, and within the world of strict moral retribution fashioned by the karma doctrine, every aspect of one's present situation is deserved. Instead of hoping to distance the powerful and wealthy from their advantages by requiring them to look *back* to the source of these assets, therefore, Buddhism makes people's *future* circumstances and entitlements depend on the present use of their advantages. This motif is found in theistic traditions where future reward or punishment depend on obedience to God's will, but it becomes a major theme in Buddhist thought.

It is a fascinating exercise in comparative religious ethics to consider the strengths and weaknesses of these respective rational strategies. If the Buddhist approach carries the psychological liability of sometimes appearing to "blame" the victims of misfortune or injustice, it has some corresponding attractions. Among the poor it eases poisonous feelings of social resentment and among the rich it puts the strong desire to perpetuate one's currently experienced status in the service of sharing. Of course, while comparative analysis may expose the particular vulnerabilities or strengths of rational religious systems, the comparison of religious ideas does not mean that religions are entirely free to choose among strategies. As I have pointed out, religions are often relatively "locked into" the basic responses they develop to meet reason's deep structural needs. Once Buddhism has adopted karma as its principal retributive doctrine, it was constrained to develop its economic teaching on this basis. If intuitions based on one's own entitlement could not be demolished, they had to be put to use.

In Buddhist thought this is accomplished through unremitting emphasis on generosity and sharing. For the Buddhist laymen, the voluntary renunciation of wealth through acts of religious giving, *dana,* becomes the main expression of personal piety and the central ritual of daily life. In each morning's encounter with members of the monastic community making their begging rounds, in weekly or seasonal attendance at sermons, and in the reading of popular moral treatises like the *Vessantara jataka,*[54] with its depictions of extreme acts of generosity, Buddhist laymen are thoroughly indoctrinated in the supreme religious value of acts of selfless giving. As a spiritual discipline, generosity is first of all a mark of respect for those who have chosen the path of renunciation and a sign of acceptance of Buddhist teaching. But it is also an exercise in the lives-long discipline that will someday culminate in the attainment of nirvana. If the principle cause of social injustice is a tenacious adherence to what is "mine," it can be said that Buddhist lay piety imposes a systematic schooling in selflessness and social virtue.

Of course, this returns us to the objection that generosity in Buddhism is always directed toward the monastic community and has a religious rather than social-welfare character. But this objection assumes it is possible in this context to distinguish religious giving from acts of economic redistribution and sharing. On several counts, however, this distinction is doubtful. For one thing, within Buddhist cultures, the monastic community performs many of the vital social and welfare tasks undertaken by charitable institutions or government in other cultures. Although in most traditional Buddhist societies, the family and wider circle of relatives constitute the "welfare" institution of first resort, the monastery provides a refuge for orphans or those without family connections.[55] (The female monastic community similarly provides a refuge for unmarried women or widows.) Through its important educational services, available free to any young man, the monastic community furnishes an essential means of social mobility and status not only for those who remain in monastic life but also for those who spend only their preparatory years in study.[56] The fact that this educational system is almost entirely "financed" by individual religious mendicancy on the part of teachers and students illustrates how difficult it is to separate socially and religiously appointed generosity in this context.

But perhaps the most important welfare effect of religious support of the *sangha* is not this direct social benefit but the long-term beneficial impact on the quality of political and social life brought about by the flourishing presence of the monastic community. Within the ideal Buddhist commonwealth, *sangha* and society perform vital and complementary functions. The *sangha* serves as a "teacher" in the fullest sense of this word. It imparts Buddhist values to society and government, and seeks to create the pacific, nonviolent, and cooperative social order on which monastic life depends and which it symbolically anticipates. The example of social life set by the *sangha* in this respect is especially important. Winston King describes the monastic community as representing, in Buddhist teaching, "the nearest possible approximation to the ideal social order possible to approximate in time and space, which *all* men ought to approximate as nearly as possible in their social relations to each other."[57] By bringing masses of individuals, many of whom will become secular leaders, into contact with this community through education and preaching, Buddhism aims to permeate the social and political order with its ideals.

For its part, government is responsible for putting these ideals into practice. Through sound foreign and domestic policies, leaders must avoid war and seek to provide for all citizens a measure of material well-being. Prosperity, and even affluence, form part of this vision. As the "middle way" between asceticism and luxury, Buddhism teaches that extremes of wealth and poverty both distract from the spiritual self-discipline needed to attain the religious goal of nirvana. Hence, some theorists have argued, it is the responsibility of a Buddhist government to ensure material sufficiency for everyone in a Buddhist common-wealth, both to facilitate the giving of *dana* and as a direct contribution to the laity's spiritual progress.[58]

This, of course, is an ideal vision and one that has only been par-tially attempted in some Buddhist societies. But as systems of thought, religions must be understood in terms of their ideals. For this reason, and to enhance our understanding of the outlines of this overarching Buddhist social vision, we should look briefly at the myth of world evo-lution we find in the Aggañña suttanta.[59] Here, in a form that allows free play to the imagination, we find an essential statement of Buddhist values. Above all, we see the central and cooperative roles played by the *sangha* and monarch within a rightly ordered commonwealth. What follows is a synopsis of the myth as it begins at the end of a previous cycle of cosmic evolution:

When, after a very long period the world cycle passed away, beings were mostly reborn in the World of Radiance where, made of mind, they dwelled "feeding on rapture, self-luminous, traversing the air, continuing in glory."[60] After a long time, the world began to reevolve. Beings who had deceased from the world of radiance were usually reborn as humans, although self-luminous humans, traversing the air, made of mind, without sexual differentiation, feeding on rapture.

The world was then watery and dark, neither sun nor moon nor stars having yet come into being. In time, just as a scum forms over the surface of boiled milky rice, the earth appeared over the waters. It was endowed with the color of pure butter and the flavor of honey. Spurred on by a "greedy disposition," one human being tasted the savory earth with his finger. Others followed him and, "suffused with the savour, . . . craving entered into them."[61] They began then to break off large lumps of this food. As a result, they became permeated with the earth material, their luminance faded away and the sun, moon, and stars appeared to replace the beings' vanished light.

For a long time, these beings continued to eat the savory earth. Their bodies thus became more solid, and differences in comeliness became manifest. Some beings were well favored, some were ill favored. Those who were well favored gloated pride-fully over their state and "despised" those who were less favored.[62] This vanity and conceit caused the savory earth to disappear.

A new form of nourishment now appeared in mushroom-like growths with the color of butter and the flavor of honey. But these caused the bodies of the human beings to become even more solid and more different from one another. Once again, this occasioned pride on the part of the better favored, and with this, the mushroom growths ceased, to be replaced by sweet tasting creeping plants.

Like the foods before them, these plants increased humans' bodily solidity and differences in physical appearance among individuals became even more manifest. Pride also increased and the plants vanished, giving way to a fragrant, huskless rice. This was so abundant that when gathered in the evening for supper, a new crop was ready to be harvested the next morning for breakfast. Eating this rice, however, accentuated human solidity and differentiation. As a result, the distinction between males and females appeared, sexual lust arose and with it, immoral conduct. To conceal their immoral behavior, beings constructed huts.

Now some being "of a lazy disposition" asked, "Why do I wear myself out fetching rice for supper in the evening, and in the morning for breakfast? What if I were to fetch enough rice for supper and breakfast together?"[63] He acted on this idea and others followed his example, storing up rice for four and then eight days. As a result, powder and husks enveloped the grain and the reaped and cut stems of the plants did not grow again. "The rice stubble stood in clumps."[64]

Lamenting their condition and the degenerated state to which "evil and immoral customs" had led them, the beings now resolved to divide off the rice fields and set boundaries thereto. But with this, some being "of greedy disposition," while watching over his own plot, stole another's plot and made use of it. The others seized and remonstrated him, but he persisted in his behavior until the others were forced to strike him with their hands, with clods, or with sticks. Thus "did stealing appear, and censure and lying and punishment."[65]

Gathering together to bewail these things, the community resolved to elect one among them to censure what should rightly be censured. They chose the most attractive and most capable of their number for this task and agreed to give him a proportion of their rice in payment for his services. This king "chosen by the whole people" was given the name Mahā Sammata (the Great Elect).[66]

With the selection of this royal person there arose the social circle of nobles. The origin of the members of this group was identical to that of other human beings but, like the king, they were appointed to political service. In time, a second group, the Brahman renouncers, also emerged, consisting of those individuals who had forsaken the world of evil deeds for forest meditation. Even-

tually, some among these proved incapable of meditation and set-
tled in the outskirts of villages where they made books. "At that
time they were looked upon as the lowest; now they are thought
the best."[67] Eventually, the two remaining groups of the caste order
emerged: the "Vessas" [Vaisyas], who adopted the married state
and set on foot various trades and the "Suddas" [Sudras], a hunter
caste. No group emerged from physically distinct types: all shared
a common human nature.

Having depicted the full evolution of the world order as we know it, the
suttanta describes a final important historical event:

> Some "Khattiya" [Kshatriya] "misprizing his own norm" went
> forth into the homeless life resolved to become a recluse. He was
> followed by like-minded Brahmans, Vessas, and Suddas. Whoever
> among these has destroyed "the intoxicants," has "laid down the
> burden," and "through knowledge made perfect is free" is declared
> chief among their number.[68]

Obviously, one must be careful in reading or interpreting a myth
like this. To a large extent it is a whimsical, ironic effort, partly meant
to poke fun at Hindu-Brahmanic pretensions and at the Brahmanic
account of the creation of the world and the social order.[69] Nevertheless,
within this irony we find a serious effort to stake out a specifically Buddhist conception of society, of human nature and human destiny.

Pivotal moral issues rest on the myth's rejection of the Hindu
understanding of caste. As presented in the Vedas and lawbooks, Hindu
social theory is based on inherited organic-spiritual distinctions among
human beings. Louis Dumont captures this in the title of his study of
the caste order, *Homo Hierarchicus.*[70] Caste and its relationship to
rational morality is an enormously complicated subject, requiring independent treatment. On the face of it, caste in Hinduism seems to repu-
diate the concept of basic moral equality that I have said is a fundamental feature of moral and religious rationality. In other ways, it can
be interpreted as an effort, perhaps not wholly successful, to fashion a
cooperative and mutually protective social order within a historical situation of vast differences in culture and power. Without attempting to
resolve this matter here, it can be said that because of its obvious moral
liabilities, the Hindu conception of caste predictably generated enormous religious opposition over the centuries both inside and outside
Hinduism. This opposition took powerful form in the Buddhist idea

that one's true caste status was determined, not by one's birth, but by the degree of one's moral and religious excellence. In the Aggañña suttanta, we see the essence of these Buddhist objections to the inherited inequalities of the Hindu caste system.

These objections take several forms. The various social orders of the caste system, we are told, do not reflect any inherited (or ontological) differences among human beings, nor do they stem from a divinely effected act of creation as claimed in the vedic Purūsha-sukta.[71] Instead, whatever caste or class groups there are reflect functional specialization. These groups possess no enduring moral significance. The worth of an individual is not the result of caste position or birth, but of individual moral integrity. It follows that the religious salvation offered by membership in the Buddhist *sangha* is open to members of all caste groups.

The rejection of permanent caste inequalities is also evidenced in the *suttanta*'s sardonic criticism of human pride. We learn that differences in "comeliness" are one unfortunate consequence of a process whereby human beings become progressively coarser and more distinct from one another. Instead of lamenting this development, however, the more attractive individuals regard their relative advantage as an excellent reason for disdaining their "inferiors." Of course, this pride only serves to accelerate the degenerative process. I said earlier that because of the teaching of karma, Buddhism does not generally seek to combat human claims to entitlement by denying their validity, as do the Western traditions. But here, in connection with the effort to denounce the pride and arrogance perceived among Brahmanic defenders of the Hindu caste system, Buddhist thinking also tries to set entitlements on their head.

In terms of economic life, the myth represents a stinging critique of uncontrolled material acquisition and of some of the institutions and practices associated with private property. In typically Buddhist fashion, the "first sin" that precipitates decline in the human condition is the lust for sense pleasures and material satisfactions. Beings that began as luminous spiritual entities are seen greedily to ingest base material that coarsens their natures. Greed and hunger produce even more greed and hunger. This process continues remorselessly until it corrupts almost every dimension of human life. Material lust gives rise to sexual lust, nature becomes debased as her uncultivated bounty gives way to sterility, and the struggle over increasingly scarce resources produces, in turn, private property, theft, violence, and a punitive political order. Private property seems not to be included among the root causes of moral degeneration—as in Christian thinking, it is a desperate response to a deteriorating situation—but it clearly belongs to a badly corrupted stage of human existence.

The parallels here to the Genesis account of human prehistory and to later Christian employments of this account are obvious, as are the contrasts. No God enters to punish human wrongdoing, and the cardinal sin is not pride or the desire to become God but physical appetite and craving.This reflects Buddhism's unique diagnosis of the cause of human evil and suffering. But where the material order is concerned, the lesson of these traditions is remarkably similar: human greed is its own undoing. Nature is viewed as having been constituted to supply human material needs, but when people strive for more than their proper share, they invariably end up with less. Disordered self-assertion diminishes nature's abundance, corrupts the human body, promotes strife and violence among persons, makes private property necessary, and leads to the need for a coercive and hierarchical state.

In this connection, it is worth noting that the passage in the suttanta dealing with rice's lost fecundity after an episode of hoarding has a striking parallel in Exodus 16. In the biblical text we read of God's bestowal of manna to the wandering Hebrews. Each family is provided daily with what it can eat and no more. Despite an explicit prohibition against saving up the foodstuff, some gather more than their share. They promptly find that the excess has been infested with maggots, while those who violate God's prohibition against gathering on the sabbath are unable to find any food at all. The specific religious dimensions of the Hebrew and the Buddhist texts clearly differ. The Israelites' behavior is another instance of their lack of faith in God and their disobedience of his commandments. But in moral terms, the lessons of the two passages are the same: unnecessary, selfish hoarding is counterproductive. Those who try to buttress their position by acquisitiveness and those who are greedy and lazy jeopardize everyone, including themselves.

Textual parallels like these are important data for comparative religious ethics. The challenge is to understand why they exist in such widely different and historically unrelated traditions. A grasp of the deep structure of moral and religious reason provides an answer. In both mythic episodes, we find a criticism of the kind of "me first" attitude that runs fundamentally counter to moral cooperation. By depicting the consequences of such selfishness in terms of its impact on nature (infertility, the vanishing of a natural bounty), these myths show the wider implications of conduct that threatens social cooperation and turns person against person.

If much of the Aggañña suttanta is critical in its stance, calling into question existing social realities and practices by viewing them as the consequence of human wrongdoing, the myth also contains a strong positive vision. This is suggested at the end with the appearance of the "Khattiya" recluse, the Buddha, who points the way to salvation and establishes the Buddhist monastic community for this purpose. Like the Brahman renouncers before them, these recluses abandon private property and the struggle for material gain; they subsist only on the modest daily offerings of the householders. But unlike the Brahman renouncers, this company draws its members from all castes and classes. Free of the sins of pride and greed, its members are able to resist the degenerative process of becoming. On the worldy side, they are assisted in this by the wise ministrations of the righteous Buddhist monarch, the Mahā Samatta, who owes his authority to the free consent of all and who "censures what should rightly be censured." Together, king and *sangha* work to reverse the historical process of social decline and reconstitute the primordial state of blissful, self-sufficient equality.

The parallels between this myth and themes in other traditions we have examined suggest that Buddhism, no less than the biblically influenced traditions, possesses an important ethic of social responsibility and sharing. Like these traditions, it respects the psychology of human productivity by tolerating private property. But it retains a moral vision of equal human entitlement to the goods of the earth. It also reinforces this vision with strategies designed to bring acquisitiveness under control and to ensure everyone's access to the earth's basic resources. In all these respects, Buddhist social teaching confirms the presence and the importance of a universal structure of moral reasoning about economic life.

In communicating these basic ideas, Buddhism employs some ideas similar to, as well as others very different from, those found in other traditions. As moral teachers, religions frequently display ideas unique to themselves side by side with conceptions strikingly parallel to those found elsewhere. The interest of comparative religious inquiry lies in perceiving what is unique and what is shared. It is important to see the degree of initiative and creativity that religious traditions are able to bring to the working out of a common rational agenda. But this agenda must also be kept in mind. It furnishes the guide that enables us to see the universal in the particular, the common human thread amidst so much bewildering diversity.

8

Morality in Popular Religious Literature: The Art of Judgment in Vālmīki's Rāmāyaṇa

Moviegoers watching an adventure film starring John Wayne or Clint Eastwood would hardly regard this experience as religious, but it has much in common with attending a traditional religious drama or listening to a recitation of epic poetry. In all these cases, the audience encounters a narrative that both stimulates and satisfies their deepest moral yearnings. They see the righteous undergo hardship and suffering, including rejection and scorn by the society they benefit. They witness the temporary flourishing and prosperity of the wicked, along with the unbearable arrogance and pride this brings. And, in the end, they see moral retribution upheld. In a more or less violent finale the weakness and impotence of the wicked are exposed and the power of righteousness is dramatically displayed.

This outline can be discerned in any number of traditional religious narratives. We find it, for example, in many specific episodes in the Hebrew Bible, from the Exodus story through the tales of Ruth or Esther. In complex ways, it furnishes the basic structure of the Christian Gospels, and it underlies much postbiblical epic Christian literature from the *Song of Roland* or *El Cantar de Mio Cid* to Arthurian romance. In China we saw this structure in the earliest efforts to "record" the history of the Shang and Chou dynasties, and it reappears in later epic novels like *Journey to the West* or the *Investiture of the*

195

Gods that draw on these early sources.[1] In India, this same moral outline underlies the plot and dramatic impetus of the two great epics of Indian literature, the Mahābhārata and the Rāmāyaṇa.[2]

Works of this sort are often described as "didactic" and, to the extent that this literature is morally instructive, the description is accurate. But if "didactic" is used pejoratively to signify a wooden impartation of accepted social norms and values, then the term is unfortunate for at least two reasons. First, because the appeal of this literature lies as much in what it assumes its audience to know as in what is imparted. Many of these stories were able to teach precisely because they drew on the powerful set of beliefs shared by human beings everywhere, convictions that form the essential "deep structure" of moral and religious reason. Literature of this sort is instructive not because it communicates these beliefs but because it upholds and vindicates them. Second, this literature does far more than merely impart social norms or display character ideals. Instead, it usually undertakes the more complex task of exploring how norms and ideals are embodied in the difficult circumstances of real life. Religious narratives like this commonly take their characters and the audience through a series of complex "cases for decision" whose purpose is to demonstrate the making of impartial moral choices in conflict-ridden situations. If these stories are instructive, this is not so much because they impart some list of standard moral rules or virtues, but because they furnish an occasion for exercising what might be called the "art of moral judgment."

No single literary creation exemplifies these qualities of religious narrative literature better than Vālmīki's Rāmāyaṇa, an epic poem in Sanskrit of some 50 thousand lines that has been at the heart of Indian and South Asian culture for more than two millennia.[3] Apart from the Bible and the Qur'ān, probably no work of religious and moral instruction has had a greater cultural impact. From India to Indonesia, it is hard to avoid this tale. Episodes from it, or from any of the numerous adaptations it has inspired, are sculpted or painted on temple walls, recited or mimed annually in village festivals, and performed in polished stage and dance presentations in urban centers. All over South Asia today and, until recently, in China as well, the adventures of King Rāma, his faithful wife Sītā, his devoted brother Lakṣmaṇa, and their wily friend Hanumān have formed a store of shared delight.[4] Although Westerners tend to think of Indian religion in terms of major "philosophical" writings like the Upanishads, the Bhagavad Gītā or the Buddhist sutras, it is arguable that the Rāmāyaṇa, through the Vālmīki original and its many vernacular retellings, has probably had the most pronounced effect of any single text in forming religious and cultural ideals in India and in the lands shaped by its civilization.[5]

To the extent that its leading characters represent virtual stereotypes of good or bad behavior, it is easy to characterize the Rāmāyaṇa as a didactic tale. Together, these characters almost define the positive and negative moral paradigms of their society. Rāma exemplifies the dutiful son, the righteous ruler, the loving husband and brother, the courageous warrior and the generous victor. Sītā is the adoring, faithful, and brave wife; Lakṣmaṇa, the devoted brother; Hanumān the stalwart friend. Rāma's principal foe, Rāvaṇa, the demon King of Lankā, is the antitype of these virtues: he is violent, lustful, and heedless of his subjects' welfare. Much of the emotional power of the narratives derives from this stereotyping. Rāma's undoubted righteousness sharpens the pathos of his unmerited suffering and rejection. Sītā's fidelity through the severest trials renders the tests of purity to which she is subjected pitiful.

But to point to the stereotypical role of the principal characters is only to scratch the surface of the Rāmāyaṇa's moral and religious appeal or of its instructive power. That good sons obey their fathers, that married love is faithful under duress, that responsible rulers do not selfishly imperil their realm—these are moral truisms. If the Rāmāyaṇa teaches its audience, it is not by imparting these self-evident truths. Rather, the text derives its genuinely instructive power in the two ways I have mentioned. Deep religious aspirations are nourished as righteousness is tested and vindicated; and by means of a series of agonizing decisions on which the plot turns, the method and complexity of moral judgment is illuminated and explored. Throughout, the power of the narrative lies not in the stereotypes it upholds. Rather, it is the transparent moral significance of these stereotypes that renders them suitable vehicles of religious assurance and complex moral instruction. By tracing this process of moral instruction in a text as rich as the Rāmāyaṇa, we can gain insight into a genre of literature that has been an important, but relatively little studied, part of human religious life.

The Basic Narrative

In its broad outlines the story recounted by the Rāmāyaṇa has an engaging simplicity and emotional power.[6] At the request of his elderly father, King Daśaratha, Rāma, the oldest of four sons, is about to be anointed as heir-apparent to the kingdom of Kosala. Although Rāma is only a young man, his valor and integrity are so well known that this decision by the king causes rejoicing in the king's retinue and among the citizens of the royal city of Ayodhyā. But, at the last moment, evil and intrigue upset the happy course of events. Kaikeyī, the youngest and loveliest of Daśaratha's three wives, is falsely persuaded by a hunchbacked maidservant, Mantharā, to believe that Rāma's installation will lead to Kaikeyī's subjection and the banishment of her son, Bharata.[7] At the wicked maidservant's urging, Kaikeyī asks the old king to grant her the two "boons" he had promised when she had once saved his life during a battle. Moved by love, in an act reminiscent of Herod's vow to Salome in the Christian Gospels, the king grants her the boons and Kaikeyī makes her fatal request: she asks that Rāma be exiled to the forest for fourteen years and that Bharata be installed as king.

Believing that he must keep his word, but struck by grief, the elderly king summons Rāma and informs him of Kaikeyī's request. Rāma immediately agrees that the queen's wishes must be respected. In a series of exchanges, Kausalyā, Rāma's mother, and his brother Lakṣmaṇa urge Rāma to disobey the king and install himself as monarch, but Rāma rejects their entreaties. His wife Sītā, whose hand he had won twelve years before in a mighty test of strength, does not try to persuade Rāma to stay, but she begs to accompany him on his forest wanderings. Rāma initially resists her appeals, but he finally yields, and the royal pair, accompanied by Lakṣmaṇa, embark on their exile.

All Ayodhyā mourns their departure, and a vast crowd of citizens tries to follow the trio into the forest. Engaging in a series of minor deceptions to free themselves from their loyal subjects, the three penetrate the wilderness and take up with a virtuous band of ascetics. Following their departure, Daśaratha dies of grief and remorse, and Bharata refuses to assume power. He visits Rāma in the forest and tries to persuade him to return. Unsuccessful, Bharata procures a pair of Rāma's sandals which he sets on the throne as a symbol of his brother's rule. Henceforth, Bharata merely serves as regent awaiting his brother's return.

For some years, Rāma, Sītā, and Lakṣmaṇa lead a joyful pastoral existence. But the brothers' warrior skills are eventually put to the test. The ascetics come under attack by vicious *rākṣasas,* ogre-demons. Although Sītā implores Rāma not to use force, since he has adopted the "harmless" life of an ascetic, Rāma insists that he must remain true to his Kshatriya (warrior) duty. He and Lakṣmaṇa take up their bows to defend the innocent sages. A series of bloody battles with the *rākṣasas* ensues, including a prolonged struggle with a hideous ogress named Śūr-paṇakhā. Smitten by love for Rāma, she tries to force herself on him. After some jocular play by the brothers, which only inflames her anger, she jealously attacks Sītā and must finally be subdued by Lakṣmaṇa, who, being unwilling to kill a woman, merely cuts off her nose and ears and drives her away. The enraged Śūrpaṇakhā then summons the aid of her demon brother Khara and his hosts. In a series of mighty battles, Rāma and Lakṣmaṇa annihilate the demon army.

But Śūrpaṇakhā is also a sister of Rāvaṇa, the powerful, "ten-headed" *rākṣasa* ruler of the southern island of Lāṅkā (perhaps modern Sri Lanka or some smaller coastal island). When she informs Rāvaṇa in his redoubt of her humiliation and the destruction of so many of his demon-followers by the royal brothers, Rāvaṇa, perceiving a threat to his rule, is stirred to action. Against the advice of his counselor Mārīca, who has met Rāma in battle, he arrives at a plan to defeat his young foe. Mārīca is asked to assume the guise of a beautiful golden deer to lure the brothers away from Sītā's side, so that Rāvaṇa will then be able to carry Sītā off. Rāvaṇa believes Rāma will be so demoralized by the loss of his wife that if he tries to recover her, he will be easily vanquished.

Mārīca, knowing Rāma's might firsthand and convinced of the recklessness of this plan, strenuously protests against it, but he is unable to change Rāvaṇa's mind and finally yields to the ruler's wishes. The plan proceeds flawlessly. Sītā is entranced by the golden deer and she urges a reluctant Rāma to pursue it. Then, made anxious about Rāma's fate by the demon's spurious cry for help from the forest, she forces Lakṣmaṇa to leave her side and search for his brother. While they are gone, Rāvaṇa, in the guise of a mendicant, abducts Sītā and carries her off in his aerial chariot. The vulture king Jatāyu witnesses the abduction and tries to intervene, but he is slain in an epic battle and Rāvaṇa is able to carry Sītā off to his island stronghold in distant Lāṅkā. There, he installs Sītā with his many wives in the Aśoka garden and gives her one year to decide her fate: either she will join Rāvaṇa's harem as a principal consort or she will be "minced by steel knives" and served for breakfast to the demon. In the meanwhile, Sītā's chastity is protected by the God Brahmā, who, following a previous incident of rape by Rāvaṇa, had threatened to destroy the demon if he ever again attacked a woman.

When Rāma learns of the kidnapping he is almost paralyzed with grief. He despairs of ever finding his wife and he alternates between vio-

lent rage and impulses to self-destruction. But he is bouyed in this difficult moment by Lakṣmaṇa, and the two set off in search of Sītā. They
soon encounter Sugrīva, a young prince of the Vānar line. (With some
uncertainty, the Rāmāyaṇa variously depicts the Vānars as either intelligent monkeys or as a somewhat uncivilized forest-dwelling tribal people.[8]) Sugrīva recounts his own mistreatment at the hands of his elder
brother, Vālin. On an expedition during which he was followed by Sugrīva, Vālin had engaged a demon foe in a cave. After a year of waiting
for Vālin to emerge from the cave, and in the certainty that he had perished in a noisy battle below, Sugrīva returned to their Vānar territory,
Kiṣkindhā, and assumed rule (including possession of Vālin's wife,
Tārā). To everyone's surprise, Vālin survived the ordeal, and on his
return he angrily confiscated Sugrīva's possessions and wives and drove
him off to the forest.

Sharing the common plight of banishment, Rāma and Sugrīva now
forge an alliance. Rāma will help restore Sugrīva to the throne, and Sugrīva, in turn, will lend his Vānar forces to the search for Sītā. Rāma
promptly keeps his side of the bargain. In one of the most morally
ambiguous moments of the epic, Rāma intrudes in a one-to-one combat
between Vālin and Sugrīva. Shooting Vālin at a distance with an arrow,
he kills the monarch and saves the life of his embattled ally. Once
restored to the throne, Sugrīva, in seemingly typical Vānar fashion,
proves less than serious about his obligations. Following the rainy season, when battle should resume, he idles in his court and has to be
reminded by an angry Lakṣmaṇa of his promise to help recover Sītā.

Sugrīva rallies. An enormous Vānar host is assembled for the
search. Troops are dispatched to all points of the compass, and a party
of the southern contingent, led by one of Sugrīva's chief lieutenants,
Hanumān, learns of Sītā's presence in Lankā. In one of the most splen-
did moments of the epic, Hanumān, who is sometimes described as the
child of the wind god, springs in a single bound across the straits sepa-
rating Lankā from the mainland. Taking the form of a tiny monkey, he
reconnoiters Rāvaṇa's city and discovers a desperate Sītā in the Aśoka
grove. He urges her to return immediately with him to the mainland,
but she fears she cannot survive the leap across the waters, and she also
protests that womanly virtue forbids her to cling to another man. Assur-
ing Sītā that he will soon return with Rāma and the Vānar troops, Hanumān allows himself to be captured by Rāvaṇa. He is marched through
the city, taunted, tormented, and his monkey tail is set aflame. But Hanumān promptly outwits his captors. He uses the occasion to set fire to

parts of Lāṅkā before jumping back to bring Rāma and Sugrīva news of his expedition.

Rāma, Lakṣmaṇa, and Sugrīva prepare for battle, aided by Vibhīṣaṇa, a brother of Rāvaṇa who had defected after an impassioned effort to convince the demon to return Rāma's wife. With the help of allies, a causeway is constructed to the island. A series of mammoth battles ensues during which magical weapons and spells are used. First one side then another prevails. In a final bloody contest, Rāma singlehandedly defeats and kills Rāvaṇa. Sītā is reunited with her husband, but, in a surprising development, Rāma appears to spurn her, insisting that his royal duty will not allow him to take back a woman who has been another man's captive. To prove her purity, Sītā subjects herself to a trial by fire, from which she emerges unscathed. Rāma declares his abiding faith in Sītā's purity and explains that his conduct was necessary to restore her public reputation. Vibhīṣaṇa is installed as king of Lāṅkā. Fourteen years have now passed and Rāma is free to repossess his throne. The happily reunited couple, along with Lakṣmaṇa, Vibhīṣaṇa, and the leading Vānar allies, mount Rāvaṇa's aerial chariot for a triumphant return to Ayodhyā. Bharata gladly welcomes his brother, and Rāma begins a blessed ten-thousand-year rule, Rāmarājya, during which poverty, disease, and crime are unknown.

To this basic plot, found in the central five books *(kaṇḍas)* of Vālmīki's Rāmāyaṇa, tradition appended a variety of materials. A preliminary book, most of which is regarded as a later addition, recounts several fabulous narratives and brings to the fore a theme of Rāma's divinity that is less pronounced in the earlier strata. According to this, Rāma is an avatar, or incarnation, of the great god Vishnu, sent to earth, as are all Vishnu's avatars, to remedy wrongdoing and to maintain the order of the world. In this instance, Vishnu must take mortal form in order to vanquish Rāvaṇa who, in a previous encounter with the gods, had been promised that he would never again be killed by one of their number. A final book, which is also almost universally regarded by scholars as a latter addition,[9] repeats Rāma's public repudiation of Sītā, but this time the outcome is less happy: deeply wounded, Sītā, like Persephone, descends to reign as a goddess in the underworld, and Rāma, before returning to heaven as Vishnu, lives out his terrestrial life in grief.

Faced with the important theological and moral differences between the core and the added material, an earlier generation of scholars sought to impose an evolutionary model on the Rāmāyaṇa. The more "human" epic of the core books, they argued, represents the true voice of the narrative, and perhaps even reflects an historical kernel in the remembered exploits of some military hero or ruler, while the later material was merely a series of less authentic and even fantastic "religious" embellishments.[10] But this approach not only ignores the anticipation of later themes in the core material, it misses the deep religious intentionality of even the earliest narrative. As Frank Whaling argues in a perceptive discussion of the epic, Rāma's semidivine status is already embodied in the earliest discernible treatments of his character and his fate.[11] From the outset, Rāma displays an almost superhuman level of moral attainment. His selflessness, his devotion to duty, and his compassion distinguish him from ordinary mortals and explain his appeal and renown.

Rāma and Reason's Deep Structure

This tendency to divinize Rāma—accentuated by the later bhakti, or devotional, tradition, which came to see Rāma as a source of religious salvation—makes sense when the epic is viewed in terms of the deep structure of moral and religious reason. Rāma's character represents the ideal expression of virtue and his career the hoped-for trajectory of moral life in this world. Rāma exemplifies not just this or that standard of conduct, whether it be the ethic of a warrior, ruler, or ascetic, but the very essence of commitment to morality. In each of his choices, he displays a willingness to put the demands of duty before personal well-being, with the result that he often suffers. Indeed, Rāma so consistently faces hardship that Whaling is led to identify suffering as the distinguishing characteristic of his choices. But this somewhat misses the point, since Rāma is not an ascetic and never deliberately seeks out misfortune. Indeed, it is fair to say that Rāma's life is a paean to happiness, whether in the joys of married life or the satisfactions of esteemed rule. But Rāma is committed, above all, to dharma, or moral duty, a commitment, the epic tells us, which can lead to suffering.[12] In facing the anguished conflict between self-interest and duty, therefore, Rāma fully participates in our human condition. He also points beyond us and reveals his divinity by maintaining a standard of nearly absolute moral perfection.

If Rāma's choices illustrate the ideal of moral commitment, his career traces the hoped-for trajectory of genuine virtue in the face of worldly reverses. Rāma certainly suffers for his choices, often far more than he or his followers anticipate. He willingly undertakes exile, and although at first the joys of pastoral life seem to make this only a slight sacrifice, in the loss of his beloved Sītā, Rāma experiences a despair so profound as to leave no question that he knows what it means to suffer in duty's name. But even this degree of suffering, the epic insists, can be overcome. Moral reward and punishment must not be doubted. When Rāma wavers, the usually less mature Lakṣmaṇa remains confident and courageous. Together, the pair strive on to victory. In the demise of Rāvaṇa and the establishment of Rāmarājya, the penalty of wickedness and the blessed fulfillment of righteousness are symbolized. If Rāma's selfless conduct conveys the essence of the "moral point of view," his resulting ordeal and triumph affirm the reality of moral retribution despite the strongest assaults against it.

In all these respects, the narratives, whether early or late, employ Rāma to convey and fulfill some of our deepest moral aspirations. Rāma's eventual divinization is thus a natural outcome of the central moral role he is given in the earliest texts. Indeed, if we keep in mind the deep structure of religious and moral reason, and the tensions within it, we can even begin to understand the curious appended tale of Sītā's second repudiation. To some extent, this episode detracts from the otherwise happy ending of the epic. But it also is an opportunity to reexplore the intensity of the moral demand. While righteousness must be seen as triumphant, fidelity to human experience requires that this ultimate confidence not obscure the real suffering moral commitment can bring. Both themes are everywhere in the epic, with the anguish of Rāma's ordeals as clearly depicted as the joy of his victories. But in retrospect, we can see that Rāma's suffering in the name of righteousness, his full participation in the human moral condition, despite his excellence and divinity, are what fired the Indian imagination and what contributed to the unique appeal of the narrative. Small wonder that when later contributors were given the opportunity to embellish the story, they wished to further represent Rāma's moral willingness to undergo suffering. While not substantially weakening any confidence in moral retribution—because the wicked have been vanquished and because, as god and goddess, Rāma and Sītā's terrestrial sufferings are soon transcended—the appended conclusion shifts the focus from moral vindication to the more human reality of suffering in duty's name.

The themes of Rāma's fellow humanity and moral nobility established in the earliest texts also lead to the powerful theme of compassion and mercy developed by the later bhakti tradition. In this later devotional tradition, Rāma comes to be viewed as a powerful savior, able to cleanse the sins of even wicked followers who seek him with love. We know that the idea of forgiveness of sins is an essential component of reason's deep structure, and we also know this theme to be in tension with the retributive, or "justice-oriented," dimensions of the moral life. This is true not only on the religious plane, where we meet the question of how we dare anticipate forgiveness without subverting the structure of justice as we understand it, but also on the human moral and legal levels, where the question arises of how wrongdoers can fairly be spared punishment.

In the earliest core of the Rāmāyaṇa, these matters are given attention in various ways. Repeatedly, and against the advice of others, Rāma forgives wrongdoers. When he is approached by Rāvaṇa's brother Vibhīṣaṇa, Rāma is counseled to slay the defector on the spot, but he insists that even a demon must be allowed to repent and join the side of the righteous. Later, following Rāvaṇa's defeat, Rāma again defies counsel and permits full mourning rites for his slain foe. This element of mercy in Rāma's character is rendered more believable by the fact that Rāma is always depicted as participating in the struggle and hardship of human moral existence. Although he never fails in his duty, various episodes present Rāma as at least sharing in the possibility of human moral weakness. In the encounter with the demonness Śūrpaṇakhā, for example, Rāma indulges in a bit of "innocent" play with the ogress, falsely flattering her and then deflecting her advances by stating the the unwed Lakṣmaṇa would make a better mate. As it turns out, not only does this exchange involve a minor lie—Lakṣmaṇa is married—but it has disastrous consequences, since it leads to the combat that ends in Śūrpaṇakhā's mutilation and the incitement of Rāvaṇa to revenge. Later, in the episode of the golden deer, when Rāma reluctantly yields to Sītā's unwise request to pursue the suspect animal, he shows himself, like his father, dangerously susceptible to the power of love, kāma. And when he finally faces the loss of Sītā, Rāma almost succumbs to a morally paralyzing despair. In each of these instances, Rāma reveals a very human and almost laudable propensity to moral weakness, a participation in the human moral condition that softens the sternness of his character. It also makes his moral compassion understandable, and prepares the way for the extreme emphasis on forgiveness developed by the later devotional tradition.[13]

The demanding nature of the moral life, the certainty of retribution and the possibility of forgiveness—these are the leading motifs of the epic. They constitute its principal religious message, a message that is instructive less because of any new information conveyed than because of its ability to engage the deep structure of moral and religious reason understood by the epic's audience. In light of this, it is not surprising that Rāma's career, his integrity, his cohumanity, his suffering and his ultimate divinization as a source of transcendent compassion reveal so many parallels to the narratives of other religious traditions, not least of all Christianity. These parallels need not be explained by cultural borrowing or coincidence, but by the indwelling structure of moral and religious concepts shared by all human beings to which the creators of epic literature make appeal.

Cases for Decision

But these religious elements constitute only one part of the epic's moral significance. On the level of normative teaching, the Rāmāyaṇa derives its instructional power from its realistic presentation of an agonizing series of moral decisions. Remarkably for a martial tale, much of the narrative's attention is given over to these decisions, with a great deal of the poem devoted to lengthy debates among characters on the appropriate course of action in each case. Reading these debates, one senses the deepest fascination on the part of both the author(s) and the audience with the question of how we are to reason our way through life's difficult moral choices.

The emphasis given moral decision making in the epic runs counter to an important current in contemporary moral discussion, which emphasizes the role of paradigmatic individuals and models of virtue in the instructive enterprise of religious literature. Some students of ethics and comparative ethics, troubled by the emphasis on moral principles and methods of moral reasoning that has dominated Western ethical theory during the modern period, have recently argued that the major ethical import of traditional moral and religious literature lies in its depiction of model persons, rather than its presentation of abstract norms or moral methodologies.[14] Some of these writers have also perceived in this literature a way of returning to an "ethics of character" that they believe has been eclipsed by narrow theoretical attention to moral principles and methods of moral reasoning. For these writers what is important in ethics is not the question of how right and wrong are to be determined or conduct justified, but the full-bodied exemplifications of moral excellence in the lives of persons, whether they be real individuals esteemed for their integrity or the heroes of fictional literature.[15]

Superficially regarded, the Rāmāyaṇa would seem to support this "character-oriented" approach to ethics. Through its pages march the moral paradigms that have inspired Indian society for centuries and that continue to form the moral stereotypes of the culture. Nevertheless, a careful reading suggests that, at its deepest level, the epic's chief interest is not in presenting models of virtuous conduct—though there is much of that—but in offering a detailed and penetrating analysis of the process of reasoned moral decision making. The importance of this exercise is intensified by the fact that in almost no instance are moral conflicts resolvable by a simple appeal to moral rules, since the rules here usually conflict. Nor does the presumed virtue or vice of the actors establish the rightness or wrongness of their choices. While knowledge of the actors' characters alerts us to the likely direction of their decision making, even the good sometime err. As a result, only careful attention to the reasoning process by which individuals arrive at decisions helps make clear the meaning of right or wrong choice. The Rāmāyaṇa is not an ethics text. But in its focus on the method of moral reasoning and in its depiction of the nature of properly made choices, it shares more with standard Western ethical theory than the proponents of an "ethics of character" might anticipate.

Morally right decisions, the epic seems to say, have two distinguishing features. One is the quality of being selfless, or more precisely, "disinterested." A morally sound decision is not infected by excessive self-concern or pride. While it is often permissible to act on self-interest, in a proper decision merely private willing is always first subordinated to a reasoned, impartial assessment of what constitutes the common good. Second, a morally acceptable decision is marked by care in reasoning and by the exercise of judgment. Good persons consider what they are about to do; they look at the facts carefully, try to determine the consequences of each course of action for all involved, they regard the precedents their conduct establishes and, if necessary, they appeal to wise counsel. In contrast, bad decisions are usually selfishly motivated, and even when they are prompted by moral concerns, they involve careless or hasty thinking. Bad persons allow themselves to be swept away by passion and emotion; they bend the facts to suit their needs, they reason poorly, neglect to consider the wider implications of their conduct and characteristically reject information or advice proferred by their wisest counselors.

In its focus on a method of moral reasoning, the epic also goes well beyond the mere application of moral rules to cases. By dwelling on rational decision in cases where the rules conflict, the epic points us back to a more basic decision process from which the rules arise and to which we must return whenever rules counsel opposing courses of action. The emphasis on this process also helps explain the pragmatic or "consequentialist" quality of so much moral debate in the epic, something that has often surprised commentators expecting a more elevated style of moral discourse.

To understand this concern with consequences, it helps to keep in mind that moral reasoning inherently involves impartially assessing conduct in terms of its impact on everyone we affect. If certain rules must ordinarily be obeyed regardless of the immediate consequences—as when we must tell the truth or keep promises even if it is disadvantageous for whomever our decision directly affects—this is because respect for these rules as public standards of conduct is overwhelmingly advantageous to the moral community as a whole. But when such rules conflict, we are thrust back to the more basic process of impartially assessing the global impact of what we propose to do. We must identify who will be affected by our decision, appreciate the basic value of each form of conduct as a public practice for the community as a whole, and carefully attend to factual and other matters that help determine which course is most conducive to human flourishing or least destructive in terms of the competing values in peril. On the normative level, therefore, the deepest lesson of the Rāmāyaṇa is not that we should adhere to this or that principle at all costs, but that in the difficult circumstances of human life, when moral rules and roles inevitably abandon us, we must be willing to look at things dispassionately, to deliberate carefully, and to fold into our decision a wise reckoning of the consequences of our decision from every point of view.

This important lesson is vividly imparted in a series of key decisions on which the plot of the epic turns. In each, the listener-reader is invited to exercise his or her own moral judgment. Sometimes we must engage in a subtle calculation of consequences or attempt to identify the relevant persons or public attitudes affected by a decision. In other instances, we must put ourselves in the shoes of a decision maker faced with competing counsel, and we must employ all our moral insight and psychological discernment to see which advice is worth heeding. If we do this successfully, we are able to anticipate the direction of the plot, and we are given a chance to measure and savor our own good judgment. Like so many texts of this kind, in other words, the Rāmāyaṇa fosters a kind of intellectual audience participation that is the chief source of its instructional power.

Although moral decisions are everywhere in the epic, several key instances of moral choice stand out. They are frequently signaled by the long debates surrounding them. Several are clustered in the events of Rāma's exile. They include Daśaratha's poor decision to grant the fatal boon to Kaikeyī and Rāma's subsequent laudable decision to obey his father's wishes. During the forest wandering a series of negative examples are provided: the brothers' engagement with the demoness Śūrpaṇakhā, Sītā's urging Rāma to pursue the golden deer, and Vālin's banishment of Sugrīva. This period also comprises one positive decision of a highly complex and ambiguous nature: Rāma's decision to ally himself with Sugrīva even to the point of compromising customary military honor. Finally, beginning in the forest period but continuing through the epic's conclusion, we encounter a string of catastrophically bad decisions by Rāvaṇa. These include the initial decision to abduct Sītā, the decision not to return her before all-out war ensued, and the last fatal decision to meet Rāma in battle.

Daśaratha's Fatal Promise and Rāma's Response

If the core narrative of the Rāmāyaṇa contains a tragic figure, it is King Daśaratha, although any estimation of his fate must be tempered by the fact that he clearly brings everything on himself. In this respect he is more a pitiful than tragic figure. Unlike Rāvaṇa, Daśaratha is not motivated by ill will. In a sense, his sins are "innocent" and all too human. But they are sins nevertheless, and they are serious enough to begin the events of the epic that lead to Daśaratha's own destruction. They include sexual lust, excessive susceptibility to the power of love, and improper respect for the duties of office. But above all, it is Daśaratha's bad judgment and careless approach to fateful choices that do him in.

Daśaratha's bad judgment reveals itself in the initial grant of the boon. The monarch first makes this promise to his youngest wife following a battle in which she had saved his life by dragging him from the field and ministering to his wounds. The promise to fulfill any two of her wishes thus seems innocent enough, a simple, even morally praise-worthy act of gratitude. But this overlooks the fact that Daśaratha is king. His first responsibility is to the welfare of his people, and, in view of this, to yield such power to a young woman and cowife is clearly, in the epic's view, an imprudent act. At the very least, the epic says at this point, a king must carefully regard the possible consequences of his actions. Above and beyond the immediate moral attraction of certain courses of action—such as the display of gratitude—full responsibility entails discretion.[16]

As if to sharpen the point, the epic does not rest content with Daś-aratha's initial decision; he is given a second chance to make the choice. Kaikeyī, having been persuaded by her wicked maidservant to ask the king to redeem his pledges, feigns illness and fails to appear for her daily rendezvous with the king. The worried monarch rushes to her side, and finds her lying on the ground. She asks the king to heed her request for a favor, and, overcome with distress and love, he replies in these impas-sioned words:

> Hast thou not learnt, wild dame, till now
> That there is none so dear as Thou
> To me thy loving husband, save
> My Ráma bravest of the brave?
> By him my race's high-souled heir,
> By him whom none can match, I swear,
> Now speak the wish that on thee weighs:
> By him whose right is length of days,
> Whom if my fond paternal eye
> Saw not one hour I needs must die,—
> I swear by Ráma my dear son,
> Speak, and thy bidding shall be done.[17]

To appreciate the moral lesson conveyed by this speech, it helps to imagine ourselves as members of a traditional audience. We have been exposed to this tale from childhood, and we certainly know what lies ahead. Kaikeyī will immediately demand Rāma's banishment. Yet here, in the name of his supreme love for the young prince, Daśaratha is vowing to grant Kaikeyī anything she wishes! Certainly every listener must see how foolish this is. Does Daśaratha lack even the minimum of common sense and experience needed to tell him that a cowife might not have his precious son's interest at heart? Does he not see that his very words contain a profound contradiction, that in the name of Rāma he is giving carte blanche to someone who, however improbably, might destroy Rāma? The lesson is clear. In making moral decisions, even in the throes of crisis or under the sway of passion, be prudent. Pay attention to the facts. Consider possibly conflicting obligations. Think about your priorities. Ask how the choice you make is likely to affect them. Weigh the dangers carefully and do not neglect even remote risks if these imperil vital interests.

With ineluctable force, the narrative now proceeds. Faced with the choice of suffering personal loss and possible damage to his kingdom or violating his pledge, the king elects to keep his word and banish Rāma. Some commentators have viewed Daśaratha's decision and conduct here as a lofty display of stern adherence to duty, in the form of one's plighted word, over lesser duties or considerations of self-interest.[18] One writer even describes Daśaratha as "a unique example of adherence at all costs and in all circumstances to the moral values which give meaning and value to life."[19] There is some truth in this. When finally faced with the consequences of his previous decisions, Daśaratha must steer a tragic course between conflicting duties, and he characteristically and perhaps wisely chooses to uphold his royal honor. But to focus on this choice really misses the whole point of the episode. The lesson is not the moralistic teaching that truth and fidelity must sometimes prevail despite the consequences. Nor is it the insight that the moral life can be tragic (although both these lessons may be there). Rather, the point is that by foresight, prudence, and wise deliberation we must try to avoid making life into a series of tragic moral choices. We can do this, the epic suggests, not by ignoring consequences but by paying the utmost attention to them, not by lofty flights of moral idealism but by our refusal to be swept away by emotion and by our reliance on common sense.

Because his earlier foolishness and misjudgment necessitate it, therefore, Daśaratha's rigorous adherence to duty in keeping his word is not morally praiseworthy; it is merely the last in an unhappy sequence of events precipitated by an initial bad choice. Just the opposite is true of Rāma's decision to undergo banishment. Here moral idealism and prudence meet in the wise acceptance of an unmerited fate. Interestingly, in a departure from its usual preoccupation with the thinking behind a specific decision, the narrative is relatively silent on the reasons for Rāma's choice, and the reasons it does give do not satisfactorily explain Rāma's conduct here or elsewhere in the epic. As a result, the fuller range of considerations behind Rāma's choice must be reconstructed from other clues in the text.

The apparent surface rationale of his decision has several aspects. As a loyal son, Rāma must obey his father.[20] In addition, after Daśaratha had given her the boon, Kaikeyī asks Rāma in general terms to swear that he would uphold a solemn pledge his father had made. Rāma agrees to do so, thus uniting father and son in a sacred vow.[21] For these reasons, Rāma's decision to obey is presented in the epic as respect for truth. Rāma has given his word, and he does not contradict himself.[22] Similarly, the integrity of Daśaratha's word must be upheld. When, at one point, Bharata tries to urge Rāma to abandon the forest and return to Ayodhyā, Rāma reminds his brother of their joint obligation to the truth:

> Resolved to keep my father's word.
> And thou, my noble brother, too
> Shouldst keep our father's promise true:
> Anointed ruler of the state
> Maintain his word inviolate.[23]

There is no doubt that honesty, whether as a general commitment to truthfulness in one's utterances or as the keeping of promises, is a major value in the epic and in classical Indian culture generally.[24] It might appear, then, that the specific moral lesson conveyed by Rāma's decision again involves the stern priority of duty over consequential considerations, the importance of maintaining truthfulness and fidelity whatever the cost. Nevertheless, as Benjamin Khan points out, there are at least several instances in the Rāmāyaṇa when Rāma and other noble characters display a much more flexible attitude to truth-telling.[25] For example, when he is leaving Ayodhyā, Rāma instructs his charioteer Sumantra to pay no attention to Daśaratha's cries for them to remain. Aware that the impassioned monarch might confront the driver directly, Rāma tells Sumantra that if this occurs, he may say to the king that he did not hear his appeals.[26] During the forest encounter with the demoness Śūrpaṇakhā, Rāma puts her off with the lie that Lakṣmaṇa is single and hence a better object of her affections, while Lakṣmaṇa, in turn, lavishly praises the physical charms of the hideous creature, in a speech of which the narrator says, "his mocking words were aught but true."[27] Sītā, too, engages in deception when she misleads the women in Rāvaṇa's harem about Hanumān's identity.[28] In another instance, an

esteemed Brahman counselor instructs envoys sent to summon Bharata
not to reveal, even if asked, the fact of Rāma's banishment.[29]

It might be said that these episodes involve only minor "white"
lies, but this should not obscure the fact that a measure of expediency
and contextual reasoning enters into each decision. Rāma is willing to
deceive his father to spare his feelings or to protect the charioteer, and
Sītā is willing to be evasive in an effort to protect Hanumān. In all these
cases, moral judgment involves not unyielding respect for this or that
moral rule, but a complex situational decision made by each individual
in which various considerations play a role and in which the final judgment is a matter of impartially sustainable choice. Indeed, Rāma suggests as much later in the epic when, in response to criticisms of his
conduct by Vālin, he states,

> Fine are the laws which guide the good,
> Abstruse, and hardly understood;
> Only the soul, enthroned within
> The breast of each, knows right from sin.[30]

These remarks are not a defense of moral relativism or of the subjectivity of moral decision making. More deeply than anyone, Rāma appre-
ciates the objectivity of right and wrong. But he also knows that conflicting rules must be applied and interpreted in complex situations.
Doing this is the task of individual moral judgment.

In view of this, we may suppose that not only a concern for truthfulness but a complex evaluative judgment underlies Rāma's decision
to respect his father's pledge to Kaikeyī. Although we are given little
direct explanation of the hero's reasoning in this matter, from other passages we can identify the considerations that move him. For example,
we can understand Rāma's choice by considering one alternative he
rejects: violent resistance to his father's will. In a lengthy series of
appeals, Lakṣmaṇa urges his brother not to submit in cowardly fashion
to the dictates of fate but to take matters in his own hands and seize the
throne from his father or Bharata. However, Lakṣmaṇa's angry words
form the best case against this course of action. Disparaging their father
as a senseless old man, a slave to passion, Lakṣmaṇa exhorts his brother
to violence:

> Come, Ráma, ere this plot be known
> Stand by me and secure the throne.

Stand like the King who rules below,
Stand aided by thy brother's bow:
How can the might of meaner men
Resist thy royal purpose then?
My shafts, if rebels court their fate,
Shall lay Ayodhyá desolate.
Then shall her streets with blood be dyed
of those who stand on Bharat's side:
None shall my slaughtering hand exempt,
For gentle patience earns contempt.[31]

Lakṣmaṇa clearly numbers among those who would "destroy a city to save it." In his anger and martial pride, he fails to realize the essential fact that this course of action, although possibly the only one open to those who would oppose Daśaratha, may unleash a civil war so bloody that even the victors will rue having entered the battle. While there is no evidence that this understanding plays a role in Rāma's conscious decision to obey Daśaratha, he clearly rejects Lakṣmaṇa's counsel. Furthermore, throughout the epic Rāma repeatedly displays a keen, pragmatic sense of what is required for tranquil and prosperous rule. Lakṣmaṇa's thoughtless diatribe, therefore, can be seen as a bit of poor counsel well disregarded by a wise ruler. In its place, Rāma seems to realize that there are moments when a violent course to power is simply self-defeating.

The same kind of wise, factually informed, and sensitive understanding may be seen to underlie Rāma's insistence on the importance of obedience to his father and fidelity to their jointly plighted words. Within this political culture, the virtues of fidelity and obedience are absolutely central to successful rule. If a monarch cannot count on these virtues in his advisors, subordinates, and subjects, the very foundations of his realm are threatened. Rāma is keenly aware of this. Rebuking an advisor who would have him disobey Daśaratha, Rāma remarks,

This world of ours is ever led
To walk the ways which others tread,
And as their princes they behold,
The subjects too their lives will mould.
That truth and mercy still must be
Beloved of kings is Heaven's decree
Upheld by truth the monarch reigns,
And truth the very world sustains.[32]

Whatever their intrinsic worth, therefore, truth-telling and the keeping of solemn promises also play an important role within Rāma's total vision of what is needed for successful rule.

Rāma's political sagacity also helps explain his perplexing behavior near the end of the epic, when, following Rāvaṇa's defeat, he appears to spurn Sītā. Some commentators have seen this as a clumsy addition to an earlier happier ending, but the episode, apart from its dramatic value as a culminating trial for Sītā, is in direct continuity with Rāma's attention to political responsibility throughout the epic. When Sītā emerges safe from the flames she has invoked as a test of her purity, Rāma joyously welcomes her back. He had no doubt that she remained true to him, Rāma says, but adds that

> 'Twas meet that mid the thousands here
> The searching fire my queen should clear.[33]

There are several indications that this remark is not an editorial after-thought, but a firm part of the Vālmīkian text. Although it is not clear whether Rāma is to be understood as aware of the threat by Brahmā that protected Sītā's chastity, he has received a report on Sītā's condition from Hanumān who, during his visit to the Aśoka grove, had seen her bitterly reject the demon's advances. Rāma understands, however, that his personal confidence in Sītā does not remove the need for a public test. Without this manifest proof of her purity, Rāma perceives that his ability to rule would be jeopardized by slanderous rumors. Royalty, he understands, must not only do right but must appear to do right. In fact, in the appended final book, ugly gossip circulating on the couple's return to Ayodhyā is what prompts Rāma to ask Sītā to repeat her trial. To the modern reader, these episodes may be disturbing, steeped as they are in traditional notions of female and male honor.[34] But within the social and political thought world of the Rāmāyaṇa, they are a further sign of the sagacity and wisdom that Rāma brings to the complex decisions that mark his career.[35] Throughout, the lesson of Rāma's conduct is not that this or that value must always be upheld, for he sometimes puts truthfulness aside, but rather that, in making sound decisions, what is crucial is a high degree of moral judgment. This involves an appreciation of the considerations that underlie abiding moral values, including the inherently—and sometimes actually—public nature of our choices. It also includes a willingness to resist the passions of the moment or the immediate lure of self-interest, and a keen sense of the important facts of the matter.

Decisions in the Forest

The period of wandering in the forest provides further illustrations of this art of moral judgment. Two of these, the brothers' decision to taunt Śūrpaṇakhā and Sītā's urging of Rāma to pursue the golden deer, are relatively innocent, but they have important consequences and play a major role in the plot. The encounter with Śūrpaṇakhā has its humorous side—we laugh at the image of this unsightly monster smitten with love for Rāma and Lakṣmaṇa and believing their high-flown praise of her beauty. The brothers' banter with this aspiring female sexual offender is hardly wicked; Śūrpaṇakhā pushes herself on them and deserves no better treatment. But even here a powerful lesson about moral judgment is conveyed. When Śūrpaṇakhā, "inflamed with love," sees Sītā at Rāma's side and rushes to devour her rival, the brothers are driven to action. Remarking on this dangerous turn of events, a chastened Rāma points up the lesson:

> Ne'er should we jest with creatures rude,
> Of savage race and wrathful mood.[36]

The point is that, although levity may be delightful, when the stakes are very high and you risk antagonizing a foe with powerful friends, it can become a dangerous indulgence. The brothers' failure here was their inadequate estimation of the possible consequences of their seemingly harmless conduct. When dealing with portentous matters, the epic seems to say, prudence dictates extreme caution in every move one makes.

Sītā displays a similar failure in judgment when she urges Rāma to pursue the spurious golden deer. If the brothers succumb momentarily to a certain youthful masculine bravado and love of mirthful play, Sītā's error is thoroughly and traditionally "feminine": she is entranced by the allure of a beautiful possession. Dismissing Lakṣmaṇa's "prudent speech" of warning that the animal may be the demon Mārīca, she presses her request on Rāma who, leaving Lakṣmaṇa to protect Sītā, undertakes the pursuit, confident of his ability to defend himself against any foe. But Sītā's "feminine" craving for a possession soon gives way to "feminine" emotional distress and fear. When Mārīca isues a false cry for help in Rāma's voice, Sītā is seized with terror. Accusing Lakṣmaṇa of wishing his brother's death and coveting her for himself, she forces him to leave her side.

The brothers' indiscretions play a minor role in these immediate events leading up to Sītā's abduction. Rāma may be guilty of some imprudence in heeding her request to capture the deer, while Lakṣmaṇa, his honor in question, may be blamed for breaking the promise he made to Rāma to guard Sītā. But each strives to make the best decision he can, and the major responsibility for her misfortunes lies with Sītā. Despite her impassioned commitment to Rāma, she allows a momentary selfish impulse to cloud her judgment. In this respect, her mistake more closely parallels Daśaratha's than the brothers'. Their moral errors have involved inattention to responsibility and a miscalculation of risks, whereas Daśaratha and Sītā fail to be clear about their own priorities. The two demonstrably love Rāma above everything, but in a moment of passionate desire they each take steps that jeopardize him. Sītā's response to the spurious cry for help highlights this. Abruptly made to see the implications of her previous choice, Sītā instantly realizes her true priorities. Above anything else, including her own safety, Rāma must be saved. But Sītā's recognition of her values comes too late and only contributes to the developing misfortune. The moral lesson? Be clear about your priorities; respect them in choosing and acting, despite the allure of more immediate attractions; and never allow events to become a tragic reminder of what those priorities are.

The Vālin Episode

If the forest wanderings repeatedly illustrate bad judgment in relatively easy instances of moral decision, they also provide two illustrations of consummately good judgment in two complex and difficult cases. These include Rāma's decision to make an alliance with the exiled Vānar king Sugrīva and his decision to intrude in the combat between Sugrīva and Vālin. As I mentioned, Rāma's conduct in these episodes has been widely regarded among interpreters of the epic as morally problematical.[37] His alliance with Sugrīva is criticized on the grounds that the young Vānar monarch had wrongly usurped the throne and had no right to regain it. According to the traditional rules governing royal succession, the elder brother inherits the throne (hence, the injustice in Kaikeyī's demand that Bharata rule). Sugrīva's assumption of power is regarded as a violation of proper order, as is his appropriation of Vālin's beautiful wife, Tārā. This suggests that Vālin may have justly banished Sugrīva and that Rāma's alliance with the exiled monarch was, at best, an exercise in realpolitik at the expense of moral principle.[38]

These criticisms, I think, are ill founded and reflect a lack of appreciation of the subtlety and incisiveness of Rāma's judgment. Although the intrigues of the Vānar court are meant to challenge our skills of moral analysis, there are a number of clues in the text suggesting that Sugrīva had rightfully assumed power and that Rāma's alliance with him is fully just. For one thing, the narrator takes pains to indicate Sugrīva's loyalty and devotion to his brother. We are told that Sugrīva had spent a lonely and anguished year waiting for Vālin to emerge from the cave into which he had followed the demon and that Sugrīva only departed long after hearing terrible noises of battle and seeing a bloody froth suggesting Vālin was dead. We also learn that Sugrīva had initially tried to keep Vālin's fate secret and had refused to assume the throne, doing so only after the lords independently learned of Vālin's seeming demise and urged Sugrīva, in defense of the city, to serve as ruler. When Vālin unexpectedly returned, Sugrīva also immediately offered to step down and restore the throne to his brother.

If all this counts as evidence of Sugrīva's integrity, further proof is that the most vigorous defenses of Vālin and the most stinging criticisms of Sugrīva's conduct are made to issue from Sugrīva's own mouth during a long funeral oration for his dead brother. These remarks are often turned against Sugrīva by commentators who take them at face value.[39] But they are really a sign that Sugrīvas's moral sensitivity, unlike Vālin's, extends to self-criticism and remorse. Vālin's comportment, in contrast, is generally reprehensible. He brings misfortune on himself by abandoning his royal duties and impetuously running off in the night to combat the demon; he displays a bloodthirsty rage on his return, killing all the lords who had supported Sugrīva; and he hastily and angrily banishes his brother, in the process defying prevailing sexual mores by taking his living brother's wife as his own.[40] This shows Vālin to be a lawless and impulsive individual, who has forfeited his claim to respect or his title to rule. The fact that Rāma immediately allies himself with Sugrīva thus is another important illustration of good judgment. Faced with a tough decision that rests, as many do, on an independent determination of others' moral character, Rāma reads the facts as carefully as circumstances allow and applies a sensitive understanding of right and wrong to assess the competing claims. Events soon support the wisdom of his decision.

An understanding of the epic's preoccupation with bad versus good judgment also helps make sense of the morally dubious episode in which Rāma intrudes in the one-to-one combat between the Vānar brothers. Superficially regarded, Rāma's conduct here appears to be a gross violation of martial honor. Nor is Rāma's case apparently strengthened when later, in response to the dying Vālin's reproaches, he is made to offer morally questionable reasons for his conduct. These include Vālin's susceptibility to punishment for his wrongful appropriation of his brother's wife (a charge that might, to a lesser extent, also be leveled at Sugrīva) and the assertion that Rāma's family possesses sovereignty in the region, with a corresponding obligation to punish miscreants. Most threadbare of all is Rāma's assertion that since the Vānars are subhuman creatures, they do not merit protection by the usual rules of martial combat and may be treated as a hunter treats his prey. This statement flies in the face of all the evidence in the epic that the Vānars are formidable allies, assumed to be capable of moral conduct and worthy of moral respect![41]

Some scholars have attributed these less-than-persuasive justifications to later editorial embarassment over a more primitive episode,[42] and they try to defend Rāma's conduct, if at all possible, on the grounds of military necessity or expediency.[43] But all these discussions miss the point that Rāma's behavior occurs in a context, and one in which all my previous remarks about the centrality of wise judgment to the epic are pertinent. For the real point of the episode is that Vālin, despite his later protestations of being wronged, really brings about his own downfall by reckless and thoughtless conduct. To begin with, Vālin is amply warned. In a long discourse that displays the epic's fascination with the process of counsel and deliberation, Vālin's faithful wife Tārā tries to draw her husband's attention to the impending danger. Observing that Sugrīva, who had already been trounced in a preliminary engagement, has nevertheless returned, she draws the conclusion

> A heart so bold that will not yield,
> But yearns to tempt the desperate field,
> Such loud defiance, fiercely pressed,
> On no uncertain hope can rest.
> So lately by thine arm o'erthrown,
> He comes not back, I ween, alone.
> Some mightier comrade guards his side,
> And spurs him to this burst of pride.[44]

To this, Tārā adds the vital information, gleaned from her son, that Rāma and Lakṣmaṇa have entered into league with Sugrīva. But Vālin dismisses all of this. Spurning her advice, he insists on his right to avenge dishonor. Furthermore, he says, he is confident that even if Rāma is on Sugrīva's side he will stay out of the fight: one "so pure and duteous," he says, "all sin will shun."[45]

Vālin's midjudgment thus compounds itself. Surely, if Rāma is as pure as Vālin acknowledges, he would not have allied himself with a wrongdoer. The inescapable conclusion from Tārā's information, therefore, is either that Vālin must re-examine the justice of his cause or reassess his confidence that Rāma will stay aloof from this particular battle (for if Rāma is so unjust as to help a sinner, what hope can there be that he will fight fairly?).[46] Vālin fails to consider any of this. Pulling Tārā's arms from around his neck, he defiantly rushes off to battle. Only against this background can we understand the moral worthlessness of his later protestations that he has been wronged. Besides the fact that these protestations presumptuously appeal to a code of martial honor ("Rāma owed it to me to face me squarely in open combat") that may not, as Rāma insists, be applicable to a criminal wrongdoer, they come from the mouth of one whose bad moral judgment has led to his own destruction. In evaluating this episode in the epic, therefore, it is not enough to look at Rāma's defense of his conduct. This, in fact, is merely the conclusion to an episode whose primary purpose is to illustrate a complex instance of unwise and imprudent decision making.

Rāvaṇa's Course of Misjudgment

Kaikeyī, Daśaratha, and Vālin all suffer the penalty for indiscretion. But they are minor offenders compared to Rāvaṇa, whose misconduct and misjudgment, if the pun be allowed, reach epic proportions. Although in his strength and grandeur Rāvaṇa has a certain appeal—we sympathize with his grieving wife Mandodarī when she weeps over his fallen body on the battlefield—he makes almost every mistake possible and serves throughout as the consummate antitype of royal virtue in matters of deliberation.

Rāvaṇa's errors begin with his decision to abduct Sītā. Despite the insane passion for her that soon dominates him, Rāvaṇa is initially moved less by lust than by what might be called "geopolitical" considerations. Taunted by Śūrpaṇakhā over the royal brothers' destruction of so many of his demon followers, Rāvaṇa feels he must act to protect his realm. Nevertheless, he is clearly warned against this course by Mārīca, who has already faced Rāma in battle. Mārīca's level-headed words of advice, in contrast to Śūrpaṇakhā's impassioned and vengeful urgings to war, vividly illustrate the central place given deliberation and counsel in the epic:

> Summon each lord of high estate,
> And chief, Vibhíshaṇ, to debate.
> With peers in lore of counsel tried
> Consider, reason, and decide.
> Scan strength and weakness, count the cost,
> What may be gained and what be lost.
> Examine and compare aright
> Thy proper power and Ráma's might,
> Then if thy weal be still thy care
> Thou wilt be prudent and forbear.
> O giant King, the contest shun,
>   Thy force is all too weak
> The lord of Kośal's mighty son
>   In deadly fray to seek.
> King of the hosts that rove at night,
>   O hear what I advise:
> My prudent counsel do not slight;
>   Be patient and be wise.[47]

Although Rāvaṇa hears out Mārīca, he quickly rejects his advice. Indeed, he has some advice of his own, and in angry tones he spells out to Mārīca the kind of behavior he expects from advisors and friends:

> 'Tis thine, when questioned, to explain
> The hope and fear, the loss and gain,
> And, when thy king thy thoughts would know,
> The triumph or the danger show.
> A prudent counsellor should wait,
> And speak when ordered in debate,
> With hands uplifted, calm and meek,
> If honour and reward he seek.
> Or, when some prudent course he sees
> Which, spoken, may his king displease,
> He should by hints of dexterous art
> His counsel to his lord impart.
> But prudent words are said in vain
> When the blunt speech brings grief and pain.

A high-souled king will scarcely thank
The man who shames his royal rank.[48]

In view of the generally respectful and concerned nature of Mārīca's previous words, Rāvaṇa's statement here amounts to the advice not to tell him what he does not want to hear. And, in fact, Rāvaṇa then states flatly that he wishes not advice but obedience:

> I asked thee not my strength to scan,
> Or loss and profit in the plan.
> I only spoke to tell the deed
> O mighty one, by me decreed,
> And bid thee in the peril lend
> Thy succour to support thy friend.[49]

Rāvaṇa always displays this attitude toward counsel. Nowhere in the epic is more room given to deliberation than in the episodes surrounding the monarch's various decisions. Each move is preceded by numerous long speeches by advisors, with wise and loyal friends often pitted against sycophants and flatterers. Yet in every case the pattern is the same. Rāvaṇa begins by seeking advice and concludes by heaping abuse on those who refuse to feed his passions or ratify his designs. In every instance, the monarch's will and brute force replace wisdom. For example, this episode closes with Rāvaṇa threatening Mārīca to either cooperate with his plans or die. Mārīca replies that he will die in any case, whether at Rāvaṇa's or Rāma's hands, but in an act of loyalty he consents to do the king's bidding. Thus, Rāvaṇa misses a final chance for wisdom: a more temperate ruler would see Mārīca's self-sacrificial act as proof of the sincerity of his advice and of the fact that, right or wrong, he is motivated by concern for the realm and for his friend, not personal interest or fear.

The same intense focus on the process of reasoned deliberation and the same unfortunate outcome mark the final series of military encounters between the forces of Rāvaṇa and Rāma. Surveying the burning ruins of Lankā in the wake of Hanumān's departure, the demon king summons his counselors and reviews the task before them:

> Now ponder well the work that lies
> Before us, ponder and advise.
> With deep-observing judgment scan
> The peril, and mature a plan.

> From counsel, sages say, the root,
> Springs victory, most glorious fruit.
> First ranks the king, when woe impends
> Who seeks the counsel of his friends,
> Of kinsmen ever faithful found,
> Or those whose hopes with his are bound,
> Then with their aid his strength applies,
> And triumphs in his enterprise.
> Next ranks the prince who plans alone,
> No counsel seeks to aid his own,
> Weighs loss and gain and wrong and right,
> And seeks success with earnest might.
> Unwisest he who spurns delays,
> Who counts no cost, no peril weighs,
> Speeds to his aim, defying fate,
> And risks his all, precipitate.[50]

This from the mouth of one who, spurning delay and stating that he wanted only obedience, sent a trusted friend and counselor off to his death! Of course, it is possible that by now Rāvaṇa has learned his lesson; that he will pay more careful attention to the advice he receives. But this is not what happens. Regarding the debate ahead, Rāvaṇa identifies three different outcomes of deliberation: "a best, a worst, a middle kind." In the best case, he says, all counselors "from first to last agree"; in a middle kind, strong debate leads eventually to consensus. But it is the last possibility that Rāvaṇa fears:

> Worst of the three is this, when each
> Assails with taunt his fellow's speech;
> When all debate, and no consent
> Concludes the angry argument.[51]

It is telling that Rāvaṇa never suggests what a monarch must do when faced with this "worst" case scenario of divided counsel. Clearly, such an outcome demands the most refined skills of analysis. A ruler confronted with advisors in sharp disagreement must review their arguments in the light of his own understanding of the facts; he must assess the judgment of each counselor and, to distinguish simple flattery from conviction, he must seek to detect the motivation behind each advisor's words. The fact that Rāvaṇa never perceives his responsibility in these terms shows that he utterly lacks independent resources for judgment. As a result, when the anticipated "worst case" occurs and his advisors disagree, Rāvaṇa handles the task of choosing in the same irrational, impulsive manner as before. During the ensuing debates, all his younger advisors counsel war. Brandishing their spears, maces, and swords they loudly assure Rāvaṇa of victory. Only Rāvaṇa's brother, Vibhīṣaṇa, dissents. Approaching Rāvaṇa respectfully, "skilled in the arts of soft address,"[52] he reviews the disasters that have befallen the realm since Sītā was abducted. He emphasizes Rāma's invincibility and, for the safety of the realm, begs the king to return Rāma's wife. But Vibhīṣaṇa's modest approach—the very manner earlier recommended by Rāvaṇa to Mārīca—and his evident concern for his brother's welfare do no good. Barely listening, Rāvaṇa heaps scorn on him and accuses him of cowardice and perfidy. A humiliated Vibhīṣaṇa then stalks out of the room, takes leave of Laṅkā, and offers his services to the forces of Rāma and Sugrīva. With this defection, wisdom symbolically departs from Rāvaṇa's camp. Governed now by power and martial virtue alone, the demon forces plunge onward through a series of military encounters and defeats that conclude with Rāvaṇa's death on the battlefield.

These long debates in Rāvaṇa's camp epitomize the epic's concern with moral judgment. In a narrow sense, they show an interest in political morality and the question of righteous rule. But, more broadly, this focus on the processes of political or military deliberation is only a vehicle for considering the larger issue of the nature of reasoned moral judgment as a whole. Much like Plato, who employed the "large letters" of politics to analyze the structure of the individual soul, the Rāmāyaṇa uses these long debates on strategy to explore rational moral decision generally, whether exercised in individual or political contexts. In all instances, the epic seems to say, sound moral judgment requires skills ranging from the simple to the complex: a respect for logic and consistency in one's thinking; attention to facts and a willingness to understand causal relations; discernment in the analysis of character and in the assessment of likely consequences of one's acts; an ability to subordinate impulse to reason; and, above all, a constant effort to achieve objectivity in the face of the many forces, whether personal or social, that distort and bias judgment.

Of course, the individual facing moral choice rarely has at hand the counselors available to a political leader, so it might seem that, in this sense, political decision making differs from individual judgment (although one subpoint of the epic is that even in making personal choices, we should try to consult others who might be more objective). But it is precisely here that the "large letters" of these political-military debates are instructive. For what the epic seems to be saying is that in moments of moral decision, each of us is a bit like Rāma, Daśaratha, Vālin, or Rāvaṇa. Our "counselors" are the contending voices within us concerning the policies and courses of action we face. Each course has its reasons and its motives, and in our minds, each "argues its case." Our task as rational and moral decision makers is to assess this "counsel." Carefully surveying the risks and gains on each side, we must try to determine whether a course is motivated by strong impulses that might distort our understanding, of the facts or lead us to forget our priorities. When our interior "counselors" disagree or when powerful forces urge action but the risks are great, we must be careful to pay special attention to those isolated and sometimes muted voices within us that recommend caution. Human rational and moral existence is a perilous enterprise, the epic seems to say. Tragedy dogs our every step, but it is not inevitable. Although misjudgment can lead us to share Rāvaṇa's fate, through the exercise of discretion and judgment we may emerge from life's course as triumphant as Rāma.

I began this chapter by observing that, the world over, the literary creations of human religious communities reveal a set of universal considerations identified by the deep structure of moral and religious reason. Traditional religious narratives like the Rāmāyaṇa, as well as others from our own cultural past, may often portray a world whose surface values seem very different from our own. For example, a modern reader is likely to perceive Rāma's loyalty to Daśaratha, or Sītā's to Rāma, as a bizarre exaggeration of more familiar virtues. But these superficial differences should not obscure the profoundly common moral world we share with those who created the Rāmāyaṇa or who have appreciated it over the centuries. Within the narrative, we find the same insistence on moral retribution, the same sense of human moral frailty, the same yearning for forgiveness that we find in the religious documents of our own culture. If Rāma is in many ways a "Christ" of Indian civilization, this is traceable to the common elements of moral and religious reasoning that find expression across distant cultural boundaries.

Beneath these surface differences in value emphasis, we also find basic agreement on the nature of moral reasoning. The need for impartiality and objectivity in judgment, concern for the public impact of our conduct and the necessity of subordinating impulse to reason in making choices are the essential lessons of traditional religious narrative. Furthermore, because moral judgment involves this difficult process of reasoning, and not simply the rules it produces (however similar the most basic rules are likely to be across cultures), it is a skill that must be taught, learned, exercised, and retaught. Hence, the suprisingly great emphasis in texts like the Rāmāyaṇa on episodes that allow listeners or readers to participate in the exercise of moral judgment.

Westerners able to follow an Indian or Thai performance of some adaptation of the Rāmāyaṇa typically experience a deep sense of community with others in the audience. We are dismayed by the momentary gains of the wicked and stirred by the victories of the righteous. We nod our heads in agreement with the wise counsel of a Vibhīṣaṇa and we think "Fool! Fool!" when Rāvaṇa abuses his selfless advisors. That this experience can be so readily shared testifies to the universality of concerns underlying religious literature of this sort. It also illustrates how this literature, by engaging our emotions and our intellects, has been able for centuries to play a leading role in humanity's moral education.

Conclusion

Several years ago, while teaching a large introductory course on comparative religion, I delivered a lecture on aspects of Buddhist teaching. One of the ideas I was dealing with struck me as so morally penetrating that I was particularly enthusiastic in my admiration for the sages who formulated it. At the end of the course, while sifting through student evaluations, I came upon a comment that at first surprised me and then made me smile. "I especially liked the lectures on Buddhism," the student wrote, "because the professor was willing to speak out on behalf of his own religion."

I am not a Buddhist. But, looking back, I am no longer surprised that what I regarded as an expression of "professional" admiration should have been taken for personal religious fervor. It is easy for an individual trained in moral philosophy, as I am, to become enthusiastic when working closely with historical religious traditions. These traditions are storehouses of moral wisdom. They deal with issues of enduring moral significance and they often explore these issues with keen insight. Since religions are also eminently *practical* exercises in moral reasoning, their first priority seems to be effectiveness in encouraging sincere moral commitment, and they are not afraid to employ whatever tools are at their disposal for this purpose. This partly explains their affinity for paradox and conceptual surprise, and their willingness to appear unreasonable if this is needed to provoke us to see the depths and difficulty of rational moral existence.

In the course of this book, I have tried to convey some of the reasons for this enthusiasm. Through various applications of the "deep structure" of moral and religious reasoning, I have sought to illustrate the value of a morally informed approach in helping us to understand the complexity of religious thought and practice. Behind this effort lie my strong conviction that religions are primarily moved by rational moral concerns and my belief that ethical theory provides the single most powerful methodology for understanding religious belief. If this has been missed by students and scholars of comparative religion, it is because they have usually been unfamiliar with the full structure of moral reasoning. If it has been missed by philosophers, it is because they have sometimes been inattentive to the serious problems of rational moral commitment that religious traditions try to address. In all these cases, without a full appreciation of the complex deep structure of religious and moral reason, many students of religion have been unable to perceive the driving, moral intentionality beneath surface religious ideas, especially those that seem remote from or even opposed to moral reason. Worse, they have often been distracted by these surface ideas and have erroneously concluded that religion primarily involves the nonrational or irrational dimensions of human life. Divine command ethics and the many themes subordinating morality to "higher" goals of salvation or liberation exemplify surface ideas of this sort. One of my most important aims in this book has been to develop the underlying logic of these complex and seemingly antirational conceptions.

I have also tried to show how an understanding of basic concepts or methods of moral reasoning helps illuminate obscure or puzzling aspects of religious life. My application of the reasoning behind the moral point of view to ritual, and my use of impartial reasoning to explain religious norms for economic life are examples. It may seem odd that a methodology rooted in philosophy and ethical theory should be of value to comparative inquiry, since this is a domain we ordinarily think of in terms of more descriptive approaches or of empirical disciplines like sociology and anthropology. But my effort here is not without precedent. In Richard Brandt's and John Ladd's philosophical studies of Native American religion a generation ago, we find some important, though limited, anticipations of the effort to use ethical concepts to explore specific nonliterate cultures and, through this, to contribute to anthropological research.[1] This kind of approach has been too long neglected. Religions, after all, are conceptual systems. Why should they not be illuminated by the kind of rigorous exploration of modes of reasoning in which philosophy and ethics engage? Only the assumption that moral philosophy is somehow a peculiarly "Western" discipline, with no value in understanding human reasoning generally, can justify a reluctance to employ the tools of ethics in comparative work. In opposition to this, I have maintained that moral reasoning is not culture-bound and that ethical theory can make a very important contribution to our understanding of diverse religious traditions.

In many ways, the explorations in this volume are only a beginning of the comparative task. An understanding of reason's deep structure opens up a variety of new areas for comparative study in moral terms. For example, I have repeatedly said that we can gain insight into religious development by drawing on the concepts of religious and moral reason, and I have sketched the major outlines of this process of development. During their early phases, before reflection is focused and made more complex by a class of literate religious specialists, religions typically emphasize localized agencies of moral retribution—ancestors, nature spirits, sorcerers or witches. There are a number of direct, quasi-magical conceptions of reward and punishment, as in ordeal ceremonies or procedures of truth determination. Moral and ritual infractions are relatively undifferentiated, and wrongdoing or sin may be perceived in material terms, with penalties attached to the mere performance of a wrongful act whatever the motive or intention. But, as rationalization proceeds, retribution characteristically comes to be centralized in a single, more coherent source, and purely magical tests of integrity diminish in importance. More refined moral reasoning also prompts a clearer sense of the priority of moral over ritual performance (although not to the exclusion of the latter), and wrongdoing comes to be seen primarily in terms of the humanly controllable factor of intention.

These developments, of course, do not proceed systematically, and residues of earlier notions may still be found even in well-developed literate traditions. In the Bible, for example, we find evidence of a variety of earlier conceptions, including traces of witchcraft practices and ordeal ceremonies, and these same features can be found in the Rāmayāṇa. Indeed, in some ways, the tales surrounding Rāma or Daśaratha would be very much at home in the setting of African traditional religion. This intermixing of themes in complex texts gives us an idea of the subtle and often gradual ways in which religions refine their structure of moral ideas. The fact that this refinement takes place within a thought-world shaped by a religion's earlier responses to reason's deep structural requirements—as when retributive ideas in classical Chinese monotheism were forced to develop within a framework of impersonal, political assumptions—makes the task of comparative analysis very complex. Nevertheless, this kind of morally-informed exploration of religious development is a fascinating possibility opened up by the method offered in this volume.

Other forms of comparative study suggest themselves. My discussion of ritual was already comparative, but there remains vast scope for moral analysis of the similarities and differences in the rituals of various traditions. Beyond this, the fact that ritual structures crop up in unexpected places offers an expanded domain for moral inquiry. For example, we can easily discern the outlines of van Gennep's tripartite structure of a rite of passage in the various myths of religious founders: again and again, we see phases of separation, liminality, and reincorporation depicted in the stories of these sacred lives. Moses' and Jesus' flights to the desert, Abraham's departure from his kinsmen, his and Isaac's trek to Mt. Moriah, Muḥammad's flight from Mecca, Krishna's sojourn in the Brindaban forest, the Buddha's wilderness quest for enlightenment, and Rāma's forest exile are all important examples. In each of these rites of passage, sacred personalities are reduced to the barest essentials of human life, suffer humiliations of one sort or another and struggle, spiritually or physically, with evil. But if ritual moments of liminality and *communitas* have the kind of moral importance I suggested, what are we to say about their role in these founder narratives? In what ways do these liminal experiences provide moral instruction, whether for the founders themselves or for adherents who model their lives on the founder's pattern? Although each of us can begin to fashion answers to these questions, the task of providing a comprehensive and comparative moral analysis of founder myths is an important one suggested by an understanding of religion's deep moral structure.

Beyond comparative analysis, understanding religion's moral role raises new questions for ethics and the philosophy of religion. These fields provide unique access to religious thought. Each advance in our understanding of the structure of practical reasoning, for example, furnishes new insight into religious traditions. In general, we can think of religious belief as the effort to preserve and render coherent aspects of moral life that remain incoherent within the limited domain of our experience. Thus, religions use ideas of spiritually empowered retributive agencies—ranging from ancestor spirits to complex natural-moral laws like karma—to harmonize the seemingly conflicting demands of prudential and moral reason. Divine command traditions use the idea of a supremely authoritative God, who is at once consummately individual and consummately social, as a way of ending this stalemate between prudence and morality. And religions use the ideas of a transcendent realm 'beyond morality' or of a God 'beyond human justice' to render compatible our conflicting rational demands for justice and mercy. Each of these ideas arises as a response to serious conceptual problems in morality, and other more subtle dimensions of religious belief may also be linked to complexities in moral thought and commitment. If philosophers have usually failed to perceive the rationality of religious belief, it is partly because they have regarded moral commitment as required by reason. Work in recent philosophy calling this into question only represents a more precise discovery of what religious thinkers long ago intuitively apprehended. One of the major tasks before religious studies, therefore, is to identify all the dilemmas in the moral reasoning process to which religious thinking responds. The method I have presented in this book suggests that ethical theory and comparative religion must develop hand in hand.

I am aware that to some, this rational methodology may seem a cold and clinical way of approaching a phenomenon whose meaning for them is profoundly personal. Others may object to the claim that religious thought arises primarily from rational considerations, and they may ask what becomes of the emotional or nonrational dimensions of religious life in such a view. To these objections I would make two replies. First, I have repeatedly said that religion comprises *all* aspects of human experience. We see this most clearly in religious rituals, which have given rise to so many varied aspects of culture, from poetry to theater and dance. Perceiving a central thread of reasoned morality running through ritual and other religious activities does not diminish them, in my view, but enhances our appreciation of their fully human significance.

Second, I would reiterate a point derived from the understanding of morality I have tried to develop in this book. Reason is the ordering aspect of the human intellect. It does not and cannot deny our many nonrational needs, passions, or desires, since these form the stuff of human existence, but it does seek to render their pursuit harmonious, within each of us as individuals and among us as members of communities. Because religion represents a moral activity, it necessarily delves into and seeks to bring together the rational and nonrational sides of our experience. It also willingly employs all aspects of our experience to foster its moral purposes. Thus, religions employ forms of mysticism or the most emotionally charged human experiences to convey and encourage the kind of moral self-transcendence at which they aim.

In this book, we have seen repeated illustrations of religions' efforts to bring together the rational and nonrational dimensions of human life. They include the inspired performances of the African spirit medium, God's terrifying call to sacrifice in Genesis 22, the intense emotion of the early Christian baptismal rite, and the interweaving of passionate love and duty in the exemplary lives of Rāma or Sītā. These sacred events, stories, and personalities display the heights and depths of human experience. They also symbolize religion's goal of fostering a mode of life in which order and vitality, reason and passion, are joined.

Notes

Introduction

1. I draw the concept of a "deep" (as opposed to "surface") structure from contemporary linguistics, where it has been applied to distinguish the universal "forms of thought" underlying languages from the specific expressions of these forms in learned and historically developed language systems. For a discussion of this, see Noam Chomsky, *Cartesian Linguistics* (New York: Harper & Row, 1966), pp. 31–51.

2. New York: Oxford University Press, 1978.

Chapter 1

1. *Grundlegung zur Metaphysik der Sitten,* p. 421; *Foundations of the Metaphysics of Morals,* tr. Lewis White Beck (Indianapolis: Bobbs-Merrill, 1969), p. 39.

2. Kant mentions this problem in criticizing the "negative golden rule" (*Grundlegung,* p. 430; *Foundations,* p. 48 n. 14).

3. For a fuller discussion of these matters see John Rawls, *A Theory of Justice* (Cambridge: Harvard University Press, 1971), sec. 40 ("The Kantian Interpretation of Justice as Fairness") and "Kantian Constructivism in Moral Theory: The Dewey Lectures 1980" *Journal of Philosophy* 77 (1980): 515–572. Also, Thomas Hill, "The Kingdom of Ends," in *Proceedings of the Third International Kant Congress* (Dordrecht: D. Reidel, 1972), 307–315.

4. See, for example, David Richards, *A Theory of Reasons for Action* (Oxford: Clarendon Press, 1971); Bernard Gert, *The Moral Rules* (New York: Harper & Row,

1970) and Rawls, *Theory of Justice.* For sensitive applications of this procedure to new areas of choice, see Sissela Bok, *Lying* (New York: Pantheon Books, 1978) and *Secrets* (New York: Pantheon Books, 1982). A Rawlsian procedure is applied to the difficult issue of paternalism by Karen M. Tait and Gerald Winslow in their article, "Beyond Consent: The Ethics of Decision Making in Emergency Medicine," in *Medical Ethics,* ed. Nathalie Abrams and Michael Buckner (Cambridge: MIT Press, 1983), pp. 285–289.

5. This is perhaps the appeal of the utilitarian formula advanced by John Stuart Mill requiring us to promote "the greatest amount of happiness altogether" (see *Utilitarianism,* ch. 2). One serious problem with utilitarianism, however, is that it confuses what is a subordinate decision rule for certain instances of moral choice with the supreme principle of morality, which requires impartial rational choice.

6. Rawls, for example, provides an argument for the appropriateness of a "maximin" decision rule where the choice of basic and enduring principles for a social order is concerned, but he acknowledges that this rule is not appropriate for all cases of rational or moral choice (*Theory of Justice,* sec. 26).

7. For a series of discussions of the issue of ethical relativism, see John Ladd, ed., *Ethical Relativism* (Belmont, Calif.: Wadsworth, 1973).

8. This aspect of morality is discussed in David Heyd, *Supererogation* (New York: Cambridge University Press, 1982). Also, J. O. Urmson, "Saints and Heroes," in *Essays in Moral Philosophy,* ed. A. I. Melden (Seattle: University of Washington Press, 1958), pp. 198–216.

9. "Treatise on the Law," *Summa Theologiae,* pts. 1a–2ae, ques. 95, art. 6.

10. This idea is insightfully developed by Reinhold Niebuhr in his classic study *Moral Man and Immoral Society* (New York: Charles Scribner's Sons, 1932).

11. *The Abolition of Man* (New York: Macmillan, 1947), p. 28.

12. A similar point is made by Basil Mitchell in his *Morality: Religious and Secular* (Oxford: Clarendon Press, 1980), p. 141.

13. For an example of this kind of misleading argument see Kurt Baier, *The Moral Point of View* (Ithaca, N.Y.: Cornell University Press, 1958), ch. 12. Baier's discussion is criticized by Kai Nielsen in his article, "Why Should I Be Moral?" *Methodos* 15 (1963): 275–306.

14. Kant similarly criticizes the effort to answer this question by appeal to the satisfactions created by heeding one's conscience. Rejecting the Stoic effort to ground moral obedience in these satisfactions, he remarks in the *Critique of Practical Reason,* "A man, if he is virtuous, will certainly not enjoy his life without being conscious of his righteousness in each action, however favorable fortune may be to him in the physical circumstances of life; but can one make him virtuous before he has so high an estimation of the moral worth of his existence merely by commending to him the contentment of spirit which will arise from the consciousness of righteousness for which he as yet has no sense?" (tr. Lewis White Beck [Indianapolis: Bobbs-Merrill, 1956]), p. 120.

15. Stephen Toulmin, in *An Examination of the Place of Reason in Ethics* (Cambridge: Cambridge University Press, 1960), ch. 14, seems to hold this view.

16. Claude Lévi-Strauss, "The Structural Study of Myth," in *Structural Anthropology,* tr. Claire Jacobson and Brooke Grundfest (New York: Basic Books, 1963), pp. 217ff.

17. Although Kant's characteristic moral understanding of religion was already evident in the *Critique of Pure Reason,* the full outlines of Kant's view are made

apparent only in his later writings on religion, especially the *Critique of Practical Reason, Religion within the Limits of Reason Alone,* and the *Critique of Judgment.*

18. In theistic systems, doctrines of grace not only offer an escape from suffering for those conscientious individuals who have come to question their own righteousness, but these doctrines also have the incidental effect of explaining the continuing flourishing of the wicked, which can be attributed to God's mercy and to his willingness to suffer human sin. See, for example, *The Midrash on Psalms,* William G. Braude, tr. (New Haven: Yale University Press, 1959), pp. 423f. (Ps. 37:3).

19. This is the point of Kant's famous argument for freedom of the will in the *Critique of Practical Reason* and of his claim there that "freedom and unconditional practical law reciprocally imply each other" (*Practical Reason,* p. 29).

20. This understanding is forcefully expressed within the Pauline tradition of Christian thought. See, for example, Augustine's discussion in his *Confessions* (bk. 8, especially ch. 9) of the conflict within the human intellect and will.

21. As important as their stress on freedom is, existentialist writers sometimes carry this insistence so far that they overlook the valid role of reason in the choice of normative rules for conduct. This is true, for example, of Jean Paul Sartre's discussion of norms in his classic essay "Existentialism is a Humanism," in *Existentialism from Dostoevsky to Sartre,* ed. Walter Kaufman (New York: New American Library, 1975), pp. 345–369. Although he criticizes normative theories of ethics, including Kant's, Sartre clearly presumes certain standards of right and wrong conduct, and the problematical cases he presents as undermining normative theories are simply very difficult instances of moral decision on any theoretical account.

22. Tr. Theodore M. Green and Hoyt H. Hudson (New York: Harper & Row, 1960), pp. 17–20.

23. Kierkegaard utilizes this essentially Kantian understanding of the unyielding "ideality" of ethics to develop his defense of the Christian doctrine of original sin in *The Concept of Anxiety,* tr. Reidar Thomte (Princeton: Princeton University Press, 1980), pp. 16f.

24. This understanding, too, is a staple of the Pauline-Lutheran tradition. But it is perhaps Kierkegaard who most insightfully perceives the paradox involved here. In the *Concluding Unscientific Postscript* he develops this idea in terms of the peculiar "catch" to guilt that makes professions of innocence amount to self-denunciation (tr. David Swenson [Princeton: Princeton University Press, 1941], p. 471).

25. 4.14.3.

26. *Aboth,* tr. J. Israelstam, pt. 4, vol. 8 of *The Babylonian Talmud,* ed. Isidore Epstein (London: Soncino, 1935), pp. 28, 44, 56–57.

27. David Little and Sumner B. Twiss express some puzzlement over the promises of reward or punishment alongside more formalistic appeals to God's will in the Gospel of Matthew. They end by dismissing the importance of these considerations in the gospel but they fail to identify the deeper logic that leads to their presence in the first place. See their *Comparative Religious Ethics* (San Francisco: Harper & Row, 1978), pp. 204f.

28. This is sometimes characterized as a "double-bind" problem in the realm of moral desert. For discussions of this, see Joel Feinberg, *Doing and Deserving: Essays in the Theory of Responsibility* (Princeton: Princeton University Press, 1970), ch. 4. Also, Steven A. Edwards, "The Inward Turn: Justice and Responsibility in the Religious Ethics of Aquinas" (Ph.D. diss., Stanford University, 1981), pp. 48–53, 160–174.

29. It sometimes confuses advanced students, too. In the effort to understand Paul's shifts between moral exhortation and denials of the importance of moral striving, for example, the great biblical scholar Albert Schweitzer was led to conclude that Paul's seeming contradictions only made sense in terms of nonrational, mystical states experienced by the apostle (*The Mysticism of Paul the Apostle,* tr. W. Montgomery [London: Adam and Charles Black, 1931]).

30. Jeffrey Stout, in his *Flight from Autonomy,* criticizes the approach I am outlining here on the grounds that it cannot explain, among other things, some scholastic Christians' approval of the use of violence against heretics ([Notre Dame, Ind.: University of Notre Dame Press, 1981], pp. 226ff.). This single counterexample is an important one, but a systematic critique of the view I present requires more than one or two counterexamples. Furthermore, the examples adduced must not be eccentric but must represent the major moral and religious tendencies of a tradition. Christian advocacy of the use of force for exclusively religious purposes, whether in war or internal repression, is a position that was contested by many generations of Christian writers and was eventually abandoned by most Christian communities. Good discussions of this tradition of thought include Roland Bainton, *Christian Attitudes toward War and Peace* (New York: Abingdon Press, 1960); Frederick H. Russell, *The Just War in the Middle Ages* (New York: Cambridge University Press, 1975) and James T. Johnson, *Just War Tradition and the Restraint of War* (Princeton: Princeton University Press, 1981).

Chapter 2

1. For discussions of these deities, see Geoffrey Parrinder, *West African Religion* (1961; reprint, New York: Barnes & Noble, 1970), ch. 4. Also, Benjamin C. Ray, *African Religions* (Englewood Cliffs, N.J.: Princtice-Hall, 1976), ch. 2. Marion Kilson provides a convenient table indicating the role of the high god and the status of its cult in various African groups ("Women in African Traditional Religions," *Journal of Religion in Africa* 8 [1976]: 135).

2. John S. Mbiti, *African Religion and Philosophy* (New York: Anchor Books, 1970), pp. 3ff., 46ff. Edward E. Evans-Pritchard, *Nuer Religion* (Oxford: Clarendon Press, 1956), pp. 7ff.

3. John Middleton, *Lugbara Religion* (London: Oxford University Press, 1960), p. 253.

4. Edward E. Evans-Pritchard, *Witchcraft, Oracles and Magic among the Azande* (Oxford: Clarendon Press, 1937), p. 110.

5. Godfrey Lienhardt, *Divinity and Experience* (Oxford: Clarendon Press, 1961), pp. 53f.

6. Robin Horton, "Types of Spirit Possession in Kalabari Region," in *Spirit Mediumship and Society in Africa,* ed. John Beattie and John Middleton (New York: Africana, 1969), p. 16.

7. Peter Fry, *Spirits of Protest* (Cambridge: Cambridge University Press, 1976), p. 19.

8. F. B. Welbourn, "Spirit Initiation in Ankole and a Christian Spirit Movement in Western Kenya," in *Spirit Mediumship,* ed. Beattie and Middleton, p. 290.

9. Introduction to *Spirit Mediumship,* ed. Beattie and Middleton, p. xxi; Mbiti, *African Religion,* pp. 6, 270; Dominique Zahan, *The Religion, Spirituality, and Thought of Traditional Africa,* tr. Kate Ezra Martin and Lawrence M. Martin (Chicago: University of Chicago Press, 1979), p. 16; Evan M. Zuesse, *Ritual Cosmos: The Sanctification of Life in African Religions* (Athens: Ohio University Press, 1979), pp. 55f. As a generalization this statement about the nonretributive role of the high god is perhaps less true of West African than East African religions. See, for example, Emanuel B. Idowu, *Oludumare: God in Yoruba Belief* and Parrinder, *West African Religion.*

10. Evans-Pritchard, *Witchcraft,* p. 489; Middleton, *Lugbara Religion,* p. 14; G. J. Wanjohi, "An African Conception of God: the Case of Gikuyu," *Journal of Religion in Africa* 9 (1978): 141.

11. Dugald Campbell, *In the Heart of Bantuland* (London: Seeley, Service, 1922), p. 245.

12. Lienhardt, *Divinity and Experience,* pp. 54ff.

13. Evans-Pritchard, *Nuer Religion,* p. 149.

14. Mbiti, *African Religion,* pp. 6, 210.

15. In some cultures, extreme immorality may lead an individual to be denied recognition as an ancestor after death, but this seems less an expression of any systematic view of eschatological punishment than one of several social disqualification for esteemed status, on a par with childlessness. See Dominique Zahan, *The Religion, Spirituality, and Thought of Traditional Africa,* pp. 49f.

16. *Nupe Religion* (London: Routledge & Kegan Paul, 1954), pp. 33, 64.

17. I draw this estimate from Robert C. Mitchell, *African Primal Religion* (Niles, Ill.: Argus Communications, 1977), p. 11. For a different estimate of the number of "tribal" groups in sub-Saharan Africa see David B. Barrett, *Schism and Renewal in Africa* (Nairobi: Oxford University Press, 1968), pp. 116, 150 n. 2.

18. Mbiti, *African Religion,* pp. 73f.

19. I. M. Lewis, "A Structural Approach to Witchcraft and Spirit Possession," in *Witchcraft Confessions and Accusations,* ed. Mary Douglas (London: Tavistock, 1970), p. 294.

20. Hugh A. Stayt, *The Bavenda* (London: Oxford University Press, 1931), p. 259.

21. *Spirits of Protest,* p. 21.

22. Middleton, *Lugbara Religion,* p. 98; Evans-Pritchard, *Nuer Religion,* p. 279.

23. Evans-Pritchard, *Nuer Religion,* pp. 148f., 159.

24. E. H. Winter, "The Enemy Within: Amba Witchcraft," in *Witchcraft and Sorcery in East Africa,* ed. John Middleton and E. H. Winter (London: Routledge & Kegan Paul, 1963), pp. 278ff.

25. *Lugbara Religion,* p. 20.

26. Ibid., pp. 34ff.

27. Mbiti, *African Religion,* p. 276.

28. Fry, *Spirits of Protest,* p. 34; Introduction to *Spirit Mediumship,* ed. Beattie and Middleton, p. xxiii.

29. Middleton, *Lugbara Religion,* p. 119; Lienhardt, *Divinity and Experience,* p. 139.

30. Middleton, *Lugbara Religion,* p. 92.

31. Lienhardt, *Divinity and Experience,* p. 86. Nadel reports similar ceremonies

among the Nupe despite his characterization of theirs as an "amoral" universe (*Nupe Religion,* p. 77).

32. Evans-Pritchard, *Witchcraft,* pp. 267, 311; also, Daryll Forde, ed., *Efik Traders of Old Calabar* (London: Oxford University Press, 1956), p. 20.

33. Much of what I say here about spirit mediums also applies to diviners and witch doctors, although these practitioners usually have less status and less moral authority and make resort to morally neutral magical preparations for the relief of suffering. See Evans-Pritchard, *Witchcraft,* pts. 2–4. Also John Beattie, "Divination in Bunyoro, Uganda" and George C. Park, "Divination and Its Social Contexts," in *Magic, Witchcraft, and Curing,* ed. John Middleton (Garden City, N.Y.: Natural History Press, 1967), pp. 211–254.

34. See Irving Zaretsky and Cynthia Shambaugh, *Spirit Possession and Spirit Mediumship in Africa and Afro-America: An Annotated Bibliography* (New York: Garland, 1978).

35. G. Kingsley Garbett, "Spirit Mediums as Mediators in Korekore," in *Spirit Mediumship,* ed. Beattie and Middleton, p. 120.

36. M. J. Field, "Spirit Possession in Ghana," in *Spirit Mediumship,* ed. Beattie and Middleton, p. 12; also, Ray, *African Religions,* p. 74.

37. Victor Turner, "Sacrifice as Quintessential Process Prophylaxis or Abandonment?" *History of Religions* 16 (1977): 189–215.

38. Horton, "Types of Spirit Possession," pp. 27f. Also, M. F. C. Bourdillon, "Religion and Ethics in Korekore Society," *Journal of Religion in Africa* 10 (1979): 81–94.

39. Fry, *Spirits of Protest,* p. 27; Introduction to *Spirit Mediumship,* p. xxiv.

40. Fry, *Spirits of Protest,* p. 37. Michael Gelfand reports that witch doctors are held to similar standards of fiscal integrity (*Witch Doctor* [London: Harvill Press, 1964], pp. 46, 93).

41. S. G. Lee, "Spirit Possession among the Zulu," in *Spirit Mediumship,* ed. Beattie and Middleton, p. 136.

42. In some African societies, a distinction is also made between group misfortunes like famine or epidemic, which are attributed to the ancestors' wrath, and some individual misfortunes that defy clear moral explanation and are attributed to witchcraft. Apparently, group misfortunes are usually seen as deserved. See T. Beidelman, "Witchcraft in Ukaguru," in *Witchcraft and Sorcery,* ed. Middleton and Winter, p. 63.

43. Evans-Pritchard, *Witchcraft,* p. 247; Middleton and Winter, *Witchcraft and Sorcery,* pp. 2ff.

44. Maximilian G. Marwick reports that among the Ceŵa, in distinction from the Azande, all mystical evildoers employ material magical substances (*Sorcery in Its Social Setting* [Manchester: Manchester University Press, 1965], pp. 81f).

45. Evans-Pritchard, *Witchcraft,* pp. 97, 121; Stayt, *Bavenda,* pp. 274f.

46. Winter, "Enemy Within," p. 292; Middleton, *Lugbara Religion,* pp. 248f.

47. Edwin Ardener, "Witchcraft, Economics, and the Continuity of Belief," in *Witchcraft Confessions and Accusations,* ed. Douglas, p. 145.

48. Fry, *Spirits of Protest,* p. 25.

49. Middleton, *Lugbara Religion,* pp. 38f.

50. Zahan, *Religion, Spirituality, and Thought,* pp. 112f.

51. It is interesting that Nadel acknowledges that witchcraft spares other spiritual

entities from moral blame and thus, in a way, upholds the integrity of the higher spiritual order. But this observation clashes with his contention that the Nupe live in an "amoral" universe. See his effort to wrestle with this apparent contradiction (*Nupe Religion*, pp. 201–206).

52. *Witchcraft*, p. 107.

53. Ibid., p. 109.

54. Ibid., p. 107.

55. Jean La Fontaine, "Witchcraft in Bugisu," in *Witchcraft and Sorcery*, ed. Middleton and Winter, p. 215.

56. Evans-Pritchard, *Witchcraft*, p. 112.

57. *Witch Doctor*, p. 48.

58. Ibid., p. 51.

59. Middleton, *Lugbara Religion*, pp. 240f.

60. Evans-Pritchard, *Witchcraft*, p. 117; Marwick, *Sorcery*, pp. 96, 243.

61. Esther Goody, "Legitimate and Illegitimate Aggression in a West African State" and G. I. Jones, "A Boundary to Accusations," in *Witchcraft Confessions and Accusations*, ed. Douglas, pp. 211, 236, 240. Also, Elizabeth Colson, "Spirit Possession in Tonga," in *Spirit Mediumship*, ed. Beattie and Middleton, p. 81; Nadel, *Nupe Religion*, p. 169; and Middleton and Winter, *Witchcraft and Sorcery*, pp. 14ff.

62. This retributive role of witchcraft in social situations where ordinary retributive instrumentalities (law, defensive violence) cannot work is underscored by Marwick's conclusion that most Cewa sorcery accusations take place within the matrilineage, the social group where judicial means of settling disputes are not available (*Sorcery*, pp. 3, 95).

63. For a clarification of this point, see Rawls, *Theory of Justice* (see ch. 1, n. 3). Also, this volume, 165–167.

64. "Witchcraft, Economics, and the Continuity of Belief," p. 146.

65. "Sorcery in Bunyoro," in *Witchcraft and Sorcery*, ed. Middleton and Winter, p. 52.

66. David Tait, "Konkomba sorcery," in *Magic, Witchcraft, and Curing*, ed. Middleton, pp. 169f.

67. Jones, "Boundary to Accusations, p. 325.

68. Beidelman, "Witchcraft in Ukaguru," p. 93.

69. Middleton, *Lugbara Religion*, pp. 17, 20.

70. Goody, "Legitimate and Illegitimate Aggression," p. 240.

71. Evans-Pritchard, *Witchcraft*, p. 101.

72. Ibid., pp. 95f. For this same ritual among the Taita, see this volume, pp. 144f.

73. Mbiti, *African Religion*, p. 114. Grace Gredys Harris states that among the Taita people of Kenya, "everyone was at times identified as bearer of the anger damaging to another living person." See her *Casting Out Anger: Religion among the Taita of Kenya* (Cambridge: Cambridge University Press, 1978), p. 146.

74. Justin S. Ukpong, "Sacrificial Worship in Ibibio Traditional Religion," *Journal of Religion in Africa* 13:3 (1982), 185f. This theme of appeal to God or to the ancestors' mercy for the relief of morally deserved misfortune is a common one in African prayer. See Aylward Shorter, *Prayer in the Religious Traditions of Africa* (New York: Oxford University Press, 1975), pp. 84–100.

75. Evans-Pritchard, *Nuer Religion*, pp. 280ff.

76. Gelfand, *Witch Doctor*, p. 35.

Chapter 3

1. For discussions of the forms of archaic Chinese religion see Fung Yu-lan, *A History of Chinese Philosophy* (Princeton: Princeton University Press, 1952), vol. 1, ch. 3; Marcel Granet, *The Religion of the Chinese People,* tr. Maurice Freedman (Oxford: Basil Blackwell, 1975), ch. 2; Ching-kung Yang, *Religion in Chinese Society* (Berkeley: University of California Press, 1961), ch. 2; and David Howard Smith, *Chinese Religions* (New York: Holt, Rinehart & Winston, 1968), ch. 1.

2. David N. Keightley, *Sources of Shang History: The Oracle Bone Inscriptions of Bronze Age China* (Berkeley: University of California Press, 1978). Also, Jack Finegan, *The Archaeology of World Religions* (Princeton: Princeton University Press, 1952), pp. 317–342.

3. For an account of Shang religion, see David N. Keightley, "The Religious Commitment: Shang Theology and the Genesis of China's Political Culture," *History of Religions* 17 (1978): 211–225. These concerns are very marked throughout *The Shoo King; or, The Book of Historical Documents,* vol. 3 of *The Chinese Classics,* tr. James Legge (London: Oxford University Press, 1865) and in the poems of *The Sheking; or, The Book of Poetry,* vol. 4 of *Chinese Classics,* tr. Legge (London: Oxford University Press, 1871). These have been more recently translated by Bernhard Karlgren as *The Book of Documents* (Stockholm: Museum of Far Eastern Antiquities, 1950) and *The Book of Odes* (Stockholm: Museum of Far Eastern Antiquities, 1950).

4. Smith, *Chinese Religions,* p. 5.

5. Paul Wheatley, *The Pivot of the Four Quarters* (Chicago: Aldine, 1971); Arthur F. Wright, *Buddhism in Chinese History* (New York: Atheneum, 1965), p. 12.

6. *Book of Odes* (tr. Karlgren), p. 31. For a discussion of the role of Heaven in such ceremonies, see Granet, *Religion of the Chinese People,* p. 166.

7. Smith, *Chinese Religions,* p. 3. However, David N. Keightley argues that some of the key moral and political presuppositions of later Chou theology are already evident in Shang religion ("Religious Commitment," 220).

8. Laurence G. Thompson, *Chinese Religion: An Introduction* (Belmont, Calif.: Dickenson, 1969), p. 47.

9. The development of this doctrine is usually attributed to the Duke of Chou, who served as regent for the son of King Wu, leader of the rebellion against Shang. The doctrine itself is enunciated in the "Great Declaration" of the *Shoo King* (tr. Legge), pp. 281–293 (*Book of Documents* [tr. Karlgren], pp. 8ff). For a discussion of these developments see H. H. Dubs, "The Archaic Royal Jou Religion," *T'oung pao* 46 (1958): 217–259 and Herrlee G. Creel, *The Origins of Statecraft in China* (Chicago: University of Chicago Press, 1970), vol. 1, ch. 5.

10. Fung, *History of Chinese Philosophy,* 1: p. 31. Also, Creel, *Origins of Statecraft,* app. C.

11. *Shoo King* (tr. Legge), bk.9, sec. 3, p. 285.

12. *Book of Documents* (tr. Karlgren), p. 45.

13. Ibid., pp. 48f.

14. Ibid., p. 9.

15. *The Religion of China,* tr. Hans H. Gerth (New York: Free Press, 1951), p. 170.

16. *Shoo King* (tr. Legge), "The Books of Shang," bk. 9, sec. 3, p. 264.

17. *Book of Odes* (tr. Karlgren), p. 249.

18. *Book of Documents* (tr. Karlgren), p. 9.

19. This contrast between the political circumstances of China and Israel is offered by Weber in *Religion of China,* pp. 23–29.

20. Reinhold Niebuhr, *The Nature and Destiny of Man* (New York: Charles Scribner's Sons, 1941), vol. 2, ch. 2.

21. A spirit of pessimism and doubt about Heaven's righteousness or its interest in human beings is found in several despairing poems of the *Book of Odes,* especially Odes 191–198 and 258 (tr. Karlgren, pp. 132–148 and 238f.). For a discussion of these developments see Dubs, "Archaic Royal Jou Religion," pp. 243ff. and Fung, *History of Chinese Philosophy,* 1: pp. 31ff.

22. These are the dates ascribed to Confucius by subsequent tradition, although they may be inaccurate by as much as a quarter of a century. For a discussion of this matter, see Herrlee G. Creel, *Confucius: The Man and the Myth* (New York: John Day, 1949), ch. 5 and *The Analects of Confucius,* tr. Arthur Waley (New York: Vintage Books, 1958), pp. 78f. All further references in the text are to Waley's translation.

23. *Analects* 7.19.

24. Ibid. 8.20.

25. Ibid. 2.11.

26. Ibid. 17.7.

27. Herrlee G. Creel, *Confucius and the Chinese Way* (New York: Harper & Row, 1949), pp. 26f.

28. *Analects* 6.4; 7.7.

29. This ideal was subsequently institutionalized with the establishment of competitive examinations for office under the Han dynasty. For discussions of this system, see Robert M. Marsh, *The Mandarins* (Glencoe: Free Press, 1961) and Ho Ping-ti *The Ladder of Success in Imperial China* (New York: Columbia University Press, 1963).

30. Anthony Cua, "Reflections on the Standard of Confucian Ethics," *Philosophy East and West* 21 (1971): 37.

31. Fung, *History of Chinese Philosophy,* 1: p. 69.

32. *Analects* 17.21; 5.18; 14.5; 5.18; 18.1.

33. Wing-tsit Chan, "The Evolution of the Confucian Concept of Jên," *Philosophy East and West* 4 (1955): 297f. Waley's translation of these terms differs from Wing-tsit Chan's.

34. *Analects* 4.6; 5.18; 7.33; 12.3; 14.2.

35. Ibid. 12.2.

36. For a discussion of the "golden rule" in other religious traditions see my *Religious Reason* (see Intro., n. 2), pp. 131, 189. Also, W. A. Spooner, "Golden Rule," in *The Encyclopedia of Religion and Ethics,* ed. James Hastings (New York: Charles Scribner's Sons, 1914), 6: pp. 310–312. More recent philosophical discussions are referred to by Marcus G. Singer in his article, "Golden Rule," in *The Encyclopedia of Philosophy,* ed. Paul Edwards (New York: Macmillan and Free Press, 1967), 3: pp. 365–367.

37. In various forms, these five relationships remain a continuing feature in Confucian thinking throughout its history. In the *Book of Documents* (tr. Karlgren, p. 4) they are presented exclusively in terms of family relationships (the individual and his father, mother, elder brother, younger brother, and son). In later renditions, they encompass duties to friends and rulers. For this later tradition, see William Theodore de Bary, "A Reappraisal of Neo-Confucianism," in *Studies in Chinese Thought,* ed. Arthur F. Wright (Chicago: University of Chicago Press, 1953), p. 88.

38. *Analects* 8.2; 12.1; 15.17,32.

39. Ibid. 3.3.

40. Ibid. 3.4, 26.

41. Wei-ming Tu, "The Creative Tension between *Jen* and *Li*," *Philosophy East and West* 18 (1967): 29–39.

42. *Confucius and the Chinese Way*, p. 94.

43. *Analects* 2.1,3; 4.11; 12.17,19; 13.4,6,12.

44. Herbert Fingarette, *Confucius: The Secular as Sacred* (New York: Harper & Row, 1972), pp. 4ff.

45. *Analects* 2.3; 4.11. In this connection I believe Wei-ming Tu introduces a false dichotomy when he states that "the point of departure in Confucianism is self-cultivation rather than social responsibility." Self-cultivation, especially by the ruler or administrator, is always essential also to sound political life. Hence, even Tu is forced to qualify his distinction by adding, "It is true that Confucian self-cultivation leads to social responsibility, and furthermore the process of self-cultivation in the Confucian sense ought to be carried out in a social context" ("The Neo-Confucian Concept of Man," *Philosophy East and West* 21 [1971]: 79).

46. Mo Tzu, born about the time of Confucius's death and an adversary of aspects of Confucian teaching, is recorded as stating that Confucius believed "Heaven to be without intelligence, and the spirits of the dead to be without consciousness" (Creel, *Confucius and the Chinese Way*, p. 114).

47. Explicit atheism may be found in the writings of the later Confucian Hsün-Tzu. See his *Basic Writings*, tr. Burton Watson (New York: Columbia University Press, 1963), esp. bk. 17. An antitheistic and naturalistic perspective also characterizes the writings of the Confucian historian Tso Chuen (*"The Ch'un Ts'ew" with "The Tso Chuen,"* vol. 5 of *Chinese Classics*, tr. James Legge [London: Oxford University Press, 1872], pp. 92, cols. 1–2; 171, col. 1; 718, cols. 1–2; 810, col. 2).

48. *Analects* 5.12.

49. Ibid. 7.20.

50. Ibid. 11.11.

51. Smith, *Chinese Religions*, p. 29.

52. For an account of these developments, see John K. Shryock, *Origin and Development of the State Cult of Confucianism* (New York: Century, 1932).

53. *Analects* 8.13; 15.8.

54. Ibid. 17.7. Waley notes that this statement contains a play on two senses of the word *shih:* either "to eat" or "to get a salary," i.e., an official position.

55. Ibid. 14.37; cf. 7.22.

56. These developments are recounted in detail by Arthur Adkins in *Merit and Responsibility* (Oxford: Clarendon Press, 1960) and *Moral Values and Political Behaviour in Ancient Greece* (New York: W. W. Norton, 1972).

57. Mencius's theory of human nature has occupied a good deal of attention among students of Confucian ethics. See, for example, Dim-Cheuk Lau, "Theories of Human Nature in *Mencius* and *Shyuntzyy*," *Bulletin of the School of Oriental and African Studies* 15 (1953): 541–565; Angus C. Graham, "The Background of the Mencian Theory of Human Nature," *Chi'ing lau hsueh-pao*, n.s., 6, 1–2 (1967): 214–271; Donald J. Munro, *The Concept of Man in Early China* (Stanford: Stanford University Press, 1969); Lee H. Yearley, "Mencius on Human Nature: The Forms of His Religious Thought," *Journal of the American Academy of Religion* 43 (1975): 185–198.

58. 2.A.6; 6.A.6. All translations are from *Mencius,* tr. Dim-Cheuk Lau (Harmondsworth, England: Penguin Books, 1970).

59. Ibid. 2.A.6.

60. Ibid. 4.A.10. For a discussion of the bases of Mencius's special view of human nature, see *Mencius,* esp. pp. 19ff.

61. Ibid. 6.A.1.

62. For a treatment of these themes in Greek and Roman philosophy, see John M. Rist, *Stoic Philosophy* (Cambridge: Cambridge University Press, 1969), chs. 1, 12 and *Human Values* (Leiden: E. J. Brill, 1982), ch. 1. Plato presents his hierarchical account of the soul in the *Phaedrus;* Aristotle develops his view of the distinctiveness and superiority of reason in the *Nicomachean Ethics,* bk. 1; Cicero deals with these themes in his *De legibus,* as does Seneca in his *Letters to Lucilius,* tr. Edward Phillips Barker (Oxford: Clarendon Press, 1932), Letter 9.

63. *Mencius* 6.A.10,12.

64. Adkins, *Merit and Responsibility,* esp. chs. 8–13.

65. *Mencius* 6.A.8.

66. Mencius's criticism of Yang Tzu may not be wholly fair. Yang Tzu appears to be less a crass egoist than an advocate of temperate self-protection and self-cultivation during times of social disorder. See *Mencius,* p. 30.

67. *Mencius* 7.A.26. Good discussions of Mohist thought include Fung, *History of Chinese Philosophy,* vol. 1, ch. 5; Angus C. Graham, *Later Mohist Logic, Ethics, and Science* (London: School of Oriental and African Studies, 1978), pp. 3–15.

68. A selection of Mo Tzu statements on "universal love" are presented in *The Works of Mencius,* vol. 2 of *Chinese Classics,* tr. Legge (Oxford: Clarendon Press, 1895), pp. 101–116.

69. The effort to ground moral judgment and moral motivation in feeling is characteristic of Bishop Butler in his Sermons on Compassion (*Sermons by Joseph Butler* [Oxford: Clarendon Press, 1896], 2: pp. 92–120). It also characterizes Hume's efforts to relate morality to sympathy (*An Enquiry Concerning the Principles of Morals,* 3d ed., ed. Lewis A. Selby-Bigge [Oxford: Clarendon Press, 1975], sec. 5, pt. 2, pp. 218ff.)

70. *Mencius* 7.A.15.

71. Ibid. 1.A.7.

72. Mencius is keenly aware of the conflict engendered by his commitment both to the five relationships and to more impersonal social obligations. Occasionally he presents hypothetical cases of conflict between these two set in the distant past. In one such case, the emperor Shun is presented as being faced with the necessity of arresting his own father on a charge of murder. Apparently unable to recommend either that Shun carry out his imperial duty or that he interfere in the process of justice on his father's behalf, Mencius solves the dilemma by presenting Shun as "casting aside" the empire and fleeing with the old man on his back to the edge of the sea (7.A.35).

73. Of course, these efforts on Mencius's part presume an interest in justifying moral commitment to the citizen and ruler. The Russian sinologist Vitaly A. Rubin, perhaps reflecting his own struggles with the Soviet regime, views this as a positive aspect of orthodox Confucianism, because it represents a valuation of the individual as a member of the political order. In contrast, Mohist thinking, says Rubin, was prepared to justify an authoritarian regime and to override individual conscience and individual rights in its effort to effect its principle of "universal love." See his *Indi-*

vidual and State in Ancient China, tr. Steven I. Levine (New York: Columbia University Press, 1976).

74. 5.26; cf. 4.6.

75. Ibid. 9.17.

76. The essay, "That the Nature is Evil," by Hsün Tzu (also known as Hsün K'wang or Hsün Ch'ing) is translated in *Works of Mencius* (tr. Legge), pp. 79–88. For a discussion of Hsün's view see *Mencius,* pp. 18–22.

77. *Works of Mencius* (tr. Legge), pp. 84ff.

78. *Mencius* 69.A.7.

79. See, for example, Confucius's disparaging remarks about his disciple Jan Ch'iu in *Analects* 11.16 and 16.1.

80. *Tao te ching,* tr. Dim-Cheuk Lau (Harmondsworth, England: Penguin Books, 1963), p. 8. All quotations are from this edition. A similar story is recorded in *The Complete Works of Chuang Tzu,* tr. Burton Watson (New York: Columbia University Press, 1968), sec. 26, pp. 297f. (hereafter cited as *Chuang Tzu*). All quotations are from this edition.

81. The literature on the authorship and dating of the *Tao te ching* and *Chuang Tzu* is extensive. Traditional teaching as recorded in the *Shih chi* holds the *Tao te ching* and the *Chuang Tzu* to be works of the early third century B.C. Western scholars have a range of views, some holding that the *Tao te ching* precedes the *Chuang Tzu,* others holding that the *Chuang Tzu* is the earlier work. Discussions of this issue may be found in Fung, *History of Chinese Philosophy,* 1: pp. 170–173, 221–223; Arthur Waley, *The Way and Its Power* (London: Macmillan, 1934), ch. 1; Henri Maspero, *Taoism and Chinese Religion,* tr. Frank Kierman, Jr. (Amherst: University of Massachusetts Press, 1981).

82. *Taoism: The Parting of the Way* (Boston: Beacon Press, 1957), p. 43.

83. The *Chuang Tzu* contains one critical mention of a follower of Confucius (sec. 12, p. 135).

84. *Tao te ching* 53.121.

85. Ibid. 17.42; 19.43; 38.82–84.

86. Ibid. 2.7,7a; 22.50b; 77.185; 24.55; 9.23; 29.68; 30.69b.

87. *Chuang Tzu,* sec. 5, p. 72; sec. 4, p. 55.

88. Even Mencius complains about the behavior of those individuals who cultivated character to attain high office but who, on reaching power, promptly abandoned their ideals. Creel, *Confucius and the Chinese Way,* p. 178.

89. *Tao te ching* 18.42.

90. *Chuang Tzu,* sec. 2, p. 44.

91. *Tao te ching* 38.83.

92. Rom. 7.8.

93. Herrlee G. Creel takes the point of view that *wu-wei* is essentially a doctrine of mystical nonactivity (*Chinese Thought from Confucius to Mao Tse-Tung* [Chicago: University of Chicago Press, 1953], pp. 112–113). In the essay, "On Two Aspects of Early Taoism," Creel supplements this judgment, stressing the copresence of a "purposive" or political dimension of *wu-wei* in the *Tao te ching* but still maintaining the existence of a quite different and unassimilable "contemplative" or mystical dimension in it (*"What Is Taoism?" and Other Studies in Chinese Cultural History* [Chicago: University of Chicago Press, 1970], pp. 37–47).

94. *Tao te ching* 57.132–133.

95. Ibid. 30.69b.
96. Ibid. 17.39,41.
97. Ibid. 27.185–185a.
98. *Chuang Tzu,* sec. 7, p. 94.
99. For these various uses of *Tao* see *Analects* 9.29. One use of the *Tao* in the *Analects* (17.19) even anticipates Taoist references to nature as self-giving and self-effacing.
100. *Chuang Tzu,* sec. 6, p. 81.
101. *Tao te ching* 1.1,2; cf. 22.72; 40.89; 45.101,103; 52.143.
102. Ibid. 51.115; 62.143.
103. Ibid. 39.85a.
104. *Chuang Tzu,* sec. 6, p. 81.
105. See Norman J. Girardot, *Myth and Meaning in Early Taoism* (Berkeley: University of California Press, 1983), ch. 2.
106. *Tao te ching* 52.118; *Chuang Tzu,* sec. 2, p. 36; sec. 6, p. 90.
107. *Tao te ching* 8.20.
108. Ibid. 37.81.
109. Ibid. 2.7,7a.
110. *Chuang Tzu,* sec. 6, p. 90.
111. Angus C. Graham sees a link between moral impartiality and the *Chuang Tzu*'s central emphasis on aware response. "In submitting to 'Respond with awareness,' says Graham, 'I have to admit that awareness from my own view point has no privileged status" ("Taoist Spontaneity and the Dichotomy of 'Is' and 'Ought'," in *Experimental Essays on Chuang-tzu,* ed. Victor H. Mair, Asian Studies at Hawaii, no. 29 [Honolulu: University of Hawaii Press, 1983], 15f).
112. For a discussion of these developments, see Anna K. Seidel, "The Image of the Perfect Ruler in Early Taoist Messianism: Lao-Tzu and Li Hung," *History of Religions* 9 (1969–70): 216–247. Also, Howard S. Levy, "Yellow Turban Religion and Rebellion at the End of the Han," *Journal of the American and Oriental Society* 76 (1956): 214–227.
113. These tensions are reflected in Chinese intellectual culture for many centuries. See Richard B. Mather, "The Controversy over Conformity and Naturalness during the Six Dynasties," *History of Religions* 9 (1969–70): 160–180.
114. *Tao te ching* 7.19.
115. Ibid.
116. *Chuang Tzu,* sec. 1, p. 34, sec. 12, p. 137.
117. For different interpretations of the *Chuang Tzu*'s relativism see Chad Hansen, "A *Tao* of *Tao* in Chuang-tzu" and Lee Yearley, "The Perfected Person in the Radical Chuang-tzu," in *Experimental Essays,* ed. Mair, 24–55, 125–139.
118. *Chuang Tzu,* sec. 2, p. 47.
119. Ibid. sec. 5, pp. 73f.
120. Ibid. sec. 6, p. 85.
121. *Tao te ching* 22.50d; 50.113; *Chuang Tzu,* sec. 17, p. 182; sec. 19, p. 198.
122. For an account of these developments, see Maspero, *Taoism and Chinese Religion,* pp. 265–272. Also, Creel, *"What is Taoism?"* chs. 1, 3, and Liu Ts'un-yan, "Taoist Self-Cultivation in Ming Thought," in *Self and Society in Ming Thought,* ed. William Theodore de Bary (New York: Columbia University Press, 1970), pp. 291–330. The speculations of the fourth century A.D. Taoist adept Ko Hung regarding

means of attaining "fullness of life" represent this direction in Taoist thinking. His treatise, the *Nei p'ien,* has been translated by James R. Ware as *Alchemy, Medicine, Religion in the China of* A.D. *320* (Cambridge: MIT Press, 1966).

123. For a comprehensive discussion of religious Taoism, see Michel Strickmann, "Taoism, History of," *Encyclopedia Britannica,* 15th ed. Macropedia, Vol. 17, pp. 1044–1050. Also Rolf A. Stein, "Religious Taoism and Popular Religion from the Second to Seventh Centuries," in *Facets of Taoism,* ed. Holmes Welch and Anna Seidel (New Haven: Yale University Press, 1979), pp. 53–81.

124. Arthur F. Wright, *Buddhism in Chinese History* (Stanford, California: Stanford University Press), p. 97.

125. Wright, *Buddhism in Chinese History;* Kenneth K. S. Ch'en, *Buddhism in China: A Historical Survey* (Princeton: Princeton University Press, 1964); Erik Zurcher, *The Buddhist Conquest of China* (Leiden: E. J. Brill, 1972); Richard Robinson and Willard Johnson, *The Buddhist Religion* (Belmont, Calif.: Wadsworth, 1982); Whalen Lai and Lewis R. Lancaster, eds., *Early Ch'an in China and Tibet,* Berkeley Buddhist Studies Series, no. 5 (Berkeley, Calif.: Asian Humanities, 1983).

126. Wolfram Eberhard, *Guilt and Sin in Traditional China* (Berkeley: University of California Press, 1967), pp. 17ff.

127. Ibid., pp. 19f.

Chapter 4

1. The view that Jewish ethics recognizes an ethic independent of revealed *halakhah* is defended by Louis Jacobs in "The Relationship between Religion and Ethics in Jewish Thought," in *Contemporary Jewish Ethics,* ed. Menachem Marc Kellner (New York: Sanhedrin, 1978), pp. 41–57. Also, Ephraim Urbach, *The Sages,* tr. Israel Abrahams (Jerusalem: Magnes Press, 1975).

2. Excellent discussions of the Christian natural law include Arthur L. Harding, ed., *Origins of the Natural Law Tradition* (Dallas: Southern Methodist University Press, 1954) and Daniel O'Connor, *Aquinas and the Natural Law* (London: Macmillan, 1968).

3. This view is advocated by Sid Leiman in his critique of Jacobs in *Contemporary Jewish Ethics,* ed. Kellner, pp. 58–60. A similar point is made by Jacob J. Petuchowski in his article, "The Dialectics of Reason and Revelation," in *Rediscovering Judaism,* ed. Arnold Wolff (Chicago: Quadrangle Books, 1965), pp. 34–37.

4. The imprint of specific biblical teachings on Roman Catholic sexual ethics, much of which claims to be theoretically grounded in natural law, can be seen in the teachings on contraception and homosexuality. See, for example, John T. Noonan, *Contraception* (Cambridge: Harvard University Press, 1965) and John Boswell, *Christianity, Social Tolerance, and Homosexuality* (Chicago: University of Chicago Press, 1980).

5. The classic criticism of divine command morality is found in Plato's *Euthyphro* dialogue. The writings of Kant, particularly his criticism of "heteronomy" in the *Foundations* (see ch. 1, n.1), establish the framework for most modern criticisms of the divine command position. A collection of leading classical and contemporary defenses of this position may be found in Jean Marie Idziak, ed., *Divine Command Morality: Historical and Contemporary Readings,* (Toronto: Edwin Mellen, 1979)

and Richard Helms, ed., *Divine Command Morality* (New York: Oxford University Press, 1981).

6. Kant is rightly regarded as responsible for the view that the "autonomy" of moral reason prohibits one's obeying any moral rule or command not capable of being authorized by one's own rational conscience. Some defenders of a revealed religious ethic find this position unacceptable. See, for example, the criticism of Kant's position advanced by Emil Fackenheim in his *Encounters between Judaism and Modern Philosophy* (New York: Basic Books: 1973), pp. 39ff. However, as even Fackenheim acknowledges, this Kantian requirement does not mean that one must *create* one's own moral rules, only that the rules one accepts, whatever their source, be capable of being appropriated by human moral reason. In *Religion within the Limits of Reason Alone,* Kant repeatedly defines *religion* as the "recognition of our moral duties as divine commands" (tr. Theodore M. Greene and Hoyt H. Hudson [New York: Harper & Row, 1960], e.g., pp. 90f., 100). Thus, for Kant, true religious obedience is based on a confident presumption of God's moral character and of the necessary integrity of his will, whereas moral "heteronomy," which Kant condemned, involves obedience to divine command as something externally imposed.

7. Lev. 20.9–10. The force of these biblical commandments was later negated by rabbinic commentators in various ways. For example, the death penalty was made progressively less applicable through the requirement that potential offenders be warned of the seriousness of their crime in advance of their committing it. The severe penalty for the rebellious son was mitigated by defining him as one so wicked and glutonous that no real youngster could qualify. For treatments of these matters see *Sanhedrin,* tr. Jacob Shachter and H. Freedman, pt. 4, vols. 5 and 6 of *Babylonian Talmud,* ed. Epstein (see ch. 1, n. 26), 40n–41a, 71a. All subsequent references to the *Babylonian Talmud* are to this edition.

8. For a good review of the treatment of Genesis 22 by biblical scholars, see John Van Seters, *Abraham in History and Tradition* (New Haven: Yale University Press, 1975), ch. 11. For a more traditional exegetical approach to the passage, see Gerhard von Rad, *Genesis: A Commentary* (Philadelphia: Westminster, 1972), pp. 237–245.

9. Søren Kierkegaard, *Fear and Trembling,* tr. Howard V. Hong and Edna H. Hong (Princeton: Princeton University Press, 1983).

10. Ibid., p. 57.

11. Ibid., p. 30.

12. Ibid., pp. 57ff.

13. Ibid., p. 57.

14. Ibid., p. 60.

15. See this volume, pp. 124f.

16. Gene Outka, "Religious and Moral Duty: Notes on *Fear and Trembling,*" in *Religion and Morality,* ed. John Reeder, Jr. and Gene Outka (New York: Doubleday, 1973), pp. 243f. Kierkegaard also mentions Abraham's faith and his belief that God could somehow restore Isaac or "another Isaac" to him (*Fear and Trembling,* p. 36). However, this theme is very much muted compared with its importance in the commentary tradition.

17. "Kierkegaard and the Midrash," *Judaism* 4 (1955): 26. Although Emil Fackenheim, in his chapter "Abraham and the Kantians," finds many features of Kierkegaard's commentary antithetical to the Jewish tradition, he also appears ultimately

to side with Kierkegaard's defense of a revealed religious ethic and of the possibility of "pristine moments of Divine Presence in which every content and all standards are called into question" (*Encounters*, p. 68).

18. Joseph H. Gumbiner, "Existentialism and Father Abraham," *Commentary* 5 (1948): 143–148; Marvin Fox, "Kierkegaard and Rabbinic Judaism," *Judaism* 2 (1953): 115–124.

19. Louis Ginzberg, *The Legends of the Jews,* 7 vols. (Philadelphia: Jewish Publication Society of America, 1913).

20. *Genesis Rabbah,* tr. H. Freedman, vols. 1–2 of *Midrash Rabbah,* ed. H. Freedman and Maurice Simon (London: Soncino, 1939), 55.1 (all subsequent references to the *Midrash Rabbah* are to this edition); Ramban (Nachmanides), *Writings and Discourses,* tr. Charles B. Chavel (New York: Shilo, 1978), 2: pp. 444f.

21. *Genesis Rabbah,* 55.1; *Numbers Rabbah,* tr. Judah J. Slotki, vols. 5–6 of *Midrash Rabbah,* 17:2; *Pesikta Rabbati,* tr. William G. Braude (New Haven: Yale University Press, 1968), p. 218. All subsequent references to the *Pesikta Rabbati* are to this translation.

22. "Kierkegaard," p. 120.

23. *Genesis Rabbah,* 57.4; Ginzberg, *Legends,* V, p. 252, n. 24. These sources also describe Job's trials as having been initially intended for Abraham. They were withheld, however, after Abraham's demonstration of obedience at Moriah.

24. *Sanhedrin,* (tr. Shachter and Freedman), 89b.

25. *Genesis Rabbah,* 55.4.

26. Ibid.

27. Ginzberg, *Legends,* I, p. 217.

28. I borrow this phrase from Halevi, "Kierkegaard and the Midrash," 21. Halevi's defense of the claim that Kierkegaard's position is consistent with Judaism sometimes appears to rest on the view that the "ethical" for Kierkegaard comprises primary loyalty to human collectivities like state or nation in opposition to more universal moral commitments. But as my own remarks indicate, I believe this is a mistaken interpretation of Kierkegaard's stated view in *Fear and Trembling*.

29. *Fear and Trembling,* p. 28.

30. *Genesis Rabbah,* 55.7.

31. Martin Buber, "Abraham the Seer," *Judaism* 5 (1955): 303.

32. *Genesis Rabbah,* 39.7; Ginzberg, *Legends,* I, pp. 217f.

33. "Kierkegaard and the Midrash," 18.

34. *Fear and Trembling,* p. 27.

35. For example, Isa. 10.4; Jer. 18.21, 19.9; Lam. 1.5.

36. *Studies in Biblical Law* (New York: Ktav, 1969), ch. 4.

37. For a fuller discussion of this, see my article "Theodicy," *Encyclopedia of Religion,* ed. Mircea Eliade (New York: Macmillan, 1987), 14:430–441.

38. *Pesikta Rabbati,* II, p. 721; *Numbers Rabbah* 17.2; *Genesis Rabbah,* 56.7.

39. *Numbers Rabbah,* 17.2. This identity between Abraham and Isaac is further reinforced by the occasional allegorization of Isaac as Abraham's "soul" (*Numbers Rabbah* 17.24).

40. *Pesikta Rabbati,* II, p. 717; *Genesis Rabbah,* 56.3.

41. The rabbis derived this number by reckoning Sarah's age at the time of Isaac's birth and her age at her death, which immediately followed on the Akedah.

42. *Genesis Rabbah,* 56.8.

43. *Pesikta Rabbati,* II, p. 717; *Genesis Rabbah,* 56.4.

44. *Pirke de Rabbi Eliezer,* tr. Gerald Friedlander (New York: Herman Press, 1965), p. 226.
45. *Pesikta Rabbati,* II, p. 717; *Genesis Rabbah,* 56.4.
46. *Pirke de Rabbi Eliezer,* p. 227; *Pesikta Rabbati,* II, p. 718.
47. *Deuteronomy Rabbah,* tr. J. Rabbinowitz, vol. 7 of Midrash Rabbah, 11.3; *Lamentations Rabbah,* tr. A. Cohen, vol. 7 of *Midrash Rabbah,* p. 46.
48. *Genesis Rabbah,* 55.4; *Sanhedrin* (Shachter and Freedman), 89b.
49. P. R. Davies and B. D. Chilton, "The Aqedah: a Revised Tradition History," *Catholic Biblical Quarterly* 40 (1978): 514–546.
50. *Lamentations Rabbah,* 1.16 (p. 133).
51. The centrality of the Akedah to the Jewish martyriological tradition is noted by two contemporary Jewish thinkers in the course of their efforts to respond to Kierkegaard's interpretation of Genesis 22. Each thinker, however, fails to relate this theme to the pervasive moralization of the episode found in classical Jewish sources. Schubert Spero sees Abraham as choosing martyrdom for Isaac, as Jewish parents have often done for their children (*Morality, Halakha, and the Jewish Tradition* [New York: Ktav, 1983], pp. 92ff.); but he misses the many other rabbinic themes relating to this story, including, for example, the themes of Isaac's voluntary participation. Emil Fackenheim alternates between religious defenses of the priority due the divine command and moral defenses of the possibility of religious self-sacrifice, which he sees the Akedah as also representing (*Encounters,* ch. 2).
52. *Fear and Trembling,* Problema III, pp. 82–120.
53. *Pesikta Rabbati,* pp. 233f.; Ginzberg, *Legends,* I, pp. 286f. It might be thought that in this connection Sarah becomes the real unwilling victim of the divine command. However, it must be remembered that Sarah's death is recounted in Genesis 23.1 immediately following the Akedah, and the rabbis—constrained by their own interpretive principle that textually related episodes are also conceptually related—were only trying to explain it. Furthermore, every effort is made here to place the blame for this unhappy turn of events on Satan, not God.
54. *The Essential Philo,* ed. Nahum N. Glatzer (New York: Schocken Books, 1971), pp. 82–138.
55. Ibid., p. 120. Philo's emphasis on the fact that Abraham was motivated by love rather than fear is also found in the rabbinic sources, for example, *Sotah,* tr. A. Cohen, pt. 3, vol. 6 of *Babylonian Talmud,* ed. Epstein (London: Soncino, 1936), 31a.
56. *Essential Philo,* p. 120. Much later, the medieval thinker Moses Maimonides, also informed by Greek philosophical thought, similarly stresses the purity of Abraham's moral motivation and the righteousness of God's conduct. See his *Guide for the Perplexed,* tr. M. Friedländer, 2d ed. (Dover, 1956), pp. 304f.
57. *Pesikta Rabbati,* p. 718.
58. *Pirke de Rabbi Eliezer,* p. 228.
59. *Pesikta Rabbati,* p. 718.
60. *Pirke de Rabbi Eliezer,* p. 228.
61. (New York: Pantheon Books, 1967).
62. Davies and Chilton disagree with Spiegel's contention that this motif is pre-Christian ("Aqedah").
63. *Religious Reason* (see Intro., n. 2), pp. 191f.
64. *Pirke de Rabbi Eliezer,* p. 228; *Numbers Rabbah,* 17.2; *Pesaḥim,* tr. H. Freedman, pt. 2, vol. 4 of *Babylonian Talmud,* ed. Epstein (London: Soncino, 1938), 54a.

65. *Aboth* (see ch. 1, n. 26), 64–65.

66. *Pirke de Rabbi Eliezer,* p. 229.

67. *Genesis Rabbah,* 56.8; *Ta'anith,* tr. J. Rabbinowitz, pt. 2, vol. 7 of *Babylonian Talmud,* ed. Epstein (London: Soncino, 1938), 4a.

68. *Ta'anith* 4a; *Genesis Rabbah,* 55.5.

69. Roland De Vaux, *Ancient Israel: Its Life and Institutions,* tr. John McHugh (New York: McGraw-Hill, 1961), pp. 442f. For a fuller discussion of views on this issue, see Van Seters, *Abraham in History and Tradition,* ch. 11.

70. See especially "The Akeda," a poem by Rabbi Ephraim ben Jacob of Bonn, reprinted and translated in Spiegel, *Last Trial,* pp. 139–151.

71. *Leviticus Rabbah,* tr. J. Israelstam and Judah J. Slotki, vol. 4 of *Midrash Rabbah,* 2.2.

72. *Zebaḥim,* tr. H. Freedman, pt. 1, vol. 1 of *Babylonian Talmud,* ed. Epstein (London: Soncino, 1948), 62a.

73. *Pesikta Rabbati,* II, p. 710; *Pirke de Rabbi Eliezer,* pp. 229f.

74. *Pesikta Rabbati,* II, p. 21.

75. Spiegel, *Last Trial,* p. 89.

76. *Leviticus Rabbah,* 29.9.

77. Even Abraham and Isaac are occasionally viewed by the rabbinic writers as having sinned. See, for example, *Shabbath,* tr. H. Freedman, pt. 2, vol. 1 of *Babylonian Talmud,* ed. Epstein (London: Soncino, 1938), 146a and *Nedarim,* tr. H. Freedman, pt. 3, vol. 5 of *Babylonian Talmud,* ed. Epstein (London: Soncino, 1936), 32a. For a fuller discussion of early Jewish thinking about the issues of sin and grace see Frederick R. Tennant, *The Sources of the Doctrine of the Fall and Original Sin* (New York: Schocken Books, 1903).

78. *Pesikta Rabbati,* II, p. 72.

79. *Sifre,* Numbers, sec. 134, ed. H. S. Horovitz (Leipzig, 1917), p. 180.

80. For a discussion of the medieval debates over the role of reason and revelation in Jewish ethics and the debates over the "reasons for the Commandments," see Julius Guttman, *Philosophies of Judaism,* tr. David W. Silverman (New York: Holt, Rinehart and Winston, 1964), pp. 134–241.

Chapter 5

1. A good review of allusions and possible allusions to the *akedah* in the New Testament is offered by Robert J. Daly in his article, "The Soteriological Significance of the Sacrifice of Isaac," *Catholic Biblical Quarterly* 39 (1977): 45–75.

2. Among the first Christian writers to discuss Genesis 22 are Tertullian, Gregory of Nyassa, St. John Chrysostom, Cyril of Jerusalem, and St. Ambrose. These discussions are much briefer than Origen's or Augustine's but are essentially similar. See, for example, Tertullian's *Disciplinary, Moral, and Ascetical Works,* tr. Rudolph Arbessman, Emily Joseph Daily, and Edwin A. Quain, *The Fathers of the Church,* vol. 40 (New York: Fathers of the Church, 1957), pp. 166f., 203 f.; St. John Chrysostom, *Commentary on Saint John the Apostle and Evangelist, Homilies 1–47,* tr. Sister Thomas Aquinas Goggin, *Fathers of the Church,* vol. 33 (New York: Fathers of the Church, 1957), pp. 426f.; and St. Ambrose, *Letters,* tr. Mary Melchior Beyenka,

Fathers of the Church, vol. 26 (New York: Fathers of the Church, 1954), p. 490. The most exhaustive compilation and discussion of the use of Genesis 22 in Christian sources is David Lerch's *Isaaks Opferung christlich gedeutet* (Tübingen: J. C. B. Mohr, 1950). He deals with the earliest sources in chs. 1–3. A much more cursory review of some of this literature is offered by Roland Bainton, "The Immoralities of the Patriarchs According to the Exegesis of the Later Middle Ages and of the Reformation," *Harvard Theological Review* 23 (1930): 39–49.

3. Origen, *Homilies on Genesis and Exodus,* tr. Ronald E. Heine, vol. 71 of *Fathers of the Church* (Washington, D.C.: Catholic University of America Press, 1982), pp. 140f.

4. Ibid., pp. 141, 145.

5. Ibid., pp. 143, 146. This allegorization is reminiscent of Philo's treatment of the text. (*Essential Philo,* [see ch. 4, n. 54], pp. 82–121).

6. Origen, *Homilies,* p. 137.

7. Ibid., p. 140.

8. *City of God,* tr. John Healey (London: J. M. Dent & Sons, 1945), bk. 16, ch. 32.

9. Ibid.

10. During this long period, Genesis 22 receives its most extensive treatment at the hands of Isadore of Seville, Peter Damian, and Bede. For a review of these discussions, see Lerch, *Isaaks Opferung,* ch. 4.

11. *Summa Theologiae* (see ch. 1 n. 9), pts. 1a–2ae, ques. 90–100. Lengthier quotations are from vols. 28 and 29 of *Summa Theologiae,* tr. David Bourke and Arthur Littledale (New York: McGraw-Hill, 1964).

12. Ques. 92, art. 1, reply obj. 4.

13. Ques. 100, art. 8, reply obj. 3.

14. Ibid.

15. Texts from these writers dealing with divine command morality are gathered in Idziak, *Divine Command Morality* (see ch. 4, n. 5).

16. *The Oxford Commentary on the Four Books of the Sentences,* bk. 3, ch. 38, ques. 1 in *Opera omnia,* 2d ed. (Paris: Vives, 1891–95). This selection translated in Idziak, *Divine Command Morality,* p. 52.

17. *The Paris Commentary on the Sentences,* bk. 4, ch. 46 in *Opera omnia.* Quotation translated in Idziak, *Divine Command Morality,* p. 54.

18. William of Ockham, *On the Four Books of the Sentences* in *Opera plurima* (Lyon, 1495, facsimile reprint, London: Gregg International, 1962). This selection is translated in Idziak, *Divine Command Morality,* pp. 55–57.

19. For an account of some of these developments, see Alexandre P. D'Entreves, *Natural Law: An Historical Survey* (New York: Harper & Row, 1965), pp. 69–72.

20. For a fuller discussion of the moral foundations of this doctrine, see my *Religious Reason* (cf. Intro., n. 2), pp. 169–182.

21. *Summa Theologiae,* pt. 1, ques. 21, 23.

22. *Exposition of the Canon of the Mass,* reading 23 in *Canonis misse expositio,* ed. Heiko A. Oberman and William J. Courtenay (Wiesbaden: Franz Steiner, 1963–67), I, p. 212. Selection translated in Idziak, *Divine Command Morality,* p. 72. The context of Biel's discussion of God's moral freedom is noted by Oberman in the course of his defense of Biel's ethics against the charge that the nominalists in general, and Biel in particular, destroyed the medieval synthesis between faith and reason.

See Oberman, *The Harvest of Medieval Theology* (Cambridge: Harvard University Press, 1963), pp. 96ff.

23. *The Bondage of the Will*, tr. J. I. Packer and O. R. Johnston (London: James Clarke: Fleming H. Revell, 1957), ch. 5, p. 209. See also his *Lectures on Romans*, tr. Walter G. Tillmanns and Jacob A. O. Preus, vol. 25 of *Luther's Works*, ed. Jaroslav Pelikan (St. Louis: Concordia, 1972), ch. 9. Both selections reprinted in Idziak, *Divine Command Morality*, pp. 93–97.

24. Tr. Ford Lewis Battles (Philadelphia: Westminster, 1960), bk. 3, ch. 23, 2.

25. *Lectures on Genesis Chapters 21–25*, tr. George V. Schick, vol. 4 of *Luther's Works*, ed. Pelikan (St. Louis: Concordia, 1964), on Gen. 22.

26. *Commentaries on the First Book of Moses Called Genesis*, 2 vol., tr. John King (Edinburgh: Calvin Translation Society, 1850). Genesis 22 is also the subject of a play written by Calvin's disciple Theodore Beza. This has been translated by Arthur Golding as *A Tragedy of Abraham's Sacrifice* (Toronto: University of Toronto Library, 1906). In all respects, it is a traditional rendition of the Genesis episode.

27. Calvin, *Commentaries*, p. 572. Luther, *Lectures on Genesis*, pp. 167ff.

28. Luther, *Lectures on Genesis*, pp. 123f., 180.

29. Excerpts from Jewish midrashim had been included by Nicolaus von Lyra (d. 1349) in a Latin translation of the Bible available to both Reformers. Calvin and Luther both make references to the "rabbis'" or "Jews'" discussions of Genesis 22, sometimes to disparage minor aspects of the midrashic interpretations. They are less willing to reveal their borrowing from these sources. See, for example, Luther, *Lectures on Genesis*, pp. 97, 113; Calvin, *Commentaries*, p. 571.

30. This, even though Calvin criticizes as "forced" Augustine's translation of "Now I know" as "Now I have made known" (*Commentaries*, p. 570).

31. Luther, *Lectures on Genesis*, p. 113; Calvin, *Commentaries*, p. 569.

32. *Lectures on Genesis*, p. 96.

33. *Commentaries*, pp. 564, 568.

34. For a discussion of these sources, see Lerch, *Isaaks Opferung*, ch. 6.

35. Kierkegaard's battle with the church of his day is recorded in *Kierkegaard's Attack upon "Christendom" 1854–1855*, tr. Walter Lowrie (Princeton: Princeton University Press, 1944). See also Neils Thulstrup and Marie M. Thulstrup, eds., *Kierkegaard and the Church in Denmark* (Copenhagen: C. A. Reitzels, 1984), pp. 227–245.

36. Kant touches briefly and approvingly on Christianity in the *Foundations*, p. 25; *Grundlegung*, pp. 408f. (see ch. 1, n.1). He devotes book 4 of *Religion within the Limits* (see ch. 4, n. 6) to an extensive criticism of orthodox Christian doctrines.

37. *Religion within the Limits*, p. 175. Kant presents an even more explicit criticism of Abraham in *The Conflict of the Faculties*, tr. Mary J. Gregor (New York: Abaris Books, 1979), p. 115.

38. For a lengthier discussion of this matter, see my "Deciphering *Fear and Trembling*'s Secret Message," *Religious Studies* 22 (1986): 95–111.

39. (Philadelphia: University of Pennsylvania Press, 1971), pp. 221–226. See, also, his article, "The View from Pisgah: A Reading of *Fear and Trembling*," in *Kierkegaard: A Collection of Critical Essays*, ed. Josiah Thompson (Garden City, N.Y.: Anchor Books, 1972), pp. 420ff. A similar interpretation is suggested by Gregor

Malantschuk in his *Kierkegaard's Truth,* tr. Howard V. Hong and Edna H. Hong (Princeton: Princeton University Press, 1971), pp. 236–243.

40. *Philosophical Fragments* (1844) emphasized the uniqueness of Jesus Christ for human redemption; *The Concept of Anxiety* (1844) is subtitled *A Simple Psychological Deliberation Oriented in the Direction of the Dogmatic Problem of Original Sin;* and *The Sickness unto Death* (1849) is a psychological exploration of selfhood and sin. Additionally, the first of the *Two Upbuilding Discourses* entitled "The Expectancy of Faith," whose publication immediately preceded *Fear and Trembling,* deals with justification through faith; and two of the *Three Upbuilding Discourses* published later in 1843 have the title "Love Will Cover the Multiplicity of Sins."

41. For a brief treatment of the father-son relationship and a bibliography of works treating this topic, see Wolfdietrich V. Kloeden, "Der Vater M. P. Kierkegaard," in *Kierkegaard as a Person,* ed. Niels Thulstrup and Marie M. Thulstrup (Copenhagen: C. A. Reitzels, 1983), pp. 14–25.

42. Thulstrup and Thulstrup, *Kierkegaard as a Person,* pp. xiif.

43. *Søren Kierkegaard's Journals and Papers,* ed. and tr. Howard V. Hong and Edna H. Hong (Bloomington: Indiana University Press, 1967–78), 6:5664. Also, Thulstrup and Thulstrup, *Kierkegaard as a Person,* p. 33.

44. *Fear and Trembling,* p. 3. This epigraph had previously been utilized by Johan Georg Hamann for his own conveyance of a secret message. See Neils Thulstrup, "His Library," in *Kierkegaard as a Person,* ed. Thulstrup and Thulstrup, pp. 95ff.

45. Like many commentators, Howard and Edna Hong regard Regine as the "secret reader" of the book (Introduction to *Fear and Trembling* and *Repetition* [Princeton: Princeton University Press, 1883], pp. xi and xiv).

46. The suggestion that this text is directed to Kierkegaard's father may be supported by the fact that Kierkegaard adds to the remark in his journals, "He who has explained this riddle has explained my life," the question "But who of my contemporaries has understood this?" (*Journals and Papers* 5:5640). In an entry for 1843 apparently intended for the title-page material for the book, but later deleted from the manuscript, Kierkegaard also records the following remarks:

> "Write."—"For whom?"—"Write for the dead, for those in the past whom you love."—"Will they read me?"—"Yes, for they come back as posterity."
>
> *An old saying.*

> "Write."—"For whom?"—"Write for the dead, for those in the past whom you love."—"Will they read me?"—"No!"
>
> *An old saying slightly altered.*

47. *Fear and Trembling,* p. 62.

48. Ibid., p. 99. At one point in his papers of 1843–44, Kierkegaard speculates on the possibility of presenting Abraham within the context of sin: "One could also have Abraham's previous life be not devoid of guilt and have him secretly ruminate on the thought that this was God's punishment, perhaps even have him get the melancholy thought that he must ask God to help make the punishment as severe as possible" (*Journals and Papers* 5:5641).

49. *Fear and Trembling,* p. 55.

50. Kierkegaard makes more explicit the connections between his use of Abraham in *Fear and Trembling,* the general condition of human sinfulness, and the overcoming of moral despair in his *Concluding Unscientific Postscript,* tr. David F. Swenson (Princeton: Princeton University Press, 1941), pp. 234, 238.

51. *Fear and Trembling,* p. 98.

52. *Religion within the Limits,* pp. 34–39. There are a number of independent indications that Kierkegaard was very familiar with Kant's discussion here. For example, Kierkegaard's treatment of Adam's sin in *The Concept of Anxiety* betrays surprising similarities to Kant's (ed. and tr. Reidar Thomte [Princeton: Princeton University Press, 1980], ch. 1). For a fuller discussion of Kierkegaard's possible engagement with Kant's *Religion within the Limits,* see my "Limits of the Ethical in Kierkegaard's *The Concept of Anxiety* and Kant's *Religion within the Limits of Reason Alone,*" in *International Kierkegaard Commentary,* ed. Robert Perkins (Macon, Ga.: Mercer University Press, 1985), pp. 63–109.

53. *Fear and Trembling,* p. 98.

54. *The Concept of Anxiety,* p. 115.

Chapter 6

1. Lewis, *Abolition of Man* (see ch. 1, n. 11), p. 28.

2. *The Elementary Forms of the Religious Life,* tr. Joseph Ward Swain (New York: Collier Books, 1961), p. 250.

3. The tendency to think of rationality solely in terms of empirical control and prediction, or as the taking of effective means to ends, is a major contributor to the tradition that relegates religion and ritual to the sphere of emotion. This tradition has no place for practical or moral rationality and hence is oblivious to the moral dimensions of ritual conduct. The tenacity of this view is demonstrated by its presence in many writings in the anthropology of religion. For example, Jack Goody, in a major review article, states without qualification, "By ritual we refer to a category of standardized behavior (custom) in which the relationship between the means and the end is not 'intrinsic', i.e. is either irrational or non-rational" ("Religion and Ritual: The Definitional Problem," *British Journal of Sociology* 12 [1961]: 159).

4. Alfred R. Radcliffe-Brown, *The Andamen Islanders* (Cambridge: Cambridge University Press, 1922), pp. 325f.; Siegfried F. Nadel, *The Foundations of Social Anthropology* (Glencoe, Ill.: Free Press, 1951), p. 138; Raymond Firth, *Elements of Social Organization,* 3d ed. (London: Watts, 1961), pp. 236ff.; Monica Wilson, *Communal Rituals of the Nyakyusa* (London: Oxford University Press, 1959), pp. 216ff. Anthony F. C. Wallace, *Religion: An Anthropological View* (New York: Random House, 1966), pp. 126ff.

5. For a review and, to some extent, a reiteration of this approach, see Tom Burns and Charles D. Laughlin, Jr., "Ritual and Social Power," in Eugene G. d'Aquili, Charles D. Laughlin, Jr., and John McManus, *The Spectrum of Ritual* (New York: Columbia University Press, 1979), pp. 249–279.

6. The most developed statements of Turner's conception of ritual are found in *The Forest of Symbols: Aspects of Ndembu Ritual* (Ithaca: Cornell University Press, 1967); *The Ritual Process: Structure and Anti-Structure* (Chicago: Aldine, 1969) and *Drama, Fields, and Metaphors: Symbolic Action in Human Society* (Ithaca: Cornell University Press, 1974).

7. *Ritual Process*, p. 106.

8. Ibid., p. 96.

9. *Dramas, Fields, and Metaphors*, p. 266.

10. *Ritual Process*, p. 105.

11. *Dramas, Fields, and Metaphors*, p. 241.

12. *Ritual Process*, p. 97.

13. *Dramas, Fields, and Metaphors*, p. 207.

14. Ibid., pp. 259f.

15. *Ritual Process*, p. 128.

16. This interpretation of Rawls is taken by Ronald Dworkin in his discussion, "The Original Position," in *Reading Rawls*, ed. Normal Daniels (New York: Basic Books, 1974), p. 51.

17. Robert Paul Wolff views both Kant's understanding of the "kingdom of ends" and Rawls's equal-liberty principle as expressions of preexisting and presumably moral commitments to the dignity of personality. See his *Understanding Rawls* (Princeton: Princeton University Press, 1977), p. 116.

18. Niebuhr, *Moral Man and Immoral Society* (see ch. 1, n. 10), p. 58.

19. *Foundations*, pp. 54f.; *Grundlegung*, p. 436 (see ch. 1, n. 1).

20. *Foundations*, p. 97 n.; *Grundlegung*, p. 430.

21. (Cambridge: Cambridge University Press, 1978), ch. 2.

22. Ibid., p. 48.

23. Ibid., ch. 5.

24. Ibid., pp. 131f.

25. Ibid., p. 136.

26. The theme of sacrifice in religion has produced an abundant literature and many theories. They include Edward Tylor's view (in his *Primitive Culture*) of sacrifice as a gift to a supernatural being to reduce its hostility; James Frazer's view of it (in *The Golden Bough*) as a magical means of rejuvenating the god; Hubert and Mauss's view (in their "Essai sur le sacrifice") of it as creating a buffer between things sacred and profane; Edward Westermarck's interpretation (in his *Origin and Development of Moral Ideas*) of sacrifice as fundamentally a means of expiation; Sigmund Freud's view of it (in *Totem and Taboo*) as linked to a primal act of parricide; and more recently René Girard's view (in *Violence and the Sacred*) of sacrifice as an outlet for endemic social violence.

27. See ch. 2, pp. 39f.

28. *Casting Out Anger*, p. 151.

29. This view of sacrifice as centrally involving self-renunciation or self-abnegation is not new. It was voiced many years ago by Tylor or by Hubert and Mauss. More recently, it has been reasserted by Victor Turner, who sees the element of self-renunciation as common to sacrifice in its various forms, from offering to expiation. In his review of discussions of sacrifice in traditional religious settings, Turner states that sacrifice represents a "destruction" of that part of the self that is pitted against the common good or that impedes the flow of giving, receiving, and giving again that is the essence of communal life in a traditional society. "To give up," he adds, "is often painful. Here to give up in sacrifice is a necessary piece of social surgery. For the Invisibles the sacrifice would be a gift; for men an atonement" ("Sacrifice" [see ch. 2, n. 37], 207).

30. Harris, *Casting Out Anger*, p. 142.

31. The distance between Jerusalem and diaspora communities led to the addi-

256 *Notes*

tion of an eighth day to the biblically mandated seven-day festival. See Theodore H. Gaster, *Passover: Its History and Traditions* (New York: Henry Schuman, 1949), p. 15.

32. Baruch M. Bokser, *The Origins of the Seder: The Passover Rite and Early Rabbinic Judaism* (Berkeley: University of California Press, 1984).

33. This preparatory period was possibly longer and more arduous in the biblical passover rite. Judah B. Segal states that the biblical ritual "was probably preceded by a preliminary period of purification lasting seven days" (*The Hebrew Passover* [London: Oxford University Press, 1963], p. 139).

34. *The Passover Seder: Afikoman in Exile* (Philadelphia: University of Pennsylvania Press, 1981), p. 45.

35. A translation of part of this Mishnah appears in Bokser, *Origins of the Seder,* ch. 3. A complete translation appears in the *Babylonian Talmud* (see ch. 4, n. 64).

36. *Mishah Pesaḥim* (tr. Bokser), 10:1.B.

37. Ibid., C.

38. *The Passover Haggadah,* tr. Jacob Sloan (New York: Schocken Books, 1969), p. 49.

39. For traditional Jewish interpretations of the Passover symbolism, see Abraham P. Bloch, *The Biblical and Historical Background of Jewish Customs and Ceremonies* (New York: Ktav, 1980), ch. 7.

40. *Passover Haggadah* (tr. Sloan), p. 21.

41. Ibid., p. 23.

42. Tr. Bokser, 10.4 There is a difference of opinion among rabbinic commentators on how this mishnaic requirement is to be interpreted. The tradition upheld by Samuel understands *humiliation* to refer to the Hebrews' oppression and inserts here the statement beginning "We were Pharaoh's slaves." A tradition upheld by Rav stresses Israel's early sins and inserts the phrase "In the beginning our fathers were idolators." It has become customary to favor the view of Samuel but to insert a statement in keeping with Rav's intepretation later in the *Haggadah*. For a discussion of this matter, see *Passover Haggadah* (tr. Sloan), p. 23.

43. *The Book of Exodus* (Philadelphia: Fortress Press, 1974), p. 200.

44. In a discussion of the Seder, Israel Scheffler states that the ritual is not a literal reenactment of the Exodus event: "The whole Seder ritual is indeed intended to foster spiritual identification with the liberated Israelites of the exodus and to kindle in participants a vivid sense of the joy of the redemption from slavery. But the various symbolic means through which the ritual strives to accomplish this goal do not add up to a literal reenactment of the portrayed historical exodus" ("Ritual and Reference," *Synthese* 46 [1981]: 434). Fredman, *Passover Seder,* p. 96, also stresses this distinction between identification and reenactment, as does Monford Harris in his article, "The Passover Seder: On Entering the Order of History," *Judaism* 25 (1976): 171. The reasons for the emphasis on this matter are not clear, although they seem to stem partly from the desire to distinguish the Seder from nonhistorical, archetypical rituals of recreation. Nevertheless, whatever theological or other motives lie behind it, this distinction is not really sustainable, since elements of the ritual, such as the evening timing of the service, the eating of matzo and other features, literally hearken back to the original Passover night. In addition, as Scheffler himself notes (p. 437, n. 24), Jewish communities have sometimes taken it upon themselves to reenact events of the Exodus.

45. *Passover Haggadah,* p. 27.

46. Ibid., p. 49.

47. *The Way of Torah,* 3d ed. (North Scituate, Mass: Duxbury, 1979), pp. 39–40.

48. Introduction to *Passover Haggadah,* p. 5.

49. *Der Stern der Erlösung,* 3:72, translated in Nachum N. Glatzer, *Franz Rosenzweig: His Life and Thought* (New York: Schocken Books, 1953), p. 319.

50. For discussions of Jewish charitable and distributive practices in general and their special relationship to Passover, see Ephraim Frisch, *An Historical Survey of Jewish Philanthropy* (New York: Macmillan, 1924), p. 9; Israel Abrahams, *Jewish Life in the Middle Ages* (London: Edward Goldston, 1932), chs. 22, 23; Salo W. Baron, *The Jewish Community* (Philadelphia: Jewish Publication Society of America, 1942), vol. 2, ch. 16; Kaufman Kohler, "The Historical Development of Jewish Charity," *Hebrew Union College and Other Addresses* (Cincinnati, 1916), pp. 229–252; and Solomon Schechter, *Studies in Judaism: Third Series* (Philadelphia: Jewish Publication Society of America, 1924), pp. 238–276.

51. Fredman, *Passover Seder,* p. 150.

52. The Eucharist following baptism, for example, has direct ritual connections to the Passover Seder. For a discussion of this relationship, see John W. Bowman, *The Gospel of Mark: The New Christian Passover Haggadah* (Leiden: E. J. Brill, 1963).

53. The earliest sources for the baptism liturgy are "Didache, or Teaching of the Apostles" in Francis X. Glimm, tr., *The Apostolic Fathers, The Fathers of the Church* (New York: Cima, 1947), I, pp. 165–184, and the "Church Order" of Hippolytus of Rome, to be found in *The "Apostolic Tradition" of St. Hippolytus of Rome,* tr. Gregory Dix (London: Society for Promoting Christian Knowledge, 1968). For a comprehensive discussion of early baptismal practice as reported in these documents and of later developments, see Josef A. Jungmann, *The Early Liturgy* (Notre Dame, Ind.: University of Notre Dame, 1959). A vivid depiction of fourth-century practice is offered by Frederik van der Meer, *Augustine the Bishop,* tr. Brian Battershaw and G. R. Lamb (New York: Harper & Row, 1961), ch. 12.

54. Joachim Jeremias, *The Origins of Infant Baptism* (Naperville, Ill.: Alec R. Allenson, 1963).

55. Hippolytus, "Apostolic Tradition," pp. 24ff; also Edward C. Whitaker, *Documents of the Baptismal Liturgy* (London: Society for Promoting Christian Knowledge, 1960), pp. 3f., 7.

56. For a discussion of this matter, see Arthur Voobus, *Liturgical Traditions in the Didache* (Stockholm: Estonian Theological Society in Exile, 1968), pp. 17ff.

57. Hippolytus, "Apostolic Tradition," pp. 34f.; Whitaker, *Documents,* pp. 3, 24.

58. It is now commonly held that Christian baptism is directly related to the Jewish practice of *tebilah,* the ritual immersion of proselytes. For a discussion of the details of this relationship, see Frank Gavin, *Jewish Antecedents of the Christian Sacraments* (New York: Ktav, 1969), pp. 26–58.

59. Gavin finds this motif of rebirth in the Jewish *tebilah,* although there appears to be no emphasis on any element of symbolic death in the rite. Gavin, *Jewish Antecedents,* p. 51.

60. This seems to be the point of 1 Pet. 3.21. For a discussion of this matter, see Whitaker, *Documents,* p. 22.

61. Leo Tolstoy's *Death of Ivan Ilyitch* provides a moving literary development of this theme.

62. Hugh M. Riley, *Christian Initiation* (Washington, D.C.: Catholic University of America Press, 1974), p. 264. In Jewish ritual immersions, the participant was required to remove all jewelry. This is formally explained by the need to expose every part of the body to the cleansing effect of the water, but it may also be understood as an expression of the *communitas* dimensions of ritual immersion in this entire tradition. See Gavin, *Jewish Antecedents*, p. 47.

63. J. Daniélou, *The Bible and the Liturgy* (Notre Dame, Ill.: University of Notre Dame Press, 1965), p. 45.

64. See Claude Lévi-Strauss, *Totemism*, tr. Rodney Needham (Boston: Beacon Press, 1963) and *The Savage Mind* (Chicago: University of Chicago Press, 1966). Although the primary emphasis of Lévi-Strauss's work has been on myth, he frequently speaks interchangeably of myth and ritual systems. Also broadly within this tradition of interpretation is Dan Sperber's effort to demonstrate the rational significance of symbolic activity. See his *Rethinking Symbolism* (New York: Cambridge University Press, 1975) and his article, "Is Symbolic Thought Prerational?" in *Between Belief and Transgression: Structuralist Essays in Religion, History, and Myth*, ed. Michel Izard and Pierre Smith (Chicago: University of Chicago Press, 1982), pp. 245–264.

65. For a review of forms and types of ritual, see Hans H. Penner, "The Concept and Forms of Ritual," *Encyclopedia Britannica*, 15th ed., Macropaedia, vol. 26, pp. 824–827.

Chapter 7

1. Major contributions to this debate include Rawls, *Theory of Justice* (see ch. 1, n. 3); Robert Nozick, *Anarchy, State, and Utopia* (New York: Basic Books, 1974); and Alan Gewirth, *Reason and Morality* (Chicago: University of Chicago Press, 1978). A selection of critical discussions of the positions explored in these texts appears in John Arthur and William H. Shaw, eds., *Justice and Economic Distribution* (Englewood Cliffs, N.J.: Prentice-Hall, 1978). In what follows, I clearly express my view that the redistributive position championed in various ways by Rawls and Gewirth remains far more persuasive than either its chief competitor, the "entitlement" position espoused by Nozick, or related libertarian positions.

2. *Theory of Justice*, sec. 15; *Reason and Morality*, p. 52.

3. Marx's colleague, Friedrich Engels, appeared to believe that social reorganization and technology would lead to exponential economic growth in communist society. See his remarks in the *Outlines of a Critique of Political Economy*, vol. 31 of Karl Marx and Friedrich Engels *Werke* (Berlin: Dietz Verlag, 1965), s. 467.

4. This idea has sometimes been sharply ridiculed by conservative theorists. For example, Nozick, in *Anarchy, State, and Utopia*, strongly objects to viewing natural abilities as a "collective asset" to be shared by members of society (pp. 228f.). But doing so is not without precedent. To some extent, publicly funded education has had a kind of indirect redistributive effect with respect to basic traits and abilities. It involves drawing on the resources and energies of the better-endowed, materialized as income, to correct personal and familial liabilities of the less-advantaged.

5. This important point is made by Normal Daniels in his article, "Meritocracy," in *Justice and Economic Distribution*, ed. Arthur and Shaw, p. 172.

6. For a fuller discussion of this, see my *Religious Reason* (see Intro., n. 2), pp. 253f.

7. In terms of numbers and location of adherents, Islam today is predominately an Asian religious tradition. Because its teachings on economic life draw on the Bible, I include it within a cultural tradition shared with Judaism and Christianity.

8. See Norman Gottwald, *The Tribes of Yahweh* (Maryknoll, N.Y.: Orbis Books, 1979), p. 690.

9. In his *Ancient Judaism,* Max Weber characterizes the prophets as antiutopian and antidemocratic demagogues (tr. and ed. Hans H. Gerth [New York: Free Press, 1952], ch. 11).

10. *Support for the Poor in the Mishnaic Law of Agriculture: Tractate Peah* (Chico, Ca.: Scholars Press, 1983), p. 18.

11. Isaiah Berlin, *Two Concepts of Liberty* (Oxford: Clarendon Press, 1958).

12. Discussions of classical Jewish approaches to the issue of social welfare include Abrahams, *Jewish Life;* Baron, *Jewish Community,* vol. 2, ch. 16; Frisch, *Historical Survey;* Kohler, *Hebrew Union College,* pp. 229–252; Solomon Schechter, *Studies in Judaism,* (for all of the above, see ch. 6, n. 50); Isadore Twersky, "Some Aspects of the Jewish Attitude toward the Welfare State," *Tradition* 5:2 (Spring 1963): pp. 238–276, 137–158. Also, Isaac Levitats, "Charity" and "Gemilut Hasadim," *Encyclopedia Judaica,* 5: 338f., 7: 374f.; Menahem Haran, "Provision for the Poor," *Encyclopedia Judaica,* 13: 850f.

13. "Some Aspects," 146.

14. *Pe'ah,* tr. S. M. Lehrman, pt. 6, vol. 2 of *Babylonian Talmud,* ed. Epstein (London: Soncino, 1948), 44.

15. *The Book of Agriculture,* tr. Isaac Klein (New Haven: Yale University Press, 1979), treat. 2, ch. 9, 3.

16. *Kethuboth,* tr. Samuel Daiches and Israel Slotki, pt. 3, vols. 3–4 of *Babylonian Talmud,* ed. Epstein (London: Soncino, 1936), 49b. Maimonides, *Book of Agriculture,* treat. 2, ch. 7, 10.

17. *Kethuboth,* 67b.

18. Maimonides, *Book of Agriculture,* treat. 2, ch. 7, 10 (quoted in Frisch, *Historical Survey* p. 79).

19. This view is forcefully stated by Rabbi Meir in *Baba Bathra,* tr. Maurice Simon and Israel Slotki, pt. 4, vols. 3–4 of *Babylonian Talmud,* ed. Epstein (London: Soncino, 1935), 10a. A similar idea is found in various Christian writings. In the "Shepherd of Hermas: Second Parable," the rich and poor are compared to an elm and a vine, as being linked together in mutual need (Glimm, Marique, and Walsh, *Apostolic Fathers* [see ch. 6, n. 53], I, pp. 288–290).

20. Luke T. Johnson views almsgiving as one of several distinct motifs in early Christian attitudes toward property, alongside more radical denunciations of wealth and appeals to common possession (*Sharing Possessions* [Philadelphia: Fortress Press, 1981], ch. 1).

21. For a discussion of this theme of identification with Christ, see William J. Walsh and John P. Langen, "Patristic Social Consciousness, The Church, and the Poor," in *The Faith That Does Justice,* ed. John C. Haughey (New York: Paulist, 1977), pp. 129–134.

22. Ibid., pp. 119–126.

23. Geo Widengren, *Mani and Manichaeism* (London: Weidenfeld & Nicolson, 1965), pp. 72f., 95f.

24. This is the major burden of Paul's letter to Philemon. For a discussion of Pauline views, see Martin Hengel, *Poverty and Riches in the Early Church* (Philadelphia: Fortress, 1974), ch. 5.

25. John G. Gager, *Kingdom and Community: The Social World of Early Christianity* (Englewood Cliffs, N.J.: Prentice-Hall, 1975), p. 106; also, Hengel, *Poverty and Riches,* ch. 9.

26. *The Social Teachings of the Christian Churches* (New York: Harper Torchbooks, 1960), I, p. 321.

27. Ibid., ch. 9.

28. Plato, *The Republic* 4.424, *Laws* 5.739; Aristotle, *Politics,* 2.5; Cicero, *De Finibus* 3.67 and *De Officio* 1.20; Seneca, *Letters to Lucilius* (see ch. 3, n. 62), letter 90; Virgil, *Georgics* 1.126ff.

29. Hengel, however, regards this influence as "questionable." (*Poverty and Riches,* p. 45).

30. Basil, *Opera Omnia,* vol. 31 of *Patrologiae graecae,* ed. J.-P. Migne (Paris, 1885), cols. 276f.; Portions of this are translated in Basil, *The Treatise "De spiritu sanctu,"* Blomfield Jackson, vol. 8 of *The Nicene and Post-Nicene Fathers, 2d ser.,* ed. Philip Schaff and Henry Wace (1895; reprint, Grand Rapids, Mich.: W. B. Eerdmans, 1952–1956), pp. lvi–lvii (henceforth NPNF); Gregory Nazianzen, *Opera Omnia,* vol. 35 of *Patrologiae graecae,* col. 892, sec. 25; Ambrose, *Principal Works,* tr. H. De Romestin, vol. 10 of NPNF, 2d ser. (1896; repr.), p. 6, para. 28 and p. 23, para. 132 and "The Hexameron" 5.15.52 in *Saint Ambrose: Hexameron, Paradise, and Cain and Abel,* tr. John Savage, vol. 42 of *The Fathers of the Church,* vol. 42 (New York: Fathers of the Church, 1961), pp. 201f. John Chrysostom, *Homilies on the Gospel of John,* tr. Philip Schaff, vol. 14 of NPNF, 1st ser. (1906; repr.), pp. 53ff. Many of these texts are gathered together in Peter C. Phan, ed., *Social Thought, Message of the Fathers of the Church,* vol. 20 (Wilmington, Del.: Michael Glazier, 1984).

31. "The Tragedy of the Commons," *Science* 162 (1968): 1243–1248.

32. Ibid., p. 1247.

33. This seems to be the view of John Chrysostom, *Homilies on the Minor Pauline Epistles,* tr. Gross Alexander, vol. 13 of NPNF, 1st ser. (1914; repr.), p. 447. According to Robert M. Grant, a similar caustic view of property is expressed in the pseudo-Clementine *Homilies* (Robert M. Grant, *Early Christianity and Society* [New York: Harper & Row, 1977], p. 184, n. 83.

34. Thomas, *Summa Theologiae,* (see ch. 1, n. 9), pts. 2a–2ae, ques. 66, art. 7.

35. Hugo Grotius, *The Rights of War and Peace,* tr. A. C. Campbell and David J. Hill (Washington: M. Walter Dunne, 1901), p. 21.

36. An illustration is Aristotle's judgment that slaves and women are inherently deficient in rational capacity (*Politics* 1. 13.1260a.12–14). In general, when Greek philosophers stressed the importance of sharing among friends, they confined this circle to members of the aristocracy.

37. Sura 3.175f.; 4.40f.; 9.34; 47. 39; 2.43,264; 4.114; 13.22; 19.55; 22.41; 23.1–4; 24.56; 41.6–7; 57.17; 58.13. All subsequent citations and quotes from the Qur'ān refer to *The Koran Interpreted,* tr. Arthur J. Arberry (New York: Macmillan, 1955).

38. Joseph Schacht, "Zakāt," in *Encyclopaedia of Islam,* vol. 4, pp. 1202–1205. Also, Azim A. Nanji, "Ethics and Taxation: The Perspective of the Islamic Tradition," *Journal of Religious Ethics* 13 (1985): 161–168; and Norman Calder, "Zakāt in Imāmī Shīʿī Jurisprudence, from the Tenth to the Sixteenth Centuries A.D.," *Bulletin of the School of Oriental and African Studies* 44 (1981): 468–480.

39. Nanji, "Ethics and Taxation," 164.

40. For a discussion of these matters see Sayed Kotb, *Social Justice in Islam,* tr. John B. Hardie (Washington: American Council of Learned Societies, 1953); Nanji, "Ethics and Taxation," and Sayyid M. Yusuf, *Economic Justice in Islam* (Lahore, Pakistan: Sh. Muhammad Ashraf, 1971).

41. Sura 59.7.

42. Kotb, *Social Justice in Islam,* p. 111.

43. Benjamin Nelson, *The Idea of Usury* (Princeton: Princeton University Press, 1949).

44. Matters of inheritance in Islamic law have their foundation in sura 4.11–12 of the Qur'ān. For a discussion of this, see Kotb, *Social Justice in Islam,* pp. 116ff.

45. Sura 24.33.

46. Sura 16.72f.

47. This was the view of al-Ash^cari in his polemic with the Mu^ctazilites. See *The Theology of al-Ashari,* tr. Richard J. McCarthy (Beirut: Imprimerie catholique, 1953), sec. 170.

48. *The Religion of India,* tr. and ed. Hans H. Gerth and Don Martindale (New York: Free Press, 1958), p. 213. Also, Arthur C. Danto, *Mysticism and Morality* (New York: Basic Books, 1972), pp. 81f.

49. *Religion of India,* p. 215.

50. Ibid., pp. 218f. Also, Melford Spiro, *Buddhism and Society,* 2d ed. (Berkeley: University of California Press, 1982), p. 67.

51. *The Dhammapada,* tr. and ed. Thera Narada (New Delhi: Sagar, 1972), p. 270.

52. Emanuel Sarkisyanz, *Buddhist Backgrounds of the Burmese Revolution* (The Hague: Martinus Nijhoff, 1965), p. 40.

53. Stanley J. Tambiah, *World Conqueror and World Renouncer* (Cambridge: Cambridge University Press, 1976), chs. 1–5. Also Sarkisyanz, *Buddhist Backgrounds,* chs. 6–7.

54. *The Perfect Generosity of Prince Vessantara,* tr. Margaret Cone and Richard Gombrich (Oxford: Clarendon Press, 1977), p. xxv.

55. Wolfram Eberhard, *Guilt and Sin in Traditional China* (Berkeley: University of California Press, 1967), p. 70.

56. For a discussion of this aspect of Buddhist monasticism, see the article by Phra Rajavaramuni in *Attitudes toward Poverty and Wealth in Theravada Buddhism,* ed. Donald Swearer and Russell Sizemore (Cambridge: Cambridge University Press, forthcoming).

57. *In Hope of Nibbana* (LaSalle, Ill: Open Court, 1964), p. 186.

58. Sarkisyanz, *Buddhist Backgrounds,* p. 14.

59. "Aggañña Suttanta," tr. by various Oriental scholars and ed. Thomas W. Rhys Davids, Sacred Books of the Buddhists (London: Humphrey Milford, 1921), pp. 77–94.

60. Ibid., p. 82.

61. Ibid.

62. Ibid., p. 84.

63. Ibid., p. 86.

64. Ibid.

65. Ibid., p. 87.

66. Ibid., p. 88.

67. Ibid., p. 90.
68. Ibid., p. 93.
69. Tambiah, *World Conqueror,* p. 9.
70. Tr. Marc Sainsbury (Chicago: University of Chicago Press, 1980).
71. Ṛg-veda 10.90. Translated in *Hinduism,* ed. Louis Renou (New York: George Braziller, 1961), pp. 64f.

Chapter 8

1. These novels are discussed by Rob Campany in his "Cosmogony and Self-Cultivation: The Demonic and the Ethical in Two Chinese Novels," *Journal of Religious Ethics* 14 (1986): 81–112.
2. The dramatic outline of evil flourishing for a time, to be finally conquered by good, has been found by George Dumézil in both the Mahābhārata and the Scandinavian *Ragnarök* myth. See his *Les Dieux des Germains* (Paris: Press universitaires de France, 1969), pp. 78–105 and *L'Idéologie des trois fonctions dans les épopées des peuples indo-europées,* vol. 1 of *Mythe et épopée* (Paris: Éditions Gallimard, 1968), p. 227.
3. Scholarly opinion now holds the core material of the Rāmāyaṇa to have been composed by a single author sometime between 750 and 500 B.C. and committed to writing at a much later date (the earliest written manuscript is dated A.D. 1020). For a recent discussion of matters of authorship and dating, see Robert P. Goldman, *General Introduction to Bālakāṇḍa,* vol. 1 of *The Rāmāyaṇa of Vālmīki,* tr. Goldman (Princeton: Princeton University Press, 1984), 14–59. Also, J. L. Brockington, *Righteous Rāma: The Evolution of an Epic* (Bombay: Oxford University Press, 1984), esp. chs. 1, 2, and 10; and Frank Whaling, *The Rise of the Religious Significance of Rāma* (Delhi: Motilal Banarsidass, 1980), 32f. n. 2.
4. For a survey of the many forms of cultural expression given the Rāmāyaṇa in Asia, from the traditional to the contemporary, see Kapila Malik Vatsyayan, *Rāmāyaṇa in the Arts of Asia* (Teheran: Asian Cultural Documentation Centre for UNESCO, 1975).
5. In India, the Rāmāyaṇa has had its most important influence, not in Vālmīki's original rendition, but in the sixteenth-century Hindi adaptation by Tulasī Dās (Tulsīdās), the *Rāmacaritamanas* (*The Holy Lake of the Acts of Rama,* tr. W. Douglas P. Hill [London: Oxford University Press, 1952]). Outside of India there exist various nationalized versions of the epic, such as the Khmer Rāmakerti or Thai Rāmakīen. Despite their many differences, these versions and adaptations generally incorporate the major episodes of moral decision drawn from Vālmīki. For discussions of these other forms of the Rāmāyaṇa, see Whaling, *Rise,* chs. 10–22 and Brockington, *Righteous Rāma,* chs. 8 and 9. Excellent discussions of the very important performance tradition of the *Rāmacaritamanas* may be found in Linda Hess and Richard Schechner, *Performative Circumstances, from the Avante Garde to the Ramlila* (Calcutta: Seagull Books, 1983) and Philip Lutgendorf, "The Life of a Text: Tulsidas' *Ramacaritmanas* in Performance" (Ph.D. diss., University of Chicago, forthcoming).
6. The first major translation of the *Rāmāyaṇa* into English was published more than a century ago by Ralph T. H. Griffith. This translation is in verse and

lacks the seventh book (*The Rámáyan of Válmíki,* 5 vols. [London: Trübner, 1870–74]). More recently the epic has been translated into prose by Hari Prasad Shastri as *The Ramayana of Valmiki,* 3 vols. (London: Shanti Sadan, 1957–1962). A new translation, under the editorship of Robert P. Goldman, is presently being prepared by Princeton University Press, although only the first book, or Bālakāṇḍa, has appeared to date. In order to preserve the flavor of the original and because no significant differences exist among the translations for the passages I have quoted, I use Griffith's poetic version for all quotations, although the corresponding references to the more recent Shastri translation are also given. For a full discussion of available translations of the Rāmāyaṇa, see H. Daniel Smith, *Reading the Rāmāyaṇa: A Bibliographic Guide for Students and College Teachers,* South Asian Special Publications no. 4 (Syracuse, N.Y.: Maxwell School of Citizenship and Public Affairs, 1983).

7. Benjamin Khan observes that "in India there is a common belief that a man with a crooked body possesses a crooked soul as well" (*The Concept of Dharma in Vālmīki Rāmāyaṇa* [Delhi: Munishi Ram Manohar Lal, 1965], pp. 189f). In the context of the epic, this spiritually and physically deformed maidservant Mantharā is something of a counterpart to the serpent in the Genesis myth of the Fall. Motivated by envy and resentment, she goads the innocent Kaikeyī into the primal wrongdoing that initiates the drama.

8. Brockington traces this equivocation to a developing disdain for the tribal peoples of the south, which led, eventually, to their being equated with animals. See his *Righteous Rāma,* p. 122.

9. For a discussion of these textual matters see Brockington, *Righteous Rāma,* pp. 13f. In almost solitary opposition to Brockington and most other commentators, Ramashraya Sharma contends that the first and seventh books are integral and original parts of the epic (*A Socio-Political Study of the Vālmīki Rāmāyaṇa* [Dehli: Motilal Banarsidass, 1971], pp. 6f).

10. This view seems to be espoused by Hermann Jacobi in his masterly treatment of the epic, *Das Râmâyaṇa: Geschichte und Inhalt nebst Concordanz der gedruckten Recensionen* (Bonn: Friedrich Cohen, 1893), p. 65.

11. *Rise,* pp. 89ff.

12. Rāma's devotion to dharma is celebrated in the traditional description of him as *rāmo dharmabhṛtāṃ,* "Rāma, best of upholders of dharma." *Dharma* has various meanings in Indian usage, including not only the overarching moral laws of the universe that bind all human beings (*sādhāraṇadharma*), but also the specific normative forms of caste and professional duty (*varṇāśramadharma*). Rāma's conduct comprises many of these normative meanings. Although much of his behavior dences conformity to his specific Kshatriya, or "warrior," dharma, his conduct also frequently exemplifies universal *sādhāraṇadharma.* For fuller discussion of these matters, see Brockington, *Righteous Rāma,* ch. 7; Whaling, *Rise,* ch. 4; and Roderick Hindery, *Comparative Ethics in Hindu and Buddhist Traditions* (Delhi: Motilal Banarsidass, 1978), pp. 102ff. For a more traditional exposition of Rāma's vaunted righteousness and dharmic excellence see C. Sivaramamurti, *Rāmo Vigrahavān Dharma: Rama Embodiment of Righteousness* (New Delhi: Kanak, 1980).

13. The theme of Rāma's saving compassion and his ability to wipe away sins becomes a major motif of Tulasī Dās's *Rāmacaritamanas.* See Whaling, *Rise,* chs. 21 and 22. However, this theme is not only anticipated in Vālmīki, it is explicitly stated in the *phalaśrutis* or "recitals of benefits" appearing near the beginning and

264   *Notes*

end of the epic, where readers are promised, among other things, material blessings, long life and the forgiveness of sins.

14. Fingarette, *Confucious* (see ch. 3, n. 44).

15. E.g., Stanley Hauerwas *A Community of Character* (Notre Dame, Ind.: University of Notre Dame Press, 1981), ch. 1; Alasdair MacIntyre, *After Virtue,* 2d ed. (Notre Dame, Ind.: University of Notre Dame Press, 1984); Gertrude E. M. Anscombe, "Modern Moral Philosophy," *Philosophy* 33 (1958): 1–19.

16. Lest there be any doubt about this, the narrative, with a pungency and irony so characteristic of popular literature, allows the point to be made by Daśaratha himself. While he is still planning the bestowal of power on Rāma, the king engages in a long discourse (Rāmāyaṇa 2.3) advising his son on the responsibilities of a ruler in which he says:

> And rule each sense with earnest will.
> Keep thou the evils far away
> That spring from love and anger's sway.
> Thy noble course alike pursue
> In secret as in open view,
> And every nerve, the love to gain
> Of ministers and subjects, strain.

17. *Rāmāyaṇa* 2.11 (tr. Griffith), vol. I, pp. 373f.; (tr. Shastri), vol. I, p. 85.

18. W. Ruben sees a conflict here between Daśaratha's spoken commitment to installing Rāma and his explicit pledge to Kaikeyī ("Vier Liebestragödie des *Ramayana,*" *Zeitschrift der deutschen morganlandischen Gesellschaft,* Wiesbaden 100 [1950]; 287–355). Sharma also views this incident as involving primarily a conflict of duties (*Socio-Political Study,* p. 299). Hindery finds the moral meaning of this episode to lie either in its upholding or condemning a kind of "Kantian" absolutism in ethics (*Comparative Ethics,* 99).

19. Shantikumar Nanooram Vyas, *India in the Rāmāyaṇa Age* (Delhi: Atma Ram & Sons, 1967), p. 295.

20. *Rāmāyaṇa* 2.19 (tr. Griffith) vol. II, p. 34, 61; (tr. Shastri), vol. I, p. 211, 224.

21. Ibid., 2.18 (tr. Griffith), vol. II, p. 30; (tr. Shastri), vol. I, p. 209.

22. Ibid.

23. Ibid., 2.107 (tr. Griffith), pp. 430f.; (tr. Shastri), vol. I, p. 412.

24. Khan, *The Concept of Dharma,* pp. 204f.

25. Ibid., pp. 140.

26. *Rāmāyaṇa* 2.40 (tr. Griffith), vol. II, p. 141; (tr. Shastri), vol. I, p. 265.

27. Ibid., 3.18 (tr. Griffith), vol. III, p. 85; (tr. Shastri), vol. II, p. 41.

28. Ibid., 5.42 (tr. Griffith), vol. IV, p. 373; (tr. Shastri), vol. II, p. 437.

29. Ibid., 2.68 (tr. Griffith), vol. II, p. 269; (tr. Shastri), vol. I, p. 330.

30. Ibid., 4.18 (tr. Griffith), vol. IV, p. 99; (tr. Shastri), vol. II, p. 211.

31. Ibid., 2.21 (tr. Griffith) vol. II, pp. 45f.; (tr. Shastri), vol. I, p. 216.

32. Ibid., 2.109 (tr. Griffith), vol. II, p. 437; (tr. Shastri), vol. I, p. 415.

33. Ibid., 6.6 (tr. Griffith), vol. V, p. 5, 282; (tr. Shastri), vol. III, pp. 341f.

34. It is noteworthy that some commentators have viewed this episode as possibly containing an implicit criticism of the prevailing social attitudes toward women's virtue that prompt the test. See, for example, the discussion by Hindery, *Comparative Ethics,* p. 113 and Vyas, *India in the Rāmāyaṇa Age,* pp. 130f. Hindery (pp.

102f.) also points out that Sītā's defense of her purity contains a relatively lofty volitional, rather than material, account of sin. Sītā's purity lies not primarily in the fact that she was sexually unmolested by Rāvaṇa, but in the fact that she never *willingly* yielded to Rāvaṇa in any way.

35. Edward Washburn Hopkins, discussing this episode in his *Ethics of India,* appears to miss this point entirely. Viewing the ordeal in terms of Rāma's desire to know whether his wife is faithful, he characterizes Rāma's conduct as "full of base suspicion and incredible brutality" ([New Haven: Yale University Press, 1924], pp. 17f.).

36. *Rāmāyaṇa* 3.18 (tr. Griffith), vol. III, p. 85; (tr. Shastri), vol. II, p. 41.

37. James Wheeler's comment is typical: "It is somewhat remarkable that Rāma appears to have formed an alliance with the wrong party, for the right of Bāli [Vālin] was evidently superior to that of Sugrīva; and it is especially noteworthy that Rāma compassed the death of Bāli by an act contrary to all the laws of fair fighting" (*History of India* [London: Trübner, 1867], p. 324). Quoted in *Rāmāyaṇa* (tr. Griffith), vol. IV, p. 418.

38. This is the view taken by Khan, *Concept of Dharma,* pp. 143–153. Whaling states that "it is not clear that Sugrīva is morally much superior to Vālin" (*Rise,* p. 27). More bluntly, J. Moussaieff Masson says that Sugrīva's account of the episode with his brother "stinks" and questions Rāma's integrity in allying himself with the wrong party in this dispute ("Fratricide among the Monkeys: Psychoanalytic Observations on an Episode in the Vālmīki Rāmāyaṇam," *Journal of the American Oriental Society* 95 (1975), 674.

39. Khan mistakenly takes Sugrīva's self-accusations as evidence of his being in the wrong in this dispute rather than as the morally proper expressions of contrition and grief that they are (*Concept of Dharma,* p. 147).

40. As Dhairyabala P. Vora points out in his *Evolution of Morals in the Epics,* Sugrīva's assumption of Vālin's wife Tārā accords with the prevailing sexual code of morality since it was permitted for a younger brother to inherit the harem of his older brother. Vālin, in contrast, was doubly in violation in seizing Sugrīva's wife Rumā, because he took the wife of a younger brother and of one still alive. ([Bombay: G. R. Bhatkal, Popular Book Depot, 1959], pp. 72f.).

41. John Cambell Oman calls Rāma's remark here "strange, indeed, when we reflect Bāli [Vālin] was the king of a magnificent city decorated with gold, silver, and ivory, and that Bāli's brother was Rāma's much decorated ally" (*The Stories of the Rāmāyaṇa and Mahābhārata* [London: George Routledge & Sons, 1895], p. 48).

42. Brockington, *Righteous Rāma,* p. 224.

43. Khan, *Concept of Dharma,* pp. 149ff.

44. *Rāmāyaṇa* 4.15 (tr. Griffith), vol. IV, p. 33; (tr. Shastri), vol. II, p. 202.

45. Ibid. 4.15 (tr. Griffith), vol. IV, p. 86; (tr. Shastri), vol. II, p. 204.

46. Masson appears to miss this dimension of the narrative when he points to Vālin's remarks here as an implicit criticism by the author of Rāma's subsequent conduct ("Fratricide among the Monkeys," 767).

47. *Rāmāyaṇa* 3.37 (tr. Griffith), vol. III, pp. 171f.; (tr. Shastri), vol. II, p. 79.

48. Ibid., 3.40 (tr. Griffith), vol. III, p. 183f.; (tr. Shastri), vol. II, p. 84.

49. Ibid.

50. Ibid., 6.6 (tr. Griffith), vol. V, pp. 16f.; (tr. Shastri), vol. III, p. 17.

51. Ibid.

52. Ibid., 6.10 (tr. Griffith), vol. V., p. 10; (tr. Shastri), vol. III, p. 23.

Conclusion

1. Richard B. Brandt, *Hopi Ethics: A Theoretical Analysis* (Chicago: University of Chicago Press, 1954); John Ladd, *The Structure of a Moral Code: A Philosophical Analysis of Ethical Discourse Applied to the Ethics of the Navaho Indians* (Cambridge: Harvard University Press, 1957).

Index